Beginning Google Maps Applications with PHP and Ajax

From Novice to Professional

Michael Purvis
Jeffrey Sambells
and Cameron Turner

Apress®

Beginning Google Maps Applications with PHP and Ajax: From Novice to Professional

Copyright © 2006 by Michael Purvis, Jeffrey Sambells, and Cameron Turner

ISBN-13 (pbk): 978-1-59059-707-1

ISBN-10 (pbk): 1-59059-707-9

Printed and bound in the United States of America 9 8 7 6 5 4 3 2

Lead Editor: Jason Gilmore
Technical Reviewer: Terrill Dent
Editorial Board: Steve Anglin, Ewan Buckingham, Gary Cornell, Jason Gilmore, Jonathan Gennick,
    Jonathan Hassell, James Huddleston, Chris Mills, Matthew Moodie, Dominic Shakeshaft, Jim Sumser,
    Keir Thomas, Matt Wade
Project Manager: Elizabeth Seymour
Copy Edit Manager: Nicole LeClerc
Copy Editor: Marilyn Smith
Assistant Production Director: Kari Brooks-Copony
Production Editor: Katie Stence
Compositor: Kinetic Publishing Services, LLC
Proofreader: Liz Welch
Indexer: Beth Palmer
Cover Designer: Kurt Krames
Manufacturing Director: Tom Debolski

Distributed to the book trade worldwide by Springer-Verlag New York, Inc., 233 Spring Street, 6th Floor, New York, NY 10013. Phone 1-800-SPRINGER, fax 201-348-4505, e-mail orders-ny@springer-sbm.com, or visit http://www.springeronline.com.

For information on translations, please contact Apress directly at 2560 Ninth Street, Suite 219, Berkeley, CA 94710. Phone 510-549-5930, fax 510-549-5939, e-mail info@apress.com, or visit http://www.apress.com.

The source code for this book is available to readers at http://www.apress.com in the Source Code section or at the official book site, http://googlemapsbook.com.

To Anne and Jim, that with God's grace,
I might one day be so loving a parent.
—Michael Purvis

Dedicated to my loving wife, Stephanie, always by my side as my navigator in life.
May we never lose our way in this crazy world.
And also to my parents, Frank and Linda,
who taught me to always look beyond the horizon.
—Jeffrey Sambells

I dedicate this book to my amazing wife, Tanya, and our son, Owen.
Tanya is the ultimate teammate and life partner—
always willing to dive into an adventure or opportunity regardless of the size.
I'd also like to thank my parents, Barry and Lorna, for supporting me
in all my ambitions and encouraging me to take risks and pursue dreams.
Without all of you, I would never have agreed to write my first book
about a moving-target topic such as Google Maps,
on a compressed timeline, with a newborn baby!
To everyone else who helped out in the last few months, thank you.
We couldn't have completed this book without your help and patience.
—Cameron Turner

Contents at a Glance

PART 1 ■■■ Your First Google Maps

PART 2 ■■■ Beyond the Basics

PART 3 ■■■ Advanced Map Features and Methods

PART 4 ■■■ Appendixes

Contents

PART 1 ■■■ Your First Google Maps

PART 2 ■■■ Beyond the Basics

PART 4 ■■■ Appendixes

Foreword

In the Beginning...

In the history of the Internet, 2005–2006 will be remembered as the year when online mapping finally came of age. Prior to 2005, MapQuest and other mapping services allowed you to look up directions, search for locations, and map businesses, but these searches were limited, usually to the companies the services had partnered with, so you couldn't search for any location. On February 8, 2005, Google changed all that. As it does with many of its services, Google quietly released the beta of Google Maps to its Labs incubator (http://labs.google.com) and let word-of-mouth marketing promote the new service.

By all accounts, Google Maps was an instant hit. It was the first free mapping service to provide satellite map views of any location on the earth, allowing anyone to look for familiar places. This started the "I can see my house from here" trend, and set the blogosphere abuzz with links to Google Maps locations around the world.

Like other mapping services, Google Maps offered directions, city and town mapping, and local business searches. However, what the Google Maps engineers buried within its code was something that quickly set it apart from the rest. Although unannounced and possibly unplanned, they provided the means to manipulate the code of Google Maps to plot your own locations. Moreover, you could combine this base mapping technology with an external data source to instantly map many location-based points of information. And all of this could be done on privately owned domains, seemingly independent of Google itself.

At first, mapping "hackers" unlocked this functionality, just as video gamers hack into games by entering simple cheat codes. They created their own mapping services using Google Maps and other sources. One of the first these was Housingmaps.com, which combined the craigslist.org housing listings with a searchable Google Maps interface. Next came Adrian Holovaty's chicagocrime.org, which offered a compelling way to view crime data logged by the Chicago Police Department. These home-brewed mapping applications were dubbed "hacks," since Google had not sanctioned the use of its code in external domains on the Web.

The major change came in June 2005, when Google officially introduced the Google Maps API, which is the foundation for this book. By releasing this API, Google allowed programmers the opportunity to build an endless array of applications on top of Google Maps. Hundreds of API keys were registered immediately after the announcement, and many sites integrating Google Maps appeared within days. The *map mashup* was born.

The Birth of the Google Maps Mania Blog

The Google Maps labs beta site had been public for barely a month when I tried it for the first time. I was fascinated. While combing through the blogosphere looking for more information, I started to see a trend toward Google Maps hacks, how-to sites, Firefox extensions, and websites indexing specific satellite images. I thought that others could benefit from an aggregation of all of these ideas into one themed blog. Thus, my Google Maps Mania blog was born.

Google Maps Mania is more accurately described as a "meta-site," as host Leo Laporte pointed out when I was a guest on his NPR G4techTV radio show in November 2005.

April 13, 2005, saw these as my first posts:

Title: Google Maps Mania

If you're like me you were absolutely floored when Google came out with the Google Maps service. Sure, it's just another mapping service. Until you realize it's full potential. The ability to toggle between regular street/road maps and a satellite view is unreal. I've started to see a lot of buzz around the blogging community about Google Maps so I've decided to help you keep up with the Google Maps related sites, blogs and tools that are cropping up. Stay tuned.

Title: Google Sightseeing

The first Google Maps related site of note is Google Sightseeing. This blog tracks interesting satellite shots as submitted by its visitors, then organizes them by interest area like buildings, natural landmarks and stadiums. It's a pretty nifty site. Google Sightseeing even posted my suggestion of Toronto's Rogers Centre (Skydome) and the CN Tower!

Title: Flickr Memory Maps

Here's a Flickr group that took off fast. Memory Maps is a Flickr group that contains maps with captions describing memories they have of those areas or specific notes about different areas. Kind of cool.

Title: Make your own multimedia Google map

Google Blogoscoped tipped me off on this link. Seems Engadget has a page which gives some pretty good directions on how to create your own annotated multimedia Google map. There is some pretty serious direction here which includes inserting pictures and movies from the annotations. I'd like to see an example of this.

Title: My GMaps

myGmaps enables you to create, save and host custom data files and display them with Google Maps. Create push-pin spots on any map of your choice. Mark your house, where an event will be held, or the route of a fun-run as a few examples. Then you can publish the map that you've created to your own website.

These postings represented an interesting cross-section of the ideas, concepts, and websites that I had come across in the two short months since Google Maps came to the Web. In the year between the start of Google Maps Mania and the release of the second-generation API (which this book is based on) in April 2006, I have made over 900 posts and attracted more than 6,000 daily readers to the blog, including the architects of the API itself. I've been Slashdotted, Dug (at Digg), and linked to from the *New York Times* site, as well as the sites of hundreds of other mainstream papers and magazines. In June 2006, Google arranged for my entire family to travel across the country so I could speak at the Google Geo Developer Day in advance of the Where 2.0 conference.

So many interesting mashups have been created using the Google Maps API that it's becoming impossible to keep up with all of them. I liken this to the early days of the Web when search directories began to manually catalog new web pages as they came online. The volume of new sites quickly became too huge to handle manually, and Google itself was born.

You can see why the Google Maps API offers the key for the next killer apps on the Web. It has been the missing link to take the Web to the next level.

This book will provide you the means to take part in this evolution of the Web. I hope to be posting about the interesting and unique map creations that you build after reading this book. Your creations will inspire others to do similar things, and together, we will continue to grow the Internet, one mapping application at a time. Let me know if you build something cool!

Mike Pegg
Google Maps Mania (http://www.gmapsmania.com)

About the Authors

MICHAEL PURVIS is a mechatronics engineering student at the University of Waterloo, Ontario. Prior to discovering web scripting, he was busy with projects of other kinds, like making a LEGO® Mindstorms kit play the game Connect Four. Since the publication of the PHP edition of this book, he has been hired for a four-month internship at Google's New York City office. On the side, he continues to maintain an active community site for classmates, built from home-brewed extensions to PunBB and MediaWiki.

He has written for *Position Is Everything*, participates in mailing list discussions, and maintains a meandering personal blog at http://uwmike.com.

Offline, he enjoys cooking, writing, cycling, and social dancing. He has worked with We-Create on a number of exciting PHP-based projects and has a strong interest in independent web standards.

JEFFREY SAMBELLS is a graphic designer and self-taught web applications developer best known for his unique ability to merge the visual world of graphics with the mental realm of code. With a Bachelor of Technology degree in Graphic Communications Management along with a minor in Multimedia, Jeffrey was originally trained for the traditional paper-and-ink printing industry, but he soon realized the world of pixels and code was where his ideas would prosper. In late 1999, he cofounded We-Create, Inc., an Internet software company based in Waterloo, Ontario, which began many long nights of challenging and creative innovation. Currently, as Director of Research and Development for We-Create, Jeffrey is responsible for investigating new and emerging Internet technologies and integrating them using web standards-compliant methods. In late 2005, he also became a Zend Certified Engineer.

When not playing at the office, Jeffrey enjoys a variety of hobbies from photography to woodworking. When the opportunity arises, he also enjoys floating in a canoe on the lakes of Algonquin Provincial Park or going on an adventurous, map-free, drive with his wife. Jeffrey also maintains a personal website at JeffreySambells.com, where he shares thoughts, ideas, and opinions about web technologies, photography, design, and more. He lives in Ontario, Canada, eh, with his wife, Stephanie, and their little dog, Milo.

■**CAMERON TURNER** has been programming computers since his first VIC 20 at age 7. He has been developing interactive websites since 1994. In 1999, he cofounded We-Create, Inc., which specializes in Internet software development. He is now the company's Chief Technology Officer. Cam obtained his Honors degree in Computer Science from the University of Waterloo with specialization in applied cryptography, database design, and computer security.

Cam lives in Canada's technology capital of Waterloo, Ontario, with his wife, Tanya, son Owen, and dog Katie. His hobbies include biking, hiking, water skiing, and painting. He maintains a personal blog at CamTurner.com, discussing nontechnical topics, thoughts, theories, and family life.

About the Technical Reviewer

 **TERRILL DENT** is enrolled in Honors Mathematics at the University of Waterloo. His major interests center around Internet culture, twentieth century history, and economic theory. Terrill.ca is home to his weblog, and MapLet.ca is the front for his web application ventures, where he lets his acute attention to detail show through. Apart from work, he busies himself with fine arts, cycling, and an occasional novel.

Acknowledgments

The authors would like to thank Mike Pegg of Google Maps Mania for giving Apress our names when contacted about doing a book on Google Maps. This book would not have been possible without his encouragement, support, generosity, and friendship.

Thanks to Terrill for finding the errors of our bleary-eyed coding sessions and helping make this book what it is today.

Thanks to Jason, Elizabeth, Marilyn, Katie, Julie, and the rest of the team at Apress. We hope that working with us has been as much fun for you as working with you was for us.

PART 1

■ ■ ■

Your First
Google Maps

CHAPTER 1

Introducing Google Maps

It's hard to argue that Google Maps hasn't had a fundamental effect on the mapping world. While everyone else was still doing grainy static images, Google developers quietly developed the slickest interface since Gmail. Then they took terabytes of satellite imagery and road data, and just gave it all away for free.

We're big fans of Google Maps and excited to get started here. We've learned a lot about the Google Maps API since it was launched, and even more during the time spent writing and researching for this book. Over the course of the coming chapters, you're going to move from simple tasks involving markers and geocoding to more advanced topics, such as how to acquire data, present many data points, and provide a useful and attractive user interface.

A lot of important web technologies and patterns have emerged in parallel with the Google Maps API. But whether you call it Ajax or Web 2.0 is less important than what it means: that the little guy is back.

You don't need an expensive development kit to use the Google Maps API. You don't need a computer science degree, or even a lot of experience. You just need a feel for what's important data and an idea of what you can do to present it in a visually persuasive way.

We know you're eager to get started on a map project, but before we actually bust out the JavaScript, we wanted to show you two simple ways of creating ultra-quickie maps: using KML files and through the Wayfaring map site.

Using either of these approaches severely limits your ability to create a truly interactive experience, but no other method will give you results as quickly.

KML: Your First Map

The map we're working on here is actually Google Maps itself. In June 2006, Google announced that the official maps site would support the plotting of KML files. You can now simply plug a URL into the search box, and Google Maps will show whatever locations are contained in the file specified by the URL. We aren't going to go in depth on this, but we've made a quick example to show you how powerful the KML method is, even if it is simple.

■**Note** KML stands for Keyhole Markup Language, which is a nod to both its XML structure and Google Earth's heritage as an application called Keyhole. Keyhole was acquired by Google late in 2004.

We created a file called `toronto.kml` and placed the contents of Listing 1-1 in it. The paragraph blurbs were borrowed from Wikipedia, and the coordinates were discovered by manually finding the locations on Google Maps.

Listing 1-1. *A Sample KML File*

```
<?xml version="1.0" encoding="UTF-8"?>
<kml xmlns="http://www.google.com/earth/kml/2">
<Document>
  <name>toronto.kml</name>
  <Placemark>
    <name>CN Tower</name>
    <description>The CN Tower (Canada's National Tower, Canadian National Tower),
    at 553.33 metres (1,815 ft., 5 inches) is the tallest freestanding structure on land.
    It is located in the city of Toronto, Ontario, Canada, and is considered the
    signature icon of the city. The CN Tower attracts close to two million visitors
    annually.

    http://en.wikipedia.org/wiki/CN_Tower</description>
    <Point>
      <coordinates>-79.386864,43.642426</coordinates>
    </Point>
  </Placemark>
</Document>
</kml>
```

In the actual file (located at `http://googlemapsbook.com/chapter1/kml/toronto.kml`), we included two more `Placemark` elements, which point to other well-known buildings in Toronto. To view this on Google Maps, paste that URL into the Google Maps search field. Alternatively, you can just visit this link:

`http://maps.google.com/maps?f=q&hl=en&q=http://googlemapsbook.com/chapter1/kml/toronto.kml`

You can see the results of this in Figure 1-1.

Figure 1-1. *A custom KML data file being displayed at maps.google.com*

Now, is that a quick result or what? Indeed, if all you need to do is show a bunch of locations, it's possible that a KML file will serve your purpose. If you're trying to link to your favorite fishing spots, you could make up a KML file, host it somewhere for free, and be finished.

But that wouldn't be any fun, would it? After all, as cool as the KML mapping is, it doesn't actually offer any interactivity to the user. In fact, most of the examples you'll work through in Chapter 2 are just replicating the functionality that Google provides here out of the box. But once you get to Chapter 3, you'll start to see things that you can do *only* when you harness the full power of the Google Maps API.

Before moving on, though, we'll take a look at one other way of getting a map online quickly.

Wayfaring: Your Second Map

A number of services out there let you publish free maps of quick, plotted-by-hand data. One of these, which we'll demonstrate here, is Wayfaring.com (Figure 1-2). Wayfaring has received attention and praise for its classy design, community features (such as commenting and shared locations), and the fact that it's built using the popular Ruby on Rails framework.

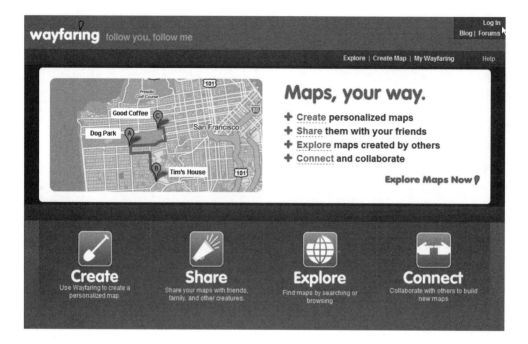

Figure 1-2. *Wayfaring.com home page*

Wayfaring is a mapping service that uses the Google Maps API and allows users to quickly create maps of anything they would like. For example, some people have made maps of their vacations; others have identified interesting aspects of their hometown or city. As an example, we'll walk you through making a quick map of an imaginary trip to the Googleplex, in Mountain View, California.

Point your browser at `http://www.wayfaring.com` and follow the links to sign up for an account. Once you've created and activated your account, you can begin building your map. Click the Create link.

Adding the First Point

We'll start by adding the home airport for our imaginary journey. In our case, that would be Pearson International Airport in Toronto, Ontario, Canada, but you could use the one closest to you. Since Pearson is an international location (outside the United States), we need to drag and zoom the map view until we find it. If you're in the United States, you could use instead the nifty Jump To feature to search by text string. Figure 1-3 shows Pearson nicely centered and zoomed.

Figure 1-3. *Lester B. Pearson International Airport, Toronto, Ontario*

Once you've found your airport, you can click Next and name the map. After clicking ahead, you should be back at the main Map Editor screen.

Select Add a Waypoint from the list of options on the right. You'll be prompted to name the waypoint. We'll call ours "Lester B Pearson International Airport." However, as we type, we find that Wayfaring is suggesting this exact name. This means that someone else on some other map has already used this waypoint, and the system is giving us a choice of using their point or making one of our own. It's a safe bet that most of the airports you could fly from are already in Wayfaring, so feel free to use the suggested one if you would like. For the sake of completeness, we'll quickly make our own. Click Next to continue.

The next two screens ask you to tag and describe this point in order to make your map more searchable for other members. We'll add the tags "airport Toronto Ontario Canada" and give it a simple description. Finally, click Done to commit the point to the map, which returns you to the Map Editor screen.

Adding the Flight Route

The next element we're going to add to our map is a route. A route is a line made up of as many points as you would like. We'll use two routes in this example. The first will be a straight line between the two airports to get a rough idea of the distance the plane will have to travel to get us to Google's headquarters. The second will be used to plot the driving path we intend to take between the San Francisco airport and the Googleplex.

To begin, click Add a Route, name the route (something like "airplane trip"), and then click your airport. A small, white dot appears on the place you clicked. This is the first point on your line. Now zoom out, scroll over to California, and zoom in on San Francisco. The airport we'll be landing at is on the west side of the bay. Click the airport here, too. As you can see in Figure 1-4, a second white dot appears on the airport and a blue line connects the two points. You can see how far your flight was on the right side of the screen, underneath the route label. Wow, our flight seems to have been over 2000 miles! If you made a mistake and accidentally clicked a few extra times in the process of getting to San Francisco, you can use the Undo Last option. Otherwise, click Save.

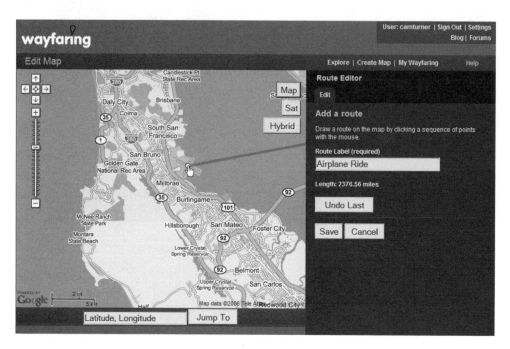

Figure 1-4. *Our flight landing at San Francisco International Airport*

Adding the Destination Point

Now that you're in San Francisco, let's figure out how to get to the Googleplex directly. Click Add a Waypoint. Our destination is Google, so we've called the new point "The Googleplex" and used the address box feature to jump directly to 1600 Amphitheatre Pky, Mountain View, CA 94043. Wayfaring is able to determine latitude and longitude from an address via a process called *geocoding*, which you'll be seeing a lot more of in Chapter 4.

To confirm you're in the right place, click the Sat button on the top-right corner of the map to switch it over to satellite mode. You should see something close to Figure 1-5.

Figure 1-5. *The Googleplex*

Excellent! Save that waypoint.

Adding a Driving Route

Next, let's figure out how far of a drive we have ahead of us. Routes don't really have a starting and ending point in Wayfaring from a visual point of view, so we can start our route from the Googleplex and work our way backwards. Switch back into map (or hybrid) mode so you can see the roads more clearly. From the Map Editor screen, select Add a Route and click the point you just added. Use 10 to 20 dots to carefully trace the trip from Mountain View back up the Bayshore Freeway (US Highway 101) to the airport. By our tracing, we end up with about 23 miles of fun driving on this California highway, as shown in Figure 1-6.

Figure 1-6. *The drive down the Bayshore Freeway to the Googleplex*

That's it. You can use the same principles to make an annotated map of your vacation or calculate how far you're going to travel, and best of all, it's a snap to share it. To see our map live, visit http://www.wayfaring.com/maps/show/17131.

Of course, since this *is* a programming book, you're probably eager to dig into the code and make something really unique. Wayfaring may be nice, but the whole point of a mashup is to automate the process of getting a lot of data combined together.

■**Tip** *Mashup* is a term that originates from DJs and other musicians who create new compositions by "mashing" together samples from existing songs. A classic example of this is *The Grey Album*, which joins the a capella versions of tracks from Jay-Z's *The Black Album* with unauthorized clips from *The White Album*, by The Beatles. In the context of this book, *mashup* refers to the mashing of data from one source with maps from Google.

What's Next?

Now that these examples are out of the way, we hope you're eager to learn how to build your own mashups from the ground up. By the end of Part 1 of this book, you'll have the skills to do everything you've just done on Wayfaring (except the route lines and distances, which are covered in Chapter 10) using JavaScript and XHTML. By the book's conclusion, you'll have learned most of the concepts needed to build your own Wayfaring clone!

So what exactly is to come? We've divided the book into three parts and two appendixes. Part 1 goes through Chapter 4 and deals with the basics that a hobbyist would need to get started. You'll make a map, add some custom pins, and geocode a set of data using freely available services. Part 2 (Chapters 5 through 8) gets into more map development topics, like building a usable interface, dealing with extremely large groups of points, and finding sources of raw information you may need to make your professional map ideas a reality. Part 3 (Chapters 9 through 11) dives into advanced topics: building custom map overlays such as your own info window and tooltip, creating your own map tiles and projections, using the spherical equations necessary to calculate surface areas on the earth, and building your own geocoder from scratch. Finally, one appendix provides a reference guide to the Google Maps version 2 API, and another points to a few places where you can find neat data for extending the examples here, and to inspire your own projects.

We hope you enjoy!

CHAPTER 2

■ ■ ■

Getting Started

In this chapter, you'll learn how to create your first Google map project, plot some markers, and add a bit of interactivity. Because JavaScript plays such a central role in controlling the maps, you'll also start to pick up a few essentials about that language along the way.

In this chapter, you'll see how to do the following:

- Get off the ground with a basic map and a Google Maps API key.

- Separate the map application's JavaScript functions, data, and XHTML.

- Unload finished maps to help browsers free their memory.

- Create map markers and respond to clicks on them with an information pop-up.

The First Map

In this section, you'll obtain a Google Maps API key, and then begin experimenting with it by retrieving Google's starter map.

Keying Up

Before you start a Google Maps web application, you need sign up for a Google Maps API key. To obtain your key, you must accept the Google Maps API Terms of Use, which stipulate, among other things, that you must not steal Google's imagery, obscure the Google logo, or hold Google responsible for its software. Additionally, you're prevented from creating maps that invade privacy or facilitate illegal activities.

Google issues as many keys as you need, but separate domains *must* apply for a separate key, as each one is valid for only a specific domain and subdirectory within that domain. For your first key, you'll want to give Google the root directory of your domain or the space in which you're working. This will allow you to create your project in any subdirectory within your domain. Visit http://www.google.com/apis/maps/signup.html (Figure 2-1) and submit the form to get your key. Throughout this book, nearly all of the examples will require you to include this key in the JavaScript `<script>` element for the Google Maps API, as we're about to demonstrate in Listing 2-1.

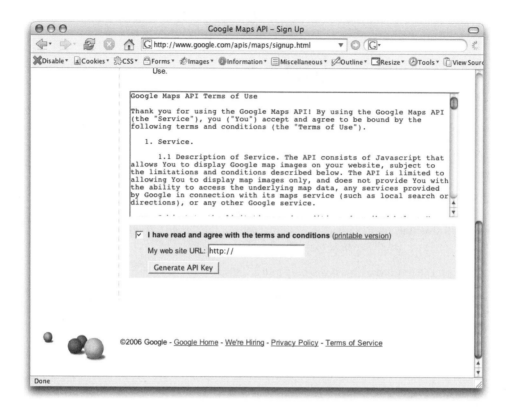

Figure 2-1. *Signing up for an API key. Check the box, and then enter the URL of your webspace.*

■**Note** Why a key? Google has its reasons, which may or may not include seeing what projects are where, which are the most popular, and which may be violating the terms of service. Google is not the only one that makes you authenticate to use an API. Del.icio.us, Amazon, and others all provide services with APIs that require you to first obtain a key.

When you sign up to receive your key, Google will also provide you with a very basic "starter map" to help familiarize you with the fundamental concepts required to integrate a map into your website. We'll begin by dissecting and working with this starter code so you can gain a basic understanding of what's happening.

If you start off using Google's sample, your key is already embedded in the JavaScript. Alternatively, you can—as with all listings—grab the source code from the book's website at `http://googlemapsbook.com` and insert your own key by hand.

Either way, save the code to a file called `index.php`. Your key is that long string of characters following `key=`. (Our key, in the case of this book's website, is `ABQIAAAA33EjxkLYsh9SEveh_MphphQP1y`➥ `R2bHJW2Brl_bW_loKXsyt8cxTKO5Zz-UKoJ6IepTlZRxN8nfTRgw`).

Examining the Sample Map

Once you have the file in Listing 2-1 uploaded to your webspace, check it out in a browser. And ta-da, a map in action!

Listing 2-1. *The Google Maps API Starter Code*

```
<!DOCTYPE html PUBLIC "-//W3C//DTD XHTML 1.0 Strict//EN"
    "http://www.w3.org/TR/xhtml1/DTD/xhtml1-strict.dtd">
<html xmlns="http://www.w3.org/1999/xhtml">
    <head>
        <meta http-equiv="content-type" content="text/html; charset=utf-8"/>
        <title>Google Maps JavaScript API Example</title>
        <script src="http://maps.google.com/maps?file=api&amp;v=2&amp;key=ABQIAAAA➥
33EjxkLYsh9SEveh_MphphQP1yR2bHJW2Brl_bW_lOKXsyt8cxTKO5Zz-UKoJ6Ie➥
pTlZRxN8nfTRgw" type="text/javascript"></script>
        <script type="text/javascript">

        //<![CDATA[

        function load() {
            if (GBrowserIsCompatible()) {
                var map = new GMap2(document.getElementById("map"));
                map.setCenter(new GLatLng(37.4419, -122.1419), 13);
            }
        }

        //]]>
        </script>
    </head>

    <body onload="load()" onunload="GUnload()">
        <div id="map" style="width: 500px; height: 300px"></div>
    </body>
</html>
```

In Listing 2-1, the container holding the map is a standard XHTML web page. A lot of the listing here is just boilerplate—standard initialization instructions for the browser. However, there are three important elements to consider.

First, the head of the document contains a critical script element. Its src attribute points to the location of the API on Google's server, and your key is passed as a parameter:

```
<script src="http://maps.google.com/maps?file=api&amp;v=2&amp;key=YOUR_KEY_HERE"➥
type="text/javascript"></script>
```

Second, the body section of the document contains a div called map:

```
<div id="map" style="width: 500px; height: 300px"></div>
```

Although it appears empty, this is the element in which the map will sit. Currently, a `style` attribute gives it a fixed size; however, it could just as easily be set it to a dynamic size, such as `width: 50%`.

Finally, back in the `head`, there's a `script` element containing a short JavaScript, which is triggered by the document body's `onload` event. It's this code that communicates with Google's API and actually sets up the map.

```
function load() {
    if (GBrowserIsCompatible()) {
        var map = new GMap2(document.getElementById("map"));
        map.setCenter(new GLatLng(37.4419, -122.1419), 13);
    }
}
```

The first line is an `if` statement, which checks that the user's browser is supported by Google Maps. Following that is a statement that creates a `GMap2` object, which is one of several important objects provided by the API. The `GMap2` object is told to hook onto the map `div`, and then it gets assigned to a variable called `map`.

■**Note** Keen readers will note that we've already encountered another of Google's special API objects: `GLatLng`. `GLatLng`, as you can probably imagine, is a pretty important class, that we're going to see a lot more of.

After you have your `GMap2` object in a `map` variable, you can use it to call any of the `GMap2` methods. The very next line, for example, calls the `setCenter()` method to center and zoom the map on Palo Alto, California. Throughout the book, we'll be introducing various methods of each of the API objects, but if you need a quick reference while developing your web applications, you can use Appendix B of this book or view the Google Maps API reference (`http://www.google.com/apis/maps/documentation/`) directly online.

Specifying a New Location

A map centered on Palo Alto is interesting, but it's not exactly groundbreaking. As a first attempt to customize this map, you're going to specify a new location for it to center on.

For this example, we've chosen the Golden Gate Bridge in San Francisco, California (Figure 2-2). It's a large landmark and is visible in the satellite imagery provided on Google Maps (`http://maps.google.com`). You can choose any starting point you like, but if you search for "Golden Gate Bridge" in Google Maps, move the view slightly, and then click Link to This Page, you'll get a URL in your location bar that looks something like this:

```
http://maps.google.com/maps?f=q&ll=37.818361,-122.478032&spn=0.029969,0.05579
```

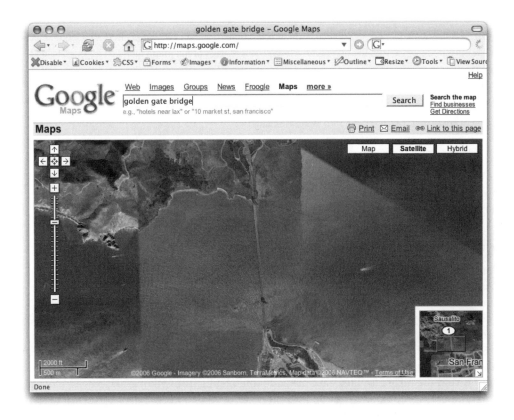

Figure 2-2. *The Golden Gate Bridge satellite imagery from Google Maps*

■Caution If you use Google Maps to search for landmarks, the Link to This Page URL won't immediately contain the latitude and longitude variable but instead have a parameter containing the search terms. To also include the latitude and longitude, you need to adjust the zoom level or move the map so that the link is no longer to the default search position.

It's clear that the URL contains three parameters, separated by ampersands:

```
f = q
ll = 37.818361, -122.478032
spn = 0.029969, 0.05579
```

The `ll` parameter is the important one you'll use to center your map. Its value contains the latitude and longitude of the center of the map in question. For the Golden Gate Bridge, the coordinates are 37.82N and 122.48W.

■**Note** *Latitude* is the number of degrees north or south of the equator, and ranges from −90 (South Pole) to 90 (North Pole). *Longitude* is the number of degrees east or west of the prime meridian at Greenwich, in England, and ranges from −180 (westward) to 180 (eastward). There are several different ways you can record latitude and longitude information. Google uses decimal notation, where a positive or negative number indicates the compass direction. The process of turning a street address into a latitude and longitude is called *geocoding*, and is covered in more detail in Chapter 4.

You can now take the latitude and longitude values from the URL and use them to recenter your own map to the new location. Fortunately, it's a simple matter of plugging the values directly into the GLatLng constructor.

Separating Code from Content

To further improve the cleanliness and readability of your code, you may want to consider separating the JavaScript into a different file. Just as Cascading Style Sheets (CSS) should not be mixed in with HTML, it's best practice to also keep JavaScript separated.

The advantages of this approach become clear as your project increases in size. With large and complicated Google Maps web applications, you could end up with hundreds of lines of JavaScript mixed in with your XHTML. Separating these out not only increases loading speeds, as the browser can cache the JavaScript independently of the XHTML, but their removal also helps prevent the messy and unreadable code that results from mixing XHTML with other programming languages. Your eyes and your text editor will love you if they don't have to deal with mixed XHTML and JavaScript at the same time.

In this case, you'll actually take it one step further and *also* separate the marker data file from the map functions file. This will allow you to easily convert the static data file to a dynamically generated file in later chapters, without the need to touch any of the processing JavaScript.

To accommodate these changes, we've separated the web application's JavaScript functions, data, and XHTML, putting them in separate files called index.php for the XHTML portion of the page, map_functions.js for the behavioral JavaScript code, and map_data.php for the data to plot on the map. Listing 2-2 shows the revised version of the index.php file.

Listing 2-2. *Extrapolated index.php File*

```
<!DOCTYPE html PUBLIC "-//W3C//DTD XHTML 1.0 Strict//EN"➥
"http://www.w3.org/TR/xhtml1/DTD/xhtml1-strict.dtd">
<html xmlns="http://www.w3.org/1999/xhtml">
<head>
    <script src="http://maps.google.com/maps?file=api&amp;v=2&amp;key=➥
ABQIAAAAfAb2RNhzPafOW1mtifapBRI9caN7296ZHDcvjSpGbL7PxwkwBS➥
ZidcfOwy4q2EZpjEJx3rc4Lt5Kg" type="text/javascript"></script>
    <script src="map_data.php" type="text/javascript"></script>
    <script src="map_functions.js" type="text/javascript"></script>
</head>
```

```
<body>
    <div id="map" style="width: 500px; height: 300px"></div>
</body>
</html>
```

Listing 2-2 is the same basic HTML document as before, except that now there are two extra `script` elements inside the `head`. Rather than referencing the external API, these reference local—on the server—JavaScript files called `map_data.php` and `map_functions.js`. For now, you'll leave the `map_data.php` file empty, but it will be used later in the chapter when we demonstrate how to map an existing list of markers. The important thing to note here is that it must be referenced first, before the `map_functions.js` file, so that the data is "available" to the code in the `map_functions.js` file. Listing 2-3 shows the revised `map_functions.js` file.

Listing 2-3. *Extrapolated map_functions.js File*

```
var centerLatitude = 37.818361;
var centerLongitude = -122.478032;
var startZoom = 13;

var map;

function init()
{
    if (GBrowserIsCompatible()) {
        map = new GMap2(document.getElementById("map"));
        var location = new GLatLng(centerLatitude, centerLongitude);
        map.setCenter(location, startZoom);
    }
}

window.onload = init;
```

Although the behavior is almost identical, the JavaScript code in Listing 2-3 has two important changes:

- The starting center point for latitude, longitude, and start zoom level of the map are stored in var variables at the top of the script, so it will be more straightforward to change the initial center point the next time. You won't need to hunt down a `setCenter()` call that's buried somewhere within the code.

- The initialization JavaScript has been moved out of the `body` of the XHTML and into the `map_functions.js` file. Rather than embedding the JavaScript in the body of the XHTML, you can attach a function to the `window.onload` event. Once the page has loaded, this function will be called and the map will be initialized.

For the rest of the examples in this chapter, the `index.php` file will remain exactly as it is in Listing 2-2, and you will need to add code only to the `map_functions.js` and `map_data.php` files to introduce the new features to your map.

■**Caution** It's important to see the difference between init and init(). When you add the parentheses after the function name, it means "execute it." Without the parentheses, it means "give me a reference to it." When you assign a function to an event handler such as document.onload, you want to be very careful that you don't include the parentheses. Otherwise, all you've assigned to the handler is the function's return value, probably a null.

Cleaning Up

One more important thing to do with your map is to be sure to correctly unload it. The extremely dynamic nature of JavaScript's variables means that correctly reclaiming memory (called *garbage collection*) can be a tricky process. As a result, some browsers do it better than others.

Firefox and Safari both seem to struggle with this, but the worst culprit is Internet Explorer. Even up to version 6, simply *closing* a web page is not enough to free all the memory associated with its JavaScript objects. An extended period of surfing JavaScript-heavy sites such as Google Maps could slowly consume all system memory until Internet Explorer is manually closed and restarted.

Fortunately, JavaScript objects can be manually destroyed by setting them equal to null. The Google Maps API now has a special function that will destroy most of the API's objects, which helps keep browsers happy. The function is GUnload(), and to take advantage of it is a simple matter of hooking it onto the body.onunload event, as in Listing 2-4.

Listing 2-4. *Calling GUnload() in map_functions.js*

```
var centerLatitude = 37.818361;
var centerLongitude = -122.478032;
var startZoom = 13;

var map;

function init() {
    if (GBrowserIsCompatible()) {
        map = new GMap2(document.getElementById("map"));
        var location = new GLatLng(centerLatitude, centerLongitude);
        map.setCenter(location, startZoom);
    }
}

window.onload = init;
window.onunload = GUnload;
```

There's no obvious reward for doing this, but it's an excellent practice to follow. As your projects become more and more complex, they will eat up available memory at an increasing rate. On the day that browsers are perfect, this approach will become a hack of yesterday. But for now, it's a quiet way to improve the experience for all your visitors.

Basic Interaction

Centering the map is all well and good, but what else can you do to make this map more exciting? You can add some user interaction.

Using Map Control Widgets

The Google Maps API provides five standard controls that you can easily add to any map:

- GLargeMapControl, the large pan and zoom control, which is used on maps.google.com
- GSmallMapControl, the mini pan and zoom control, which is appropriate for smaller maps
- GScaleControl, the control that shows the metric and imperial scale of the map's current center
- GSmallZoomControl, the two-button zoom control used in driving-direction pop-ups
- GMapTypeControl, which lets the visitor toggle between Map, Satellite, and Hybrid types

---

■**Tip** If you're interested in making your own custom controls, you can do so by extending the GControl class and implementing its various functions. We may discuss this on the googlemapsbook.com blog, so be sure to check it out.

In all cases, it's a matter of instantiating the control object, and then adding it to the map with the GMap2 object's addControl() method. For example, here's how to add the small map control, which you can see as part of the next example in Listing 2-5:

```
map.addControl(new GSmallMapControl());
```

You use an identical process to add all the controls: simply pass in a new instance of the control's class.

■**Note** What does *instantiating* mean? In object-oriented programming, a class is like a blueprint for a type of entity that can be created in memory. When you put new in front of a class name, JavaScript takes the blueprint and actually creates a usable copy (an *instance*) of the object. There's only one GLatLng class, but you can instantiate as many GLatLng *objects* as you need.

Creating Markers

The Google Maps API makes an important distinction between *creating* a marker, or pin, and *adding the marker to a map*. In fact, the map object has a general addOverlay() method, used for both the markers and the white information bubbles.

In order to plot a marker (Figure 2-3), you need the following series of objects:

- A GLatLng object stores the latitude and longitude of the location of the marker.

- An optional GIcon object stores the image that visually represents the marker on the map.

- A GMarker object is the marker itself.

- A GMap2 object has the marker plotted on it, using the addOverlay() method.

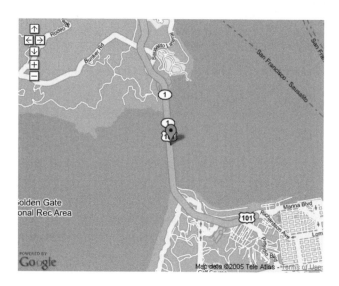

Figure 2-3. *Marker plotted in the middle of the Golden Gate Bridge map*

Does it seem like overkill? It's less scary than it sounds. An updated map_functions.js is presented in Listing 2-5, with the new lines marked in bold.

Listing 2-5. *Plotting a Marker*

```
var centerLatitude = 37.818361;
var centerLongitude = -122.478032;
var startZoom = 13;

var map;

function init()
{
    if (GBrowserIsCompatible()) {
        map = new GMap2(document.getElementById("map"));
        map.addControl(new GSmallMapControl());
        var location = new GLatLng(centerLatitude, centerLongitude);
        map.setCenter(location, startZoom);
```

```
        var marker = new GMarker(location)
        map.addOverlay(marker);
    }
}

window.onload = init;
window.onunload = GUnload;
```

■**Caution** If you try to add overlays to a map before setting the center, it will cause the API to give unpredictable results. Be careful to setCenter() your GMap2 object before adding any overlays to it, even if it's just to a hard-coded dummy location that you intend to change again right away.

See what happened? We assigned the new GLatLng object to a variable, and then we were able to use it twice: first to center the map, and then a second time to create the marker.

The exciting part isn't creating one marker; it's creating many markers. But before we come to that, we must quickly look at the Google Maps facility for showing information bubbles.

WHITHER THOU, GICON?

You can see that we didn't actually use a GIcon object anywhere in Listing 2-5. If we had one defined, it would be possible to make the marker take on a different appearance, like so:

```
var marker = new GMarker(my_GLatLng, my_GIcon);
```

However, when the icon isn't specified, the API assumes the red inverted teardrop as a default. There is a more detailed discussion of how to use the GIcon object in Chapter 3.

Opening Info Windows

It's time to make your map respond to the user! For instance, clicking a marker could reveal additional information about its location (Figure 2-4). The API provides an excellent method for achieving this result: the info window. To know when to open the info window, however, you'll need to listen for a click event on the marker you plotted.

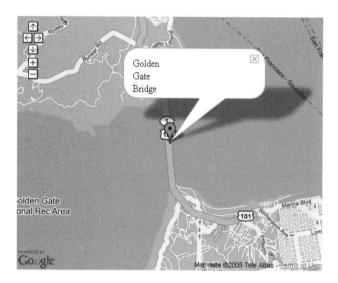

Figure 2-4. *An info window open over the Golden Gate Bridge*

Detecting Marker Clicks

JavaScript is primarily an event-driven language. The init() function that you've been using since Listing 2-3 is hooked onto the window.onload event. Although the browser provides many events such as these, the API gives you a convenient way of hooking up code to various events related to user interaction with the map.

For example, if you had a GMarker object on the map called marker, you could detect marker clicks like so:

```
function handleMarkerClick() {
    alert("You clicked the marker!");
}

GEvent.addListener(marker, 'click', handleMarkerClick);
```

It's workable, but it will be a major problem once you have a lot of markers. Fortunately, the dynamic nature of JavaScript yields a terrific shortcut here. You can actually just pass the function *itself* directly to addListener() as a parameter:

```
GEvent.addListener(marker, 'click',
    function() {
        alert("You clicked the marker!");
    }
);
```

Opening the Info Window

Chapter 3 will discuss the info window in more detail. The method we'll demonstrate here is openInfoWindowHtml(). Although you can open info windows over arbitrary locations on the map, here you'll open them above markers only, so the code can take advantage of a shortcut method built into the GMarker object:

```
marker.openInfoWindowHtml(description);
```

Of course, the whole point is to open the info window only when the marker is clicked, so you'll need to combine this code with the addListener() function:

```
GEvent.addListener(marker, 'click',
    function() {
        marker.openInfoWindowHtml(description);
    }
);
```

Finally, you'll wrap up all the code for generating a pin, an event, and an info window into a single function, called addMarker(), in Listing 2-6.

Listing 2-6. *Creating a Marker with an Info Window*

```
var centerLatitude = 37.818361;
var centerLongitude = -122.478032;
var description = 'Golden Gate Bridge';

var startZoom = 13;
var map;

function addMarker(latitude, longitude, description) {
    var marker = new GMarker(new GLatLng(latitude, longitude));

    GEvent.addListener(marker, 'click',
        function() {
            marker.openInfoWindowHtml(description);
        }
    );

    map.addOverlay(marker);
}

function init() {
    if (GBrowserIsCompatible()) {
        map = new GMap2(document.getElementById("map"));
        map.addControl(new GSmallMapControl());
        map.setCenter(new GLatLng(centerLatitude, centerLongitude), startZoom);

        addMarker(centerLatitude, centerLongitude, description);
    }
}

window.onload = init;
window.onunload = GUnload;
```

This is a nice clean function that does everything you need for plotting a pin with a click-able information bubble. Now you're perfectly set up for plotting a whole bunch of markers on your map.

A List of Points

In Listing 2-3, we introduced the variables `centerLongitude` and `centerLatitude`. Global variables like these are fine for a single centering point, but what you *probably* want to do is store a whole series of values and map a bunch of markers all at once. Specifically, you want a list of latitude and longitude pairs representing the points of the markers you'll plot.

Using Arrays and Objects

To store the list of points, you can combine the power of JavaScript's `array` and `object` constructs. An *array* stores a list of numbered entities. An *object* stores a list of keyed entities, similar to how a dictionary matches words to definitions. Compare these two lines:

```
var myArray = ['John', 'Sue', 'James', 'Edward'];
var myObject = {'John': 19, 'Sue': 21, 'James': 24, 'Edward': 18};
```

To access elements of the array, you must use their numeric indices. So, `myArray[0]` is equal to `'John'`, and `myArray[3]` is equal to `'Edward'`.

The object, however, is slightly more interesting. In the object, the names *themselves* are the indices, and the numbers are the values. To look up how old Sue is, all you do is check the value of `myObject['Sue']`.

■**Note** For accessing members of an object, JavaScript allows both `myObject['Sue']` and the alternative notation `myObject.Sue`. The second is usually more convenient, but the first is important if the value of the index you want to access is stored in *another* variable, for example, `myObject[someName]`.

For each marker you plot, you want an object that looks like this:

```
var myMarker = {
        'latitude': 37.818361,
        'longitude': -122.478032,
        'name': 'Golden Gate Bridge'
};
```

Having the data organized this way is useful because the related information is grouped as "children" of a common parent object. The variables are no longer just `latitude` and `longitude`—now they are `myMarker.latitude` and `myMarker.longitude`.

Most likely, for your application you'll want more than one marker on the map. To proceed from one to many, it's just a matter of having an *array* of these objects:

```
var myMarkers = [Marker1, Marker2, Marker3, Marker4];
```

Then you can cycle through the array, accessing the members of each object and plotting a marker for each entity.

When the nesting is combined into one step (Figure 2-5), it becomes a surprisingly elegant data structure, as in Listing 2-7.

Listing 2-7. *A JavaScript Data Structure for a List of Locations*

```
var markers = [
    {
        'latitude': 37.818361,
        'longitude': -122.478032,
        'name': 'Golden Gate Bridge'
    },
    {
        'latitude': 40.6897,
        'longitude': -74.0446,
        'name': 'Statue of Liberty'
    },
    {
        'latitude': 38.889166,
        'longitude': -77.035307,
        'name': 'Washington Monument'
    }
];
```

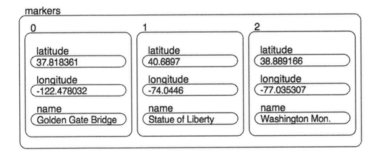

Figure 2-5. *A series of objects stored inside an array*

As you'll see in the next section, JavaScript provides some terrific methods for working with data in this type of format.

Note In this book, you'll see primarily MySQL used for storing data permanently. Some people however, have proposed the exact format in Figure 2-5 as an alternative to XML, calling it JSON, for JavaScript Object Notation. While there are some advantages, JSON's plethora of punctuation can be intimidating to a less technical person. You can find more information on JSON at http://json.org. We'll still be using a lot of JSON-like structures for communicating data from the server to the browser.

Iterating

JavaScript, like many languages, provides a for loop—a way of repeating a block of code *for* so many iterations, using a counter. One way of cycling through your list of points would be a loop such as this:

```
for (id = 0; id < markers.length; id++) {
        // create a marker at markers[id].latitude, markers[id].longitude
}
```

However, JavaScript also provides a much classier way of setting this up. It's called a for in loop. Watch for the difference:

```
for (id in markers) {
        // create a marker at markers[id].latitude, markers[id].longitude
}
```

Wow. It automatically gives you back every index that exists in an array or object, without needing to increment anything manually, or ever test boundaries. Clearly, you'll want to use a for in loop to cycle over the array of points.

Until now, the map_data.php file has been empty and you've been dealing mainly with the map_functions.js file. To show a list of markers, you need to include the list, so this is where map_data.php comes in. For this chapter, you're not going to actually use any PHP, but the intention is that you can populate that file from database queries or some other data store. We've named the file with the PHP extension so you can reuse the same base code in later chapters without the need to edit everything and start over. For now, pretend the PHP file is like any other normal JavaScript file and create your list of markers there. As an example, populate your map_data.php file with the structure from Listing 2-7.

To get that structure plotted, it's just a matter of wrapping the marker-creation code in a for in loop, as shown in Listing 2-8.

Listing 2-8. *map_functions.js Modified to Use the Markers from map_data.php*

```
var map;
var centerLatitude = -95.0446;
var centerLongitude = 40.6897;
var startZoom = 3;

function addMarker(longitude, latitude, description) {
    var marker = new GMarker(new GLatLng(latitude, longitude));

    GEvent.addListener(marker, 'click',
        function() {
            marker.openInfoWindowHtml(description);
        }
    );

    map.addOverlay(marker);
}
```

```
function init() {
    if (GBrowserIsCompatible()) {
        map = new GMap2(document.getElementById("map"));
        map.addControl(new GSmallMapControl());
        map.setCenter(new GLatLng(centerLatitude, centerLongitude), startZoom);

        for(id in markers) {
            addMarker(markers[id].latitude, markers[id].longitude, markers[id].name);
        }
    }
}

window.onload = init;
window.onunload = GUnload;
```

Nothing here should be much of a surprise. You can see that the addMarker() function is called for each of the markers, so you have three markers and three different info windows.

Summary

With this chapter complete, you've made an incredible amount of progress! You've looked at several good programming practices, seen how to plot multiple markers, and popped up the info window. And all of this is in a tidy, reusable package.

So what will you do with it? Plot your favorite restaurants? Mark where you parked the car? Show the locations of your business? Maybe mark your band's upcoming gigs?

The possibilities are endless, but it's really just the beginning. In the next chapter, you'll be expanding on what you learned here by creating your map data dynamically and learning the key to building a real community: accepting user-submitted information. After that, the weird and wonderful science of geocoding—turning street addresses into latitudes and longitudes—will follow, along with a variety of tips and tricks you can use to add flavor to your web applications.

CHAPTER 3

■■■

Interacting with the User and the Server

Now that you've created your first map (in Chapter 2) and had a chance to perform some initial experiments using the Google Maps API, it's time to make your map a little more useful and dynamic. Most, if not all, of the best Google Maps mashups rely on interaction with the user in order to customize the information displayed on the map. As you've already learned, it's relatively easy to create a map and display a fixed set of points using static HTML and a bit of JavaScript. Anyone with a few minutes of spare time and some programming knowledge could create a simple map that would, for example, display the markers of all the places he visited on his vacation last year. A static map such as this is nice to look at, but once you've seen it, what would make you return to the page to look at it again? To keep people coming back and to hold their attention for longer than a few seconds, you need a map with added interactivity and a bit of flair.

You can add interactivity to your map mashups in a number of ways. For instance, you might offer some additional detail for each marker using the info window bubbles introduced in Chapter 2, or use something more elaborate such as filtering the markers based on search criteria. Google Maps, Google's public mapping site (http://maps.google.com/) is a mashup of business addresses and a map to visually display where the businesses are located. It provides the required interactivity by allowing you to search for specific businesses, and listing other relevant businesses nearby, but then goes even further to offer driving directions to the marked locations. Allowing you to see the location of a business you're looking for is great, but telling you how to get there in your car, now that's interactivity! Without the directions, the map would be an image with a bunch of pretty dots, and you would be left trying to figure out how to get to each dot. Regardless of how it's done, the point is that interacting with the map is always important, but don't go overboard and overwhelm your users with too many options.

In this chapter, we'll explore a few examples of how to provide interactivity in your map using the Google Maps API, and you'll see how you can use the API to save and retrieve information from your server. While building a small web application, you'll learn how to do the following:

- Trigger events on your map and markers to add either new markers or info windows.

- Modify the content of info windows attached to a map or to individual markers.

- Use Google's GXmlHttp object to communicate with your server.

- Improve your web application by changing the appearance of the markers.

Going on a Treasure Hunt

To help you learn about some of the interactive features of the Google Maps API, you're going to go on a treasure hunt and create a map of all the treasures you find. The treasures in this case are geocaches, those little plastic boxes of goodies that are hidden all over the earth.

For those of you who are not familiar with *geocaches* (not to be confused with geocoding, which we will discuss in the next chapter), or *geocaching* as the activity is commonly referred to, it is a global "hide-and-seek" game that can be played by anyone with a Global Positioning System (GPS) device (Figure 3-1) and some treasure to hide and seek. People worldwide place small caches of trinkets in plastic containers, and then distribute their GPS locations using the Internet. Other people then follow the latitude and longitude coordinates and attempt to locate the hidden treasures within the cache. Upon finding a cache, they exchange an item in the cache for something of their own.

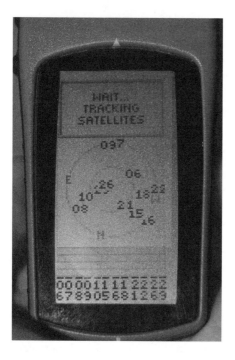

Figure 3-1. *A common handheld GPS device used by geocachers to locate hidden geocaches*

Note For more information about geocaching, check out the official Geocaching website (http://www. geocaching.com) or pick up *Geocaching: Hike and Seek with Your GPS*, by Erik Sherman (http://www.apress. com/book/bookDisplay.html?bID=194).

As you create your interactive geocache treasure map, you'll learn how to do the following:

- Create a map and add a JavaScript event trigger using the `GEvent.addListener()` method to react to clicks by the users, so that people who visit the map can mark their finds on the map.

- Ask users for additional information about their finds using an info window and an embedded HTML form.

- Save the latitude, longitude, and additional information in the form to your server using the `GXmlHttp` Asynchronous JavaScript and XML (Ajax) object on the client side and PHP on the server.

- Retrieve the existing markers and their additional information from the server using Ajax and PHP.

- Re-create the map upon loading by inserting new markers from a server-side list, each with an info window to display its information.

For this chapter, we're not going to discuss any CSS styling of the map and its contents; we'll leave all that up to you.

Creating the Map and Marking Points

You'll begin the map for this chapter from the same set of files introduced in Chapter 2, which include the following:

- `index.php` to hold the XHTML of the page

- `map_functions.js` to hold the JavaScript functionality

- `map_data.php` to create a JavaScript array and objects representing each location on the map

Additionally, you'll create a file called `storeMarker.php` to save information back to the server and another file called `retrieveMarkers.php` to retrieve XML using Ajax, but we'll get to those later.

Starting the Map

To start, copy the `index.php` file from Listing 2-2 and the `map_functions.js` file from Listing 2-3 into a new directory for this chapter. Also, create an empty `map_data.php` file and empty `storeMarker.php` and `retrieveMarkers.php` files.

While building the map for this chapter and other projects, you'll be adding auxiliary functions to the `map_functions.js` file. You may have noticed in Chapter 2 that you declared the `map` variable outside the `init()` function in Listing 2-2. Declaring `map` outside the `init()` function allows you to reference `map` at any time and from any auxiliary functions you add to the `map_functions.js` file. It will also ensure you're targeting the same `map` object. Also, you may want to add some of the control objects introduced in Chapter 2, such as `GMapTypeControl`. Listing 3-1 highlights the `map` variable and additional controls.

Listing 3-1. *Highlights for map_functions.js*

```
var centerLatitude = 37.4419;
var centerLongitude = -122.1419;
var startZoom = 12;

var map;

function init() {
    if (GBrowserIsCompatible()) {
        map = new GMap2(document.getElementById("map"));
        map.addControl(new GSmallMapControl());
        map.addControl(new GMapTypeControl());
        map.setCenter(new GLatLng(centerLatitude, centerLongitude), startZoom);
    }
}

window.onload = init;
window.onunload = GUnload;
```

Now you have a solid starting point for your web application. When viewed in your web browser, the page will have a simple map with controls centered on Palo Alto, California (Figure 3-2). For this example, the starting GLatLng is not important, so feel free to change it to some other location if you wish.

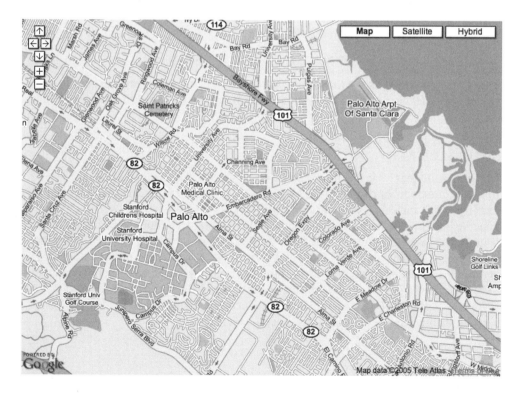

Figure 3-2. *Starting map with controls centered on Palo Alto, California*

Listening to User Events

The purpose of your map is to allow visitors to add markers wherever they click. To capture the clicks on the map, you'll need to trigger a JavaScript function to execute whenever the map area is clicked. As you saw in Chapter 2, Google's API allows you to attach these triggers, called *event listeners*, to your map objects through the use of the GEvent.addListener() method. You can add event listeners for a variety of events, including move and click, but in this case, you are interested only in users clicking the map, not moving it or dragging it around.

■**Tip** If you refer to the Google Maps API documentation in Appendix B, you'll notice a wide variety of events for both the GMap2 and the GMarker objects, as well as a few others. Each of these different events can be used to add varying amounts of interactivity to your map. For example, you could use the moveend event for the GMap2 to trigger an Ajax call and retrieve points for the new area of the map. For the geocaching map example, you could also use the GMarker's infowindowclose event to check to see if the information in the form has been saved and if not, ask the user what to do. You can also attach events to Document Object Model (DOM) elements using GEvent.addDomListener() and trigger an event using JavaScript with the GEvent.trigger() method.

The GEvent.addListener() method handles all the necessary code required to watch for and trigger each of the events. All you need to do is tell it which object to watch, which event to listen for, and which function to execute when it's triggered.

```
GEvent.addListener(map, "click", function(overlay, latlng) {
    //your code
});
```

Given the source map and the event click, this example will trigger the function to run any code you wish to implement.

Take a look at the modification to the init() function in Listing 3-2 to see how easy it is to add this event listener to your existing code and use it to create markers the same way you did in Chapter 2. The difference is that in Chapter 2, you used new GLatLng() to create the latitude and longitude location for the markers, whereas here, instead of creating a new GLatLng, you can use the latlng variable passed into the event listener's handler function. The latlng variable is a GLatLng representation of the latitude and longitude where you clicked on the map. The overlay variable is the overlay where the clicked location resides if you clicked on a marker or another overlay object.

Listing 3-2. *Using the addListener() Method to Create a Marker at the Click Location*

```
function init() {
    if (GBrowserIsCompatible()) {
        map = new GMap2(document.getElementById("map"));
        map.addControl(new GSmallMapControl());
        map.addControl(new GMapTypeControl());
        map.setCenter(new GLatLng(centerLatitude, centerLongitude), startZoom);
```

```
        //allow the user to click the map to create a marker
        GEvent.addListener(map, "click", function(overlay, latlng) {
            var marker = new GMarker(latlng)
            map.addOverlay(marker);
        });
    }
}
```

Ta-da! Now, with a slight code addition and one simple click, anyone worldwide could visit your map page and add as many markers as they want (Figure 3-3). However, all the markers will disappear as soon as the user leaves the page, never to be seen again. To keep the markers around, you need to collect some information and send it back to the server for storage using the GXmlHttp object or the GDownloadUrl object, which we'll discuss in the "Using Google's Ajax Object" section later in this chapter.

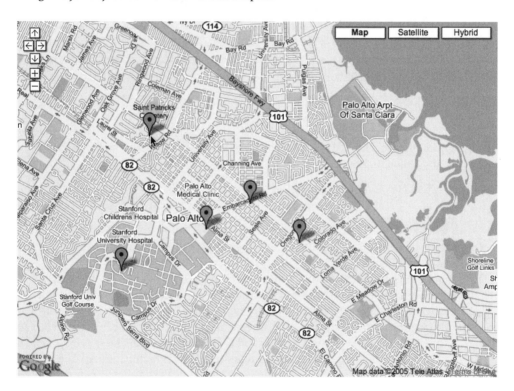

Figure 3-3. *New markers created by clicking on the map*

RETRIEVING THE LATITUDE AND LONGITUDE FROM A MAP CLICK

When you click on a Google map, the `latlng` variable passed into the event listener's handler function is a `GLatLng` object with `lat()` and `lng()` methods. Using the `lat()` and `lng()` methods makes it relatively easy for you to retrieve the latitude and longitude of any point on earth simply by zooming in and clicking on the map. This is particularly useful when you are trying to find the latitude and longitude of places that do not have readily accessible latitude/longitude information for addresses.

In countries where there is excellent latitude and longitude information, such as the United States, Canada, and more recently, France, Italy, Spain and Germany, you can often use an address lookup service to retrieve the latitude and longitude of a street address. But in other locations, such as the United Kingdom, the data is limited or inaccurate. In the case where data can't be readily retrieved by computer, manual human entry of points may be required. For more information about geocoding and using addresses to find latitude and longitude, see Chapter 4.

Additionally, If you want to retrieve the X and Y coordinates of a position on the map in pixels on the screen, you can use the `fromLatLngToDivPixel()` method of the `GMap2` object. By passing in a `GLatLng` object, `GMap2.fromLatLngToDivPixel(latlng)` will return a `GPoint` representation of the X and Y offset relative to the DOM element containing the map.

Asking for More Information with an Info Window

You could simply collect the latitude and longitude of each marker on your map, but just the location of the markers would provide only limited information to the people browsing your map. Remember interactivity is key, so you want to provide a little more than just a marker. For the geocaching map, visitors really want to know what was found at each location. To provide this extra information, let's create a little HTML form. When asking for input of any type in a web browser, you need to use HTML form elements. In this case, let's put the form in an info window indicating where the visitor clicked.

As introduced in Chapter 2, the info window is the cartoon-like bubble that often appears when you click map markers (Figure 3-4). It is used by Google Maps to allow you to enter the To Here or From Here information for driving directions, or to show you a zoomed view of the map at each point in the directions. Info windows do not need to be linked to markers on the map. They can also be created on the map itself to indicate locations where no marker is present.

Figure 3-4. *An empty info window*

You're going to use the info window for two purposes:

- It will display the information about each existing marker when the marker is clicked.

- It will hold a little HTML form so that your geocachers can tell you what they've found.

■**Note** When we introduce the GXmlHttp object in the "Using Google's Ajax Object" section later in this chapter, we'll explain how to save the content of the info window to your server.

Creating an Info Window on the Map

In Listing 3-2, you used the event listener to create a marker on your map where it was clicked. Rather than creating markers when you click the map, you'll modify your existing code to create an info window. To create an info window directly on the map object, call the openInfoWindow() method of the map:

```
GMap2.openInfoWindow(GLatLng, htmlDomElem, GInfoWindowOptions);
```

openInfoWindow() takes a GLatLng as the first parameter and an HTML DOM document element as the second parameter. The last parameter, GInfoWindowOptions, is optional unless you want to modify the default settings of the window.

For a quick demonstration, modify Listing 3-2 to use the following event listener, which opens an info window when the map is clicked, rather than creating a new marker:

```
GEvent.addListener(map, "click", function(overlay, latlng) {
    map.openInfoWindow (latlng,document.createTextNode("You clicked here!"));
});
```

Now when you click the map, you'll see an info window pop up with its base pointing at the position you just clicked with the content "You clicked here!" (Figure 3-5).

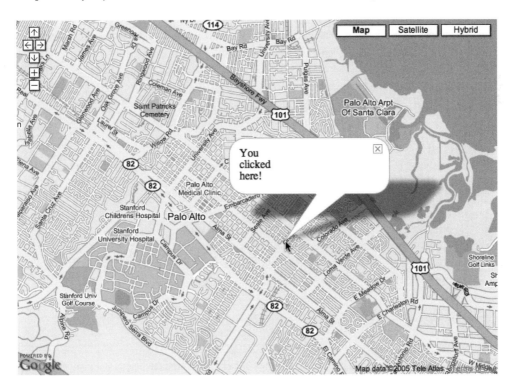

Figure 3-5. *An info window created when clicking the map*

Embedding a Form into the Info Window

When geocachers want to create a new marker, you'll first prompt them to enter some information about their treasure. You'll want to know the geocache's location (this will be determined using the point where they clicked the map), what they found at the location, and what they left behind. To accomplish this in your form, you'll need the following:

- A text field for entering information about what they found

- A text field for entering information about what they left behind

- A hidden field for the longitude

- A hidden field for the latitude

- A submit button

The HTML form used for the example is shown in Listing 3-3, but as you can see in Listing 3-4, you are going to use the JavaScript Document Object Model (DOM) object and methods to create the form element. You need to use DOM because the GMarker.openInfoWindow() method expects an HTML DOM element as the second parameter, not simply a string of HTML.

■**Tip** If you want to make the form a little more presentable, you could easily add ids and/or classes to the form elements and use CSS styles to format them accordingly.

Listing 3-3. *HTML Version of the Form for the Info Window*

```
<form action="" onsubmit="storeMarker(); return false;">
    <fieldset style="width:150px;">
        <legend>New Marker</legend>
        <label for="found">Found</label>
        <input type="text" id="found" style="width:100%;"/>
        <label for="left">Left</label>
        <input type="text" id="left" style="width:100%;"/>
        <input type="submit" value="Save"/>
        <input type="hidden" id="longitude"/>
        <input type="hidden" id="latitude"/>
    </fieldset>
</form>
```

■**Note** You may notice the form in Listing 3-3 has an onsubmit event attribute that calls a storeMarker() JavaScript function. The storeMarker() function does not yet exist in your script, and if you try to click the *Save* button, you'll get a JavaScript error. Ignore this for now, as you'll create the storeMarker() function in the "Saving Data with GXmlHttp" section later in the chapter, when you save the form contents to the server.

Listing 3-4. *Adding the DOM HTML Form to the Info Window*

```
GEvent.addListener(map, "click", function(overlay, latlng) {

    //create an HTML DOM form element
    var inputForm = document.createElement("form");
    inputForm.setAttribute("action","");
    inputForm.onsubmit = function() {storeMarker(); return false;};

    //retrieve the longitude and lattitude of the click point
    var lng = latlng.lng();
    var lat = latlng.lat();

    inputForm.innerHTML = '<fieldset style="width:150px;">'
        + '<legend>New Marker</legend>'
        + '<label for="found">Found</label>'
        + '<input type="text" id="found" style="width:100%;"/>'
        + '<label for="left">Left</label>'
        + '<input type="text" id="left" style="width:100%;"/>'
        + '<input type="submit" value="Save"/>'
        + '<input type="hidden" id="longitude" value="' + lng + '"/>'
        + '<input type="hidden" id="latitude" value="' + lat + '"/>'
        + '</fieldset>';

    map.openInfoWindow (latlng,inputForm);
});
```

■**Caution** When creating the DOM `form` element, you need to use the `setAttribute()` method to define things like `name`, `action`, `target`, and `method`, but once you venture beyond these basic four, you may begin to notice inconsistencies. For example, using `setAttribute()` to define `onsubmit` works fine in Mozilla-based browsers but not in Microsoft Internet Explorer browsers. For cross-browser compatibility, you need to define `onsubmit` using a function, as you did in Listing 3-4. For more detailed information regarding DOM and how to use it, check out the DOM section of the W3Schools website at `http://www.w3schools.com/dom/`.

After you've changed the `GEvent.addListener()` call in Listing 3-2 to the one in Listing 3-4, when you click your map, you'll see an info window containing your form (Figure 3-6).

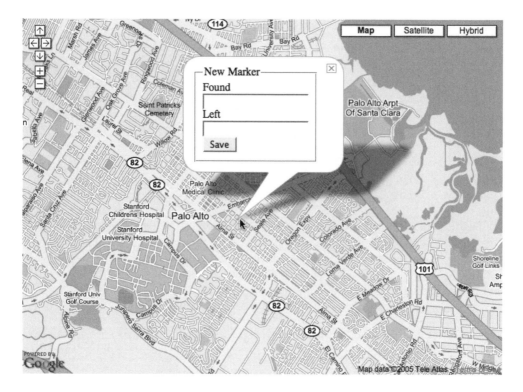

Figure 3-6. *The info window with an embedded form*

In Listing 3-4, the latitude and longitude elements of the form have been pre-populated with the latlng.lat() and latlng.lng() values from the GLatLng object passed in to the event listener. This allows you to later save the latitude and longitude coordinates and re-create the marker in the exact position when you retrieve the data from the server. Also, once the information has been saved for the new location, you can use this latitude and longitude to instantly create a marker at the new location, bypassing the need to refresh the web browser to show the newly saved point.

If you click again elsewhere on the map, you'll also notice your info window disappears and reappears at the location of the new click. As a restriction of the Google Maps API, you can have only one instance of the info window open at any time. When you click elsewhere on the map, the original info window is destroyed and a brand-new one is created. Be aware that it is not simply moved from place to place.

You can demonstrate the destructive effect of creating a new info window yourself by filling in the form (Figure 3-7), and then clicking elsewhere on the map without clicking the *Save* button. You'll notice that the information you entered in the form disappears (Figure 3-8) because the original info window is destroyed and a new one is created.

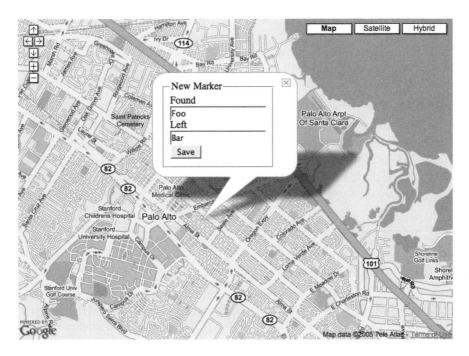

Figure 3-7. *Info window with populated form information*

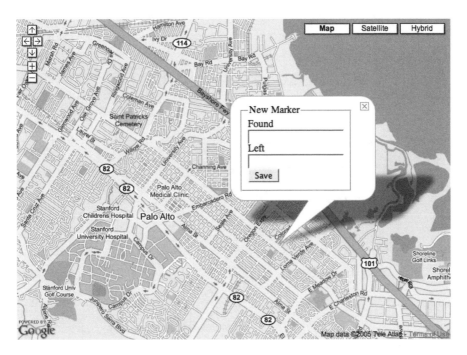

Figure 3-8. *New info window that has lost the previously supplied information*

Earlier, when you created the info window containing "You clicked here!" the same thing happened. Each marker had the same content ("You clicked here!"), so it just *appeared* as though the info window was simply moving around.

Tip If you've taken some time to review the Google Maps API in Appendix B, you might be wondering why you couldn't use the GMap2.openInfoWindowHtml() method to add the form to the info window. After all, it lets you use an HTML string rather than an HTML DOM element. The short answer is you can. In version 1 of the API, openInfoWindowHtml() required a marker to exist on the map first, whereas openInfoWindow() allowed you to open an info window at a specified point without a marker. We chose to use the openInfoWindow() method here so that you would be able to see how the DOM structure and click actions interact with the info window.

Avoiding an Ambiguous State

When creating your web applications, be sure not to create the marker until after you've verified the information and saved it to the server. If you create the marker first and the user then closes the info window using the window's close button (Figure 3-9), there would be a marker on the map that wasn't recorded on the server (Figure 3-10).

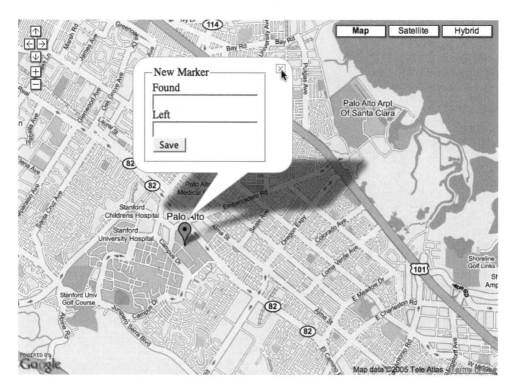

Figure 3-9. *Using the close (X) button to close the info window*

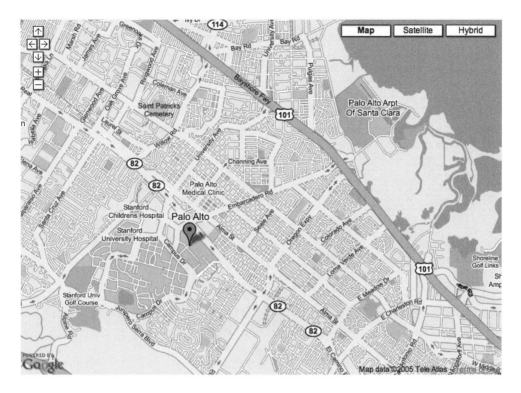

Figure 3-10. *Marker left behind by closing the window*

By creating the marker only after the data has been saved, you ensure the integrity of the map and keep the visible markers in sync with the stored markers on the server.

If you want, you can save the marker information in two steps: first send just the latitude and longitude to save the marker's location, and then send a second request to save the additional information, if any. Storing the latitude and longitude immediately may seem like a logical idea, until you realize that users may click the map in the wrong location and inadvertently add a bunch of points that don't really mean anything. For the geocaching map, you want to be sure there is information associated with each point, so you need to save all the information in one request.

■**Caution** Don't confuse the GMap2.openInfoWindow() method with the GMarker.openInfoWindow() method. The map and marker objects have similar properties and methods; however, their parameters differ. You need to use the GMap2 methods when creating info windows attached to the map itself, but if you have an existing marker, you could then use the GMarker methods to attach an info window to the marker. The GMarker methods can't be used to create an info window without a marker.

INFO WINDOWS THAT ZOOM

`GMap2.showMapBlowup()` and `GMarker.showMapBlowup()` are two other methods in the Google Maps API that will let you create info windows. These info windows are special and contain a zoomed-in view of the map. For example, `map.showMapBlowup(new GLatLng(37.4419, -122.1419), 3, G_SATELLITE_ TYPE)` will display a small satellite map at zoom level 3 centered on Palo Alto, California. If you create the map blowup in an event listener, you can zoom in on any point you click on your map.

Controlling the Info Window Size

When you add content to the info window, it will automatically expand to encompass the content you've placed in it. The content container will expand in the same way a `<div>` tag expands to its internal content. To provide a bit of control over how it expands, you can add CSS styles to the content of the info window in the same way you would in a regular HTML page.

In Listings 3-3 and 3-4, the `<fieldset>` element was assigned a width of 150px, forcing the info window's content container to 150 pixels wide (Figure 3-11). Also, the text `<input>` elements were set to a width of 100% to display a simple clean form. (For more tips and tricks regarding info windows, see Chapter 9.)

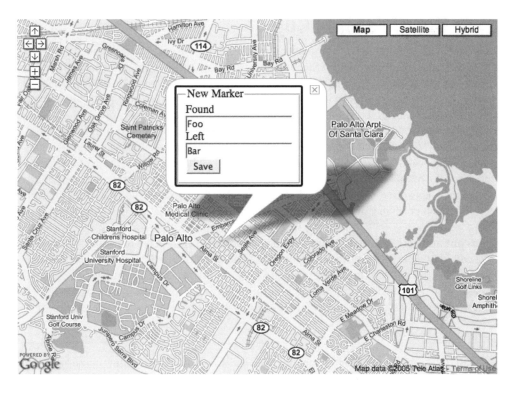

Figure 3-11. *Info window with an inner width of 150 pixels*

HOW TO CHANGE THE STYLE OF THE INFO WINDOW

Getting tired of the cartoon bubble and want to create something fancier with the info window API? Sorry, you're out of luck—well, sort of.

Currently, the Google Maps API doesn't allow you to change the style of the info window, but you could create your own using the GOverlay class. If you're interested, check out Chapter 9, where you'll learn how to create your own info window, as in the following example.

Using Google's Ajax Object

To save the markers entered by your geocaching visitors, you're going to upgrade to "Web 2.0" and use only Ajax to communicate with your server. Ajax relies completely on JavaScript running in your visitor's web browser; without JavaScript running, Ajax simply won't work. You can argue that using a strictly JavaScript-based Ajax interface might not be a good idea. You read everywhere that in order to be good coders and offer compliant services, you should always have an alternative solution to JavaScript-based user interfaces, and that's completely true, but the Google Maps API itself doesn't offer an alternative for JavaScript-disabled browsers. Therefore, if geocachers are visiting your page without the ability to use JavaScript, they're not going to see the map! Feel free to build alternative solutions for all your other web tools, and we strongly suggest that you do, but when dealing strictly with the Google Maps API, there isn't really much point in a non-JavaScript solution, since without JavaScript, the map itself is useless.

To communicate with your server, Google has provided you access to its integrated Ajax object called GXmlHttp. If you want to spend the time, you could roll your own Ajax code. If you're a fan of one of the many free libraries such as Prototype (http://prototype.conio.net), you could also use one of those. For this example, we'll stick to the Google Maps API and the GXmlHttp object, as it's already loaded for you and doesn't require you to include anything else.

■**Caution** The Google GXmlHttp object, and any other Ajax script based on the XmlHttpRequest object, allows you to query only within the domain where the map is served. For example, if your map were at http://example.com/webapp/, then the GXmlHttp.request() method can retrieve data only from scripts located in the http://example.com domain. You can't retrieve data from another domain such as http://jeffreysambells.com, as the request would break the web browser's "Same Origin" security policy (http://www.mozilla.org/projects/security/components/same-origin.html). Using a little JavaScript trickery to dynamically add <script> tags to the page does allow you to get around this policy but requires you to do special things on the server side as well. For an example of how to do this, check out the XssHttpRequest object at http://jeffreysambells.com/posts/2006/03/06/centralized_ajax_services/.

To implement the GXmlHttp object, a few things need to happen when users click the Save button:

- The information in your form needs to be sent to the server and verified for integrity.

- The information needs to be stored as necessary.

- Your server-side script needs to respond back to the client-side JavaScript to let the client know that everything was successful and send back any necessary information.

- The client-side JavaScript needs to indicate to the user that there was either an error or a successful response.

To accomplish this, let's send the information back to the server and store it in a flat XML file. Then, when responding that everything is okay, let's create a new marker on the map with the new information to confirm to the user that the data was successfully saved.

Saving Data with GXmlHttp

To send information to the server using the GXmlHttp object, first you need to retrieve the information from the form in the info window you created. Referring back to Listings 3-3 and 3-4, you'll notice that each of the form elements has a unique id associated with it. Since you're using the Ajax method to send data, the form will not actually submit to the server using the traditional POST method. To submit the data, you retrieve the values of the form by using the JavaScript document.getElementById() method and concatenate each of the values onto the GET string of the GXmlHttp request object. Then using the onreadystatechange() method of the GXmlHttp object, you can process the request when it is complete.

Listing 3-5 shows the storeMarker() and createMarker() functions to add to your map_functions.js file. Also, if you haven't already done so, create the storeMarker.php file in the same directory as your HTML document and create an empty data.xml file to store your marker data. Be sure to give the data.xml file the appropriate write permissions for your server environment.

Tip For more information about the XmlHttpRequest object and using it to send data via the POST method, see the W3Schools page at http://www.w3schools.com/xml/xml_http.asp.

Listing 3-5. *Sending Data to the Server Using GXmlHttp*

```
function storeMarker(){
    var lng = document.getElementById("longitude").value;
    var lat = document.getElementById("latitude").value;

    var getVars =  "?found=" + document.getElementById("found").value
        + "&left=" + document.getElementById("left").value
        + "&lng=" + lng
        + "&lat=" + lat ;

    var request = GXmlHttp.create();

    //open the request to storeMarker.php on your server
    request.open('GET', 'storeMarker.php' + getVars, true);
    request.onreadystatechange = function() {
        if (request.readyState == 4) {
            //the request is complete

            var xmlDoc = request.responseXML;
```

```
            //retrieve the root document element (response)
            var responseNode = xmlDoc.documentElement;

            //retrieve the type attribute of the node
            var type = responseNode.getAttribute("type");

            //retrieve the content of the responseNode
            var content = responseNode.firstChild.nodeValue;

            //check to see if it was an error or success
            if(type!='success') {
                alert(content);
            } else {
                //create a new marker and add its info window
                var latlng = new GLatLng(parseFloat(lat),parseFloat(lng));
                var marker = createMarker(latlng, content);
                map.addOverlay(marker);
                map.closeInfoWindow();
            }
        }
    }
    request.send(null);
    return false;
}

function createMarker(latlng, html) {
    var marker = new GMarker(latlng);
    GEvent.addListener(marker, 'click', function() {
        var markerHTML = html;
        marker.openInfoWindowHtml(markerHTML);
    });
    return marker;
}
```

The storeMarker() function you just added is responsible for sending the marker information to the server through Ajax. It retrieves the information from the form and sends it to the storeMarker.php script in Listing 3-6 using the GXmlHttp object. You can also see that the createMarker() function is used to create the GMarker object and populate the info window. By creating the GMarker in another function, you can reuse the same function later when retrieving markers from the server (in Listing 3-8, later in the chapter).

Listing 3-6. *storeMarker.php Server-Side Script Used to Store the Marker Information in XML Format*

```php
<?php

header('Content-Type: text/xml');

$lat = (float)$_GET['lat'];
$lng = (float)$_GET['lng'];
$found = htmlspecialchars(strip_tags(utf8_encode($_GET['found'])));
$left = htmlspecialchars(strip_tags(utf8_encode($_GET['left'])));


//create an XML node
$marker = <<<MARKER
<marker lat="$lat" lng="$lng" found="$found" left="$left"/>
MARKER;

//open the data.xml file for appending
$f=@fopen('data.xml', 'a+');
if(!$f) die('<?xml version="1.0"?>
<response type="error"><![CDATA[Could not open data.xml file]]></response>
');

//add the node
$w=@fwrite($f, $marker);
if(!$w) die('<?xml version="1.0"?>
<response type="error"><![CDATA[Could not write to data.xml file]]></response>');

@fclose($f);

//return a response
$newMarkerContent = "<div><b>found </b>$found</div><div><b>left </b>$left</div>";
echo <<<XML
<?xml version="1.0"?>
<response type="success" icon="$icon"><![CDATA[$newMarkerContent]]></response>
XML;

?>
```

For simplicity in the example, we use a flat file on the server in Listing 3-6 to store the data. This file (called data.xml) is simply a list of all the points saved to the server and resembles the following:

```
<marker lat="37.441" lng="-122.141" found="Keychain" left="Book"/>
<marker lat="37.322" lng="-121.213" found="Water Bottle" left="Necklace"/>
```

Note there is no surrounding root node, so the file is not actually valid XML. When you retrieve the XML later in the chapter, you'll be retrieving all the XML at once and wrapping it in a parent `<markers>` node, so you'll end up with a valid XML result:

```
<?xml version="1.0"?>
<markers>
    <marker lat="37.441" lng="-122.141" found="Keychain" left="Book"/>
    <marker lat="37.322" lng="-121.213" found="Water Bottle" left="Necklace"/>
</markers>
```

Since you're going to retrieve all the XML without any matching or searching to determine which bits to retrieve, it makes sense to store the data in one file in the format you want. In a real-world web application, you would probably want to store the information in a SQL database and retrieve only a smaller subset of points based on some search criteria. Once you've mastered sending and retrieving data, you could easily extend this example with a searchable SQL database, and then retrieve only the points in the latitude and longitude bounds of the viewable map area.

Checking When the Request Is Completed

When you click the Save button on the info window, the information in the form is sent back to the server using the GXmlHttp object in Listing 3-5 and awaits a response back in XML format from the PHP script in Listing 3-6. During the request, the readyState property of the request object will contain one of five possible incrementing values:

- 0, for uninitialized
- 1, for loading
- 2, for loaded
- 3, for interactive
- 4, for completed

The changes to the readyState property are monitored using the GXmlHttp. onreadystatechange() event listener (Figure 3-12). At each increment, the function you've defined for the onreadystatechange() method will be triggered to allow you to execute any additional JavaScript code you would like. For the example, you need to deal with only the completed state of the request, so your function checks to see when readyState==4, and then parses the XML document as necessary.

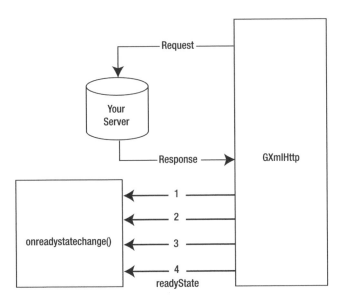

Figure 3-12. *GXmlHttp request response diagram*

■**Tip** This Ajax implementation is not actually checking to see if the request completed in a valid state. For example, if the page you requested was not found, the readyState will still be 4 at the end of the request, but no XML would have been returned. To check the state of the GXmlHttp request, you need to check the GXmlHttp.status property. If status is equal to 200, then the page was successfully loaded. A status of 404 indicates the page was not found. GXmlHttp.status could contain any valid HTTP request codes returned by the server.

Testing the Asynchronous State

Don't forget that the GXmlHttp request is asynchronous, meaning that the JavaScript continues to run while your GXmlHttp request is awaiting a response. While the PHP script is busy saving the file to the server, any code you've added after request.send(null); may execute before the response is returned from the server.

   You can observe the asynchronous state of the request and response by adding a JavaScript alert() call right after you send the request:

```
request.send(null);
alert('Continue');
return false;
```

   And another alert in the onreadystatechange() method of the request:

```
request.onreadystatechange = function() {
    if (request.readyState == 4) {
```

```
        alert('Process Response');
    }
}
```

If you run the script over and over, sometimes the alert boxes will appear in the order Process Response then Continue, but more likely, you'll get Continue then Process Request. Just remember that if you want something to occur after the response, you must use the onreadystatechange() method when the readyState is 4.

■Tip To further enhance your web application, you could use the various states of the request object to add loading, completed, and error states. For example, when initiating a request, you could show an animated loading image to indicate to the user that the information is loading. Providing feedback at each stage of the request makes it easier for the user to know what's happening and how to react. If no loading state is displayed, users may assume they have not actually clicked the button or will become frustrated and think nothing is happening.

Using GDownloadUrl for Simple Ajax Requests

If your web application doesn't require a high level of control over the Ajax request, you can use an alternative object called GDownloadUrl. You can use GDownloadUrl to send and retrieve content the same way you do with GXmlHttp; however the API is much simpler. Rather than checking response states and all that other stuff, you just supply a URL with any appropriate GET variables and a function to execute when the response in returned. This simplifies the request to the following:

```
GDownloadUrl('storeMarker.php' + getVars,  function(data,responseCode)) {
    //Do something with the data
});
```

But note that this approach doesn't give you as much control over the different states of the request.

Parsing the XML Document Using DOM Methods

When the readyState reaches 4 and your onreadystatechange() function is triggered, you need to parse the response from the server to determine if the PHP script replied with an execution error or a successful save. Referring back to Listing 3-6, the storeMarker.php source, you can see that in the event of a successful save, the type attribute of the XML response node is success:

```
<?xml version="1.0"?>
<response type="success">
    <![CDATA[<div><b>Found</b> foo</div><div><b>Left</b> bar </div>]]>
</response>
```

In the event of an error, such as the script not having permission to write to the file, the value of type is error:

```
<?xml version="1.0"?>
<response type="error">
  <![CDATA[Could not open data.xml file.]]>
</response>
```

When the web browser receives the XML from your request object, it is contained in the responseXML property. You can now search the XML using the JavaScript DOM methods and properties, such as xmlDoc.documentElement to give you the root node (in this case, the <response> node) and the getAttribute() method to retrieve the value of the type attribute of the <response> node.

In the event of an error in Listing 3-5, you simply need to call a JavaScript alert() with the content of the <response> tag to alert the user (Figure 3-13).

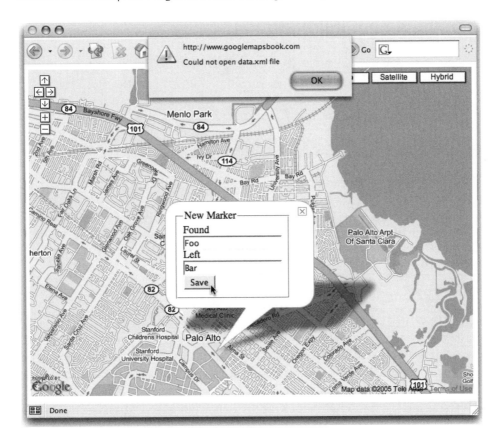

Figure 3-13. *An error in the response*

With a successful execution, you create a new marker at the latitude and longitude of the click and attach an event listener to the marker itself in order to create a new info window with the content of the response. The new marker now indicates the newly created location on the map, and when clicked, displays the information about the marker (Figure 3-14).

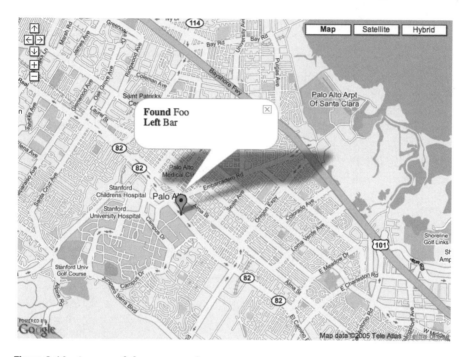

Figure 3-14. *A successful request and response*

You've probably noticed that in Listing 3-5, you've used the `marker.openInfoWindowHTML()` method rather than the `map.openInfoWindow()` method. Since you now have your marker on the map, you can apply the info window directly to it and pass in an HTML string rather than an HTML DOM element.

■**Caution** When accepting input from the users of your website, it is always good practice to assume the data is evil and the user is trying to take advantage of your system. Always filter input to ensure it's in the format you are expecting. Numbers should be numbers, strings should be strings, and unless desired, nothing should contain HTML or JavaScript code. Listing 3-6 could easily be compromised through cross-site scripting (XSS) if you don't filter out JavaScript in the user-submitted data. For more information see `http://owasp.org`.

Retrieving Markers from the Server

Your geocaching map is almost finished. So far, you've used event listeners to add marks on the map, displayed info windows to ask for more input, and saved the input back to the server using Ajax. You now want to take all the markers you've been collecting and show them on the page when users first visit.

The information to display the markers resides on the server in the data.xml file created by the storeMarkers.php script in Listing 3-5. In Chapter 2, you loaded the map data from map_data.php into the head of the index.php document using a <script> tag. You could easily do the same thing here, but for this chapter, we're going to mix things up a bit and show you a more controlled way. To gain more interactive control, you'll retrieve the data from the server using the GXmlHttp object. Using the GXmlHttp object will allow you to retrieve points at any time, not just when the page loads. For example, when you've finished this example, you could extend it further by tracking the movements of the map and retrieve the points based on the map's viewable area, as you'll see later in Chapter 7.

To start, remove the reference to map_data.php from the head of your index.php file and create the retrieveMarkers.php file in Listing 3-7 on your server in the same directory as your HTML document.

Listing 3-7. *retrieveMarkers.php Script Used to Format and Retrieve the data.xml File*

```php
<?php
header('Content-Type:text/xml');
$markers = file_get_contents('data.xml');
echo <<<XML
<markers>
$markers
</markers>
XML;
?>
```

Also, copy the retrieveMarkers() function from Listing 3-8 into the map_functions.js file. In Listing 3-8, notice the marker is created by the same createMarker() function you used in Listing 3-5. This allows you to maintain the proper scope of the data passed into the info window. If you create each marker in the retrieveMarkers() function, each marker's info window will have the html value of the last marker created in the loop. The value of html will be identical for each marker because the info window is not actually created until you click the marker and html is retrieved from the scope of the JavaScript at that time. By moving the creation into another function, you've given each instance of the function its own namespace.

Listing 3-8. *Ajax retrieveMarkers() Function*

```javascript
function retrieveMarkers() {
    var request = GXmlHttp.create();

    //tell the request where to retrieve data from.
    request.open('GET', 'retrieveMarkers.php', true);
```

```
            //tell the request what to do when the state changes.
            request.onreadystatechange = function() {
                if (request.readyState == 4) {
                    var xmlDoc = request.responseXML;

                    var markers = xmlDoc.documentElement.getElementsByTagName("marker");
                    for (var i = 0; i < markers.length; i++) {
                        var lng = markers[i].getAttribute("lng");
                        var lat = markers[i].getAttribute("lat");
                        //check for lng and lat so MSIE does not error
                        //on parseFloat of a null value
                        if(lng && lat) {
                            var latlng = new GLatLng(parseFloat(lat),parseFloat(lng));

                            var html = '<div><b>Found</b> '
                                + markers[i].getAttribute("found")
                                + '</div><div><b>Left</b> '
                                + markers[i].getAttribute("left")
                                + '</div>';

                            var marker = createMarker(latlng, html);
                            map.addOverlay(marker);
                        }
                    } //for
                } //if
            } //function

            request.send(null);
    }
```

Once you've created the retrieveMarkers.php file and copied the retrieveMarkers()
function into the map_functions.js file, you can load the markers into your map by calling the
retrieveMarkers() function. For example, to load the markers when the page loads, you'll
need to call the retrieveMarkers() function from the init() function after you create the map.

```
function init() {
    ... cut ...
    map = new GMap2(document.getElementById("map"));
    retrieveMarkers();
    ... cut ...
}
```

When the retrieveMarkers()function is executed, the server-side PHP script,
retrieveMarkers.php (Listing 3-7), will return an XML file containing the latitude and longitude
for each marker you previously saved.

```
<markers>
    <marker lat="37.441" lng="-122.141" found="Keychain" left="Book"/>
    <marker lat="37.322" lng="-121.213" found="Water Bottle" left="Necklace"/>
    ... etc ...
</markers>
```

The XML also contains the additional information you requested for each marker so that you'll be able to include it in the info window. You can search this file using the JavaScript DOM methods in the same way you did for the `storeMarker()` function in Listing 3-5, but because you have a list of markers, you'll need to loop through the object list from `xmlDoc.documentElement.getElementsByTagName("marker")` and create each marker individually.

You don't necessarily have to return XML to the `GXmlHttp` object. You can also return HTML, text, or the same JSON format introduced in Chapter 2. If you return something other than XML, you need to use the `response.responseText` property and parse it accordingly.

■Tip For more information about using Ajax, read *Beginning Ajax with PHP: From Novice to Professional*, by Lee Babin (`http://www.apress.com/book/bookDisplay.html?bID=10117`).

Adding Some Flair

You now have a fun little interactive web application that anyone with Internet access can use. Geocachers can come and see what kinds of things have been found and let others know what they've found. You could be finished with the map, but let's use the Google Maps API to add just a bit more flair.

All the red markers on the map don't really mean anything when you look at them as a whole. Without clicking on each marker to reveal the info window, there's no way to tell anything about what's there other than the location.

One of the keys to a successful web application is to provide your users the information they want both easily and quickly. For instance, if you come back to the map frequently, you would prefer to quickly pick out the points you haven't seen before, rather than hunt and examine each marker to see the information. To give the map more visual information, let's let the geocachers add a custom icon for their finds. This will make the map more visually interesting and provide quick and easy information to the viewers.

By default, Google uses an inverted teardrop pin for marking points on a map, and up until now, this is what you've been using as well. Now, using Google's `GIcon` object, you can rid your map of the little red dots and customize them to use whatever image you like. Rather than looking at a red marker, you can add a small icon of the find (Figure 3-15).

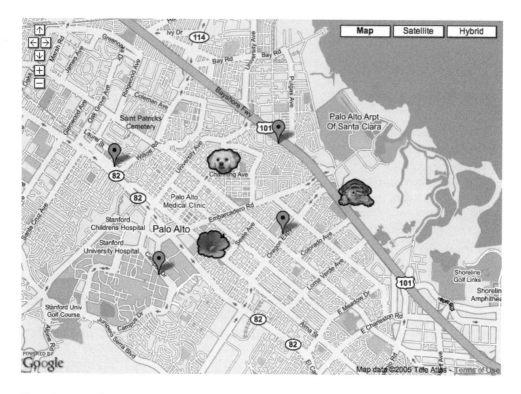

Figure 3-15. *Different marker icons on a map*

To use the GIcon object, you are required to set a minimum of three properties:

- GIcon.image: URL of the image

- GIcon.iconSize: Size of the image in pixels

- GIcon.iconAnchor: Location of the anchor point

Also, because you're currently making use of the info window for each of your markers, you must specify the infoWindowAnchor property of the icon.

To get the URL for the GIcon.image property, you'll need to ask the geocaching users where their icon is by adding another element to the info window's form, and then pass it through the GET parameters of your GXmlHttp.request. First, in the click event for the map from Listing 3-4, add the following two highlighted lines:

```
inputForm.innerHTML = '<fieldset style="width:150px;">'
        + '<legend>New Marker</legend>'
        + '<label for="found">Found</label>'
        + '<input type="text" id="found" style="width:100%"/>'
        + '<label for="left">Left</label>'
        + '<input type="text" id="left" style="width:100%"/>'
        + '<label for="left">Icon URL</label>'
        + '<input type="text" id="icon" style="width:100%"/>'
        + '<input type="submit" value="Save"/>'
```

```
         + '<input type="hidden" id="longitude" value="' + lng + '"/>'
         + '<input type="hidden" id="latitude" value="' + lat + '"/>'
         + '</fieldset>';
```

▪Tip For a complete working example of the following changes, see the final example for Chapter 3 in the book's accompanying code or online at http://googlemapsbook.com/chapter3/final.

Second, in the storeMarker() function from Listing 3-5, add the following highlighted parameter to the request:

```
var getVars =   "?found=" + document.getElementById("found").value
         + "&left=" + document.getElementById("left").value
         + "&icon=" + document.getElementById("icon").value
         + "&lng=" + lng
         + "&lat=" + lat ;
```

Now the icon's URL can be entered and passed to the server. In order to save the information in the data.xml file, add the following highlighted lines to the storeMarkers.php file in Listing 3-6:

```
$icon = $_GET['icon'];
$marker = <<<MARKER
<marker lat="$lat" lng="$lng" found="$found" left="$left" icon="$icon"/>
MARKER;
```

When the XML is retrieved from the server, it will automatically include the new icon information, so you do not need to modify the retrieveMarkers.php file in Listing 3-7. To show the new icons, you'll need to create a new GIcon object with the appropriate properties when you retrieve the markers from the server and when you create the new marker upon a successful save.

The GIcon objects are created as independent objects and passed in as the second parameter when creating a new GMarker object. The GIcon objects are reusable, so you do not need to create a new GIcon object for each new GMarker object, unless you are using a different icon for each marker, as you are doing in this example. To use the icons while retrieving the saved pins in Listing 3-8, add the icon URL as a third parameter to the createMarker() call:

```
var marker = createMarker(latlng, html, markers[i].getAttribute("icon"));
```

Then create your GIcon object in the createMarker() function and assign it to the marker with the following changes:

```
function createMarker(latlng, html, iconImage) {
    if(iconImage!='') {
        var icon = new GIcon();
        icon.image = iconImage;
        icon.iconSize = new GSize(25, 25);
        icon.iconAnchor = new GPoint(14, 25);
        icon.infoWindowAnchor = new GPoint(14, 14);
```

```
            var marker = new GMarker(latlng,icon);
        } else {
            var marker = new GMarker(latlng);
        }
        GEvent.addListener(marker, 'click', function() {
            var markerHTML = html;
            marker.openInfoWindowHtml(markerHTML);
        });
        return marker;
}
```

Additionally, when you create the new `GIcon` object in the `storeMarker()` and `retrieveMarkers()` functions, you'll need to retrieve the icon from the XML and pass the icon image into the `createMarker` call. In `storeMarker()`, add the following:

```
var iconImage = responseNode.getAttribute("icon");
var marker = createMarker(latlng, content, iconImage);
```

In `retrieveMarkers()`, add this:

```
var iconImage = markers[i].getAttribute("icon");
var marker = createMarker(latlng, html, iconImage);
```

Now when you regenerate the map and create new points, the icon from the URL will be used rather than the default red marker. The size you pick for your `GIcon` objects is based on a width and height in pixels. The preceding changes use an arbitrary `GSize` of 25 by 25 pixels for all of the icons. If the image in the URL is larger than 25 by 25 pixels, it will be squished down to fit.

Summary

Now that you have your first interactive Google Maps web application, grab a GPS and start looking for geocaches to add to your map! Get your friends involved, too, and show off what you've learned.

The ideas and techniques covered in this chapter can be applied to many different web applications, and the same basic interface can be used to mark any geographical information on a map. Want to chart the world's volcanoes? Just click away on the map and mark them down.

You may also want to build on the example here and incorporate some of the other features of the Google Maps API. For example, try retrieving only a specified list of markers, or maybe markers within a certain distance of a selected point. You could also improve the interface by adding listener events to trigger when you open and close an info window, or improve the server-side script by downloading and automatically resizing the desired icons. Later in the book, we'll discuss a variety of other ways to improve your maps.

In the next chapter, we'll show you how you can use publicly available services to automatically plot markers on your map based not just on clicks, but also on postal and street addresses.

■ ■ ■

CHAPTER 4

Geocoding Addresses

As you've probably already guessed, the heart of any mashup is correlating your information with latitudes and longitudes for plotting on your map. Fortunately, geocoding services are available to help you convert postal addresses to precise latitude and longitude coordinates. For locations in the United States and Canada, these services make geocoding addresses relatively easy and quite accurate most of the time. In other parts of the world, the job can become much harder.

In this chapter, while building a store locator map, you'll learn how to do the following:

- Create an XML file describing a set of locations and details.

- Request information from geocoding web services and process their responses.

- Learn the pros and cons of Google's new JavaScript-based geocoder, as well as suggestions on when to use it.

- Precompute and cache the latitude and longitude for the points you intend to plot.

Creating an XML File with the Address Data

In this chapter, you're going to create a simple store location map using the postal address of each location in the chain to map the markers. The important aspect about this kind of data is that it changes slowly over time. A few points are added every now and then as the chain of stores expands, but rarely are points removed. In general, it makes sense to precompute and cache information like latitude and longitude for this type of data, as you'll see in the "Caching Lookups" section later in this chapter.

For this example, we'll use the chain of stores and attractions known as Ron Jon Surf Shop, since its story appeals to our own entrepreneurial style:

> *It was 1959 and on the New Jersey shore a bright young man named Ron DiMenna was just discovering the sport of surfing with fiberglass surfboards. The pastime soon became a passion and homemade surfboards would no longer do. When his father heard that Ron wanted his own custom surfboard from California, he suggested, "Buy three, sell two at a profit, then yours will be free." His Dad was right and Ron Jon Surf Shop was born.*

http://www.ronjons.com

With permission, we've taken the addresses of all of the Ron Jon properties from the website and converted them into the sample XML data file for this chapter. Listing 4-1 shows the `ronjons.xml` file that you'll use while following the examples in this chapter. By the end of the chapter, you'll be able to create your own XML file and use the same techniques to map your own list of related addresses.

Listing 4-1. *Ron Jon Properties (from* www.ronjons.com *as of July 2006)*

```
<?xml version="1.0" encoding="UTF-8"?>
<stores>
 <store>
  <name>"The Original" Ron Jon Surf Shop</name>
  <address>901 Central Avenue</address>
  <city>Long Beach Island</city>
  <state>NJ</state>
  <zip>08008</zip>
  <phone>(609) 494-8844</phone>
  <pin>store</pin>
 </store>
 <store>
  <name>"One of a Kind" Ron Jon Surf Shop</name>
  <address>4151 North Atlantic Avenue</address>
  <city>Cocoa Beach</city>
  <state>FL</state>
  <zip>32931</zip>
  <phone>(321) 799-8888</phone>
  <pin>store</pin>
 </store>
 <store>
  <name>Ron Jon Surf Shop - Sunrise </name>
  <address>2610 Sawgrass Mills Circle</address>
  <address2>Suite 1415</address2>
  <city>Sunrise</city>
  <state>FL</state>
  <zip>33323</zip>
  <phone>(954) 846-1880</phone>
  <pin>store</pin>
 </store>
 <store>
  <name>Ron Jon Surf Shop - Orlando</name>
  <address>5160 International Drive</address>
  <city>Orlando</city>
  <state>FL</state>
  <zip>32819</zip>
  <phone>(407) 481-2555</phone>
  <pin>store</pin>
 </store>
 <store>
```

```
  <name>Ron Jon Surf Shop - Key West</name>
  <address>503 Front Street</address>
  <city>Key West</city>
  <state>FL</state>
  <zip>33040</zip>
  <phone>(305) 293-8880</phone>
  <pin>store</pin>
 </store>
 <store>
  <name>Ron Jon Surf Shop - California</name>
  <address>20 City Blvd.</address>
  <address2>West Building C Suite 1</address2>
  <city>Orange</city>
  <state>CA</state>
  <zip>92868</zip>
  <phone>(714) 939-9822</phone>
  <pin>store</pin>
 </store>
 <store>
  <name>Ron Jon Cape Caribe Resort</name>
  <address>1000 Shorewood Drive</address>
  <city>Cape Canaveral</city>
  <state>FL</state>
  <zip>32920</zip>
  <phone>(321) 328-2830</phone>
  <pin>resort</pin>
 </store>
</stores>
```

■**Caution** We've left out declaring a namespace for this XML document to keep the example simple for XML novices. For these simple examples, a namespace is not needed. However, using namespaces is generally a good idea. For more information, check out the excellent primer on namespaces, "XML Namespaces by Example," at `http://www.xml.com/pub/a/1999/01/namespaces.html`.

Using Geocoding Web Services

Converting postal addresses to precise latitude and longitude coordinates is made simple by a few good geocoding services. In this section, we're going to cover some of the most popular geocoding services we've found to date. (For an updated list of the geocoders we know about, check out our website at `http://googlemapsbook.com/geocoders.`)

However, before you dive into the available web services, there are a few server-side requirements you'll need to consider.

■**Note** There are also sources of raw information that you can use to make your own geocoding solutions. So, if you can't find a service that fits your needs, and you have a place to get some raw street data, see Chapter 11 for the basics of creating your own geocoding service.

Requirements for Consuming Geocoding Services

To consume the services, you need a web server permanently connected to the Internet, and it will need to be able to connect to the appropriate services. For the examples in this chapter, you'll be using the PHP CURL extension to retrieve the XML information from the available services, and you'll be using PHP 5's SimpleXML feature to parse the XML you retrieve.

CURL

Many of these services require you to send a carefully crafted URL request to retrieve your information. For this purpose, you'll use the CURL extension in PHP. This extension is not bundled by default with PHP; however, it is one of the most commonly installed extensions, so you should have no trouble finding a host with it available.

Basically, the PHP CURL functions are available through the use of `libcurl`, a library created by Daniel Stenberg, and allow you to connect and communicate with web servers using many different types of protocols. You'll be using a very small subset of functions here, though we encourage you to look deeper into this very useful feature by visiting `http://www.php.net/curl`.

SimpleXML

Most of the geocoding solutions we're about to investigate return an XML document as their result. To process these responses, you'll use PHP 5's SimpleXML features, which are perfectly suited to the level of complexity of the answers you'll receive. SimpleXML brings a unique perspective to XML parsing in that element names are automatically (recursively) converted into properties of an object, and attributes are accessed as if they were items in a named array. From your point of view, all of this happens when the `simplexml_load_string($string)` constructor is called; however, from a memory usage point of view, it happens on demand.

If you've never used SimpleXML, or need a refresher, we encourage you to check out a great article by Zend Technologies available at `http://www.zend.com/php5/articles/php5-simplexml.php`. This article also presents an example for PHP 4's DOM processing, in case you don't have access to PHP 5 on your server (you should really consider upgrading!).

■**Note** If you have PHP 4 and still want something like SimpleXML you might want to try MiniXML from `http://minixml.psychogenic.com`. It gets rave reviews on many forums and news groups, though we have never needed to use it ourselves. The description from their site states that: "MiniXML provides a simple, API to generating and parsing XML. Its advantages are ease-of-use and the fact that no additional libraries are required. It comes with two independent implementations, 100% PHP and 100% PERL, which you can use separately."

The Google Maps API Geocoder

We'll begin our investigation of geocoding solutions with the Google Maps API geocoder (`http://www.google.com/apis/maps/documentation/#Geocoding_Examples`). Google claims that this solution should give street-level accuracy for the United States, Canada, France, Italy, Germany, and Spain. The Google developers hope to roll out support for more countries in the near future, so before you rule them out for a particular country, you might want to check either our website (`http://googlemapsbook.com`) or the official API documentation.

Before June 2006, there was no official geocoder from Google. Many hacks used the `maps.google.com` site's built-in geocoder and screen-scraped the answer. This was an explicitly unauthorized use of the service, and while we never heard of a crackdown on people doing this, Google did frown upon it. As a result, a number of alternative services popped up to fill the void, which we'll cover later in the chapter. Despite being late to the game, Google's geocoder has a number of really interesting features that none of the others have yet, and we'll highlight them throughout the discussion.

First, we'll look at the most basic method for accessing the geocoder: the HTTP-based lookup methods. You can also access the geocoder within JavaScript, as discussed later in this section and in Chapter 10's polyline example.

Like most of the other services we'll investigate, the Google method uses Representational State Transfer (REST) requests for accessing the service. REST is basically a simple HTTP request that passes `GET` parameters by appending things like `key=value&key2=value2` to the end of the request URL. Generally, a REST service returns some form of text-based data structure like XML. Google's geocoder is (so far) unique in that it can also return Keyhole Markup Language, or KML (for use in Google Earth), and JSON directly.

THE ORIGIN OF REST

Representational State Transfer (REST) is a concept used to connect services in distributed systems like the World Wide Web. The term originated in a 2000 doctoral dissertation about the Web written by Roy Fielding, one of the principal authors of the HTTP specification, and has quickly passed into widespread use in the networking community.

Fielding's vision of REST described a strict abstraction of architectural principles. However, people now often loosely use the term to describe any simple web-based interface that uses XML and HTTP without the extra abstraction layers of approaches like the SOAP protocol. As a result, these two different uses of REST cause some confusion in technical discussions. Throughout this book, we refer to it in the looser, more common, meaning of REST.

Google has outdone many of the other geocoders on the market in that its geocoder returns an excellent answer given fairly poor input. It does not require you to separate out the street number, street name, direction (N, S, E, W, and so on), city, state, or even ZIP code. It simply takes what you give it, uses Google's extensive experience with understanding your search terms, and returns a best guess. Moreover, the service formats the input you give it into a nice, clean, consistent representation when it gives you the latitude and longitude answer. The geocoder even goes so far as to look past poor punctuation and strange abbreviations, which is great if you're taking the input from a visitor to your site.

Like most of the geocoders available on the market, Google limits the number of geocoding requests that you can make before it cuts you off. The Google limit is a generous 50,000 lookups per API key per day, provided you space them out at a rate of one every 1.75 seconds (as of the time of publishing). To maximize this limit and your bandwidth, we suggest you use the server-side caching approach discussed in the "Caching Lookups" section later in this chapter.

Google Geocoder Responses

Let's look at the Google geocoder's response for a sample query adapted from the official documentation:

```
http://maps.google.com/maps/geo?q=1600+AmPhItHEaTRe+PKway+Mtn+View+CA&output=➥
xml&key=your_api_key
```

This query returns the XML in Listing 4-2.

Listing 4-2. *Sample Response from Google's REST Geocoder*

```
<kml>
 <Response>
  <name>1600 AmPhItHEaTRe PKway Mtn View CA</name>
  <Status>
   <code>200</code>
   <request>geocode</request>
  </Status>
  <Placemark>
   <address>
    1600 Amphitheatre Pkwy, Mountain View, CA 94043, USA
   </address>
   <AddressDetails>
    <Country>
     <CountryNameCode>US</CountryNameCode>
      <AdministrativeArea>
       <AdministrativeAreaName>CA</AdministrativeAreaName>
       <SubAdministrativeArea>
        <SubAdministrativeAreaName>Santa Clara</SubAdministrativeAreaName>
        <Locality>
         <LocalityName>Mountain View</LocalityName>
         <Thoroughfare>
          <ThoroughfareName>1600 Amphitheatre Pkwy</ThoroughfareName>
         </Thoroughfare>
         <PostalCode>
          <PostalCodeNumber>94043</PostalCodeNumber>
         </PostalCode>
        </Locality>
```

```
      </SubAdministrativeArea>
     </AdministrativeArea>
    </Country>
   </AddressDetails>
  <Point>
   <coordinates>-122.083739,37.423021,0</coordinates>
  </Point>
 </Placemark>
<Response>
</kml>
```

The response has three major components:

- name: The name is exactly what you fed into the geocoder, so you know if it interpreted your URL encoding properly.

- Status: This is the response code, which indicates whether the lookup was successful or if it failed. Table 4-1 lists the possible response codes and their meanings.

- Placemark: This is available only if the geocoding was successful and contains the information you're seeking. The placemark itself contains three important components:

  - address: The address is the full, nicely formatted string that Google actually used after it cleaned up the input you gave it. This is useful for a number of reasons, including storing something clean in your database and debugging when the answers seem to come back incorrectly.

  - Point: The point is a coordinate in 3D space and represents longitude, latitude, and elevation. Elevation data may or may not be available for a given answer, so take a 0 with a grain of salt, as it is the default and is also returned if no data is available.

  - AddressDetails: This is a block of more complicated XML that uses a standard format called eXtensible Address Language (xAL). Unless you're interested in extracting the individual pieces of the address for storage in your database or formatting on your screen, you could safely ignore this chunk of XML and get away with using only the status, address, and point information.

Note Upon launch of their geocoder, Google developers stated that all elevations would return 0 and that they were unsure when they would be able to supply elevation data. Before you use any of the elevation data, check the official API documentation online or the official Google Maps API blog (http://googlemapsapi.blogspot.com/) to see which regions now have elevation data available.

Table 4-1. *Google Geocoder Response Codes*

Code	Constant Name	Description
200	G_GEO_SUCCESS	No errors occurred; the address was successfully parsed and its geocode has been returned.
500	G_GEO_SERVER_ERROR	A geocoding request could not be successfully processed, yet the exact reason for the failure is not known.
601	G_GEO_MISSING_ADDRESS	The HTTP q parameter was either missing or had no value.
602	G_GEO_UNKNOWN_ADDRESS	No corresponding geographic location could be found for the specified address. This may be due to the fact that the address is relatively new, or it may be incorrect.
603	G_UNAVAILABLE_ADDRESS	The geocode for the given address cannot be returned due to legal or contractual reasons.
610	G_GEO_BAD_KEY	The given key is either invalid or does not match the domain for which it was given.
620	G_TOO_MANY_QUERIES	You have accessed the service too frequently and are either temporarily or permanently blocked from further use.

---

xAL

Defining a uniform way to describe addresses across 200 countries is no easy task. Some countries use street names; others don't. Some place higher importance on the postal code; others insist that the street number is most important. Some divide their "administrative" zones into a two-tier system of province/city; others use more tiers like state/county/city/locality. Whatever format is chosen must take all of these situations into account. OASIS has defined a format called xAL, which stands for eXtensible Address Language (in this case). Google has adopted it as a component of the XML response that its geocoder returns.

xAL uses a hierarchical data model (XML) since it seems like such a natural fit for addresses. For example, a country has states, a state has counties, a county has cities, a city has streets, and a street has individual plots of land. Some countries omit one or more of these levels, of course, but in general, that's not a problem.

However, you should realize that the xAL specification is designed to describe the address elements, not to be specific about the formatting and presentation of the address. There is no guarantee that the use of whitespace in the different elements will be consistent or even predictable, only that each type of data will be separated in a defined way. Using an XML-based format ensures that the data can be compared, sorted, and understood using simple programmatic methods.

For more information on xAL, visit the official site at `http://www.oasis-open.org/committees/ciq/ciq.html#6` or Google for the term "xAL address."

Google Geocoder Requests

Now let's look at a simple snippet of code that uses CURL to query the HTTP-based geocoding API and SimpleXML to parse the answer. Listing 4-3 shows this code.

Listing 4-3. *Using the Google Maps API Geocoder to Locate the Stores*

```php
<?php

$api_key = "yourkey";

// Create a CURL object for later use
$ch = curl_init();
curl_setopt($ch, CURLOPT_HEADER, 0);
curl_setopt($ch, CURLOPT_RETURNTRANSFER, 1);

// Open the ronjons.xml file
$datafile = simplexml_load_file("ronjons.xml");
if (!$datafile) die("Unable to open input file!");

foreach ($datafile->store as $store) {
  // Construct the geocoder request string (URL)
  $url = "http://maps.google.com/maps/geo?output=xml&key=$api_key&q=";
  $q = $store->address.", ".$store->city.", ".$store->state.", ".$store->zip;
  $url .= urlencode($q);

  echo "\nStore: {$store->name}\n";
  echo "Source Address: $q\n";

  // Query Google for this store's longitude and latitude
  curl_setopt($ch, CURLOPT_URL, $url);
  $response = curl_exec($ch);

  // Use SimpleXML to parse our answer into something we can use
  $googleresult = simplexml_load_string($response);
  echo "Status: ".$googleresult->Response->Status->code."\n";
  if ($googleresult->Response->Status->code != 200)
      echo "Unable to parse Google response for {$store->name}!\n";
  else foreach ($googleresult->Response as $response) {
    foreach ($response->Placemark as $place) {
      list($longitude,$latitude) = split(",",$place->Point->coordinates);
      echo "Result Address: ".$place->address."\n";
      echo "  Latitude: $latitude\n";
      echo "  Longitude: $longitude\n";
    } // for each placemark
  } // for each Google result
} // for each store

// Close the CURL file and destroy the object
curl_close($ch);
?>
```

In this example, first we use `curl_setopt()` to define CURL's behavior while talking with Google. This includes telling CURL that we don't care about HTTP headers in $googleresult with the option `CURLOPT_HEADER = 0`, and instructing CURL to buffer the response (instead of sending it directly to the output buffer) with `CURLOPT_RETURNTRANSFER = 1`.

Next, we open your data file and parse it using SimpleXML. The resultant object is then used in the loop, which in turn creates a REST request URL for each store. Also note that you must use PHP's `urlencode()` function on the query portion of the string to ensure that the information is transmitted cleanly to the service.

___

Caution Remember that SimpleXML and XML in general are case-sensitive. The fact that our input XML is all lowercase means that we loop using `$datafile->store` (lowercase s), while the Google response uses title case, and therefore our inner loop uses `$googleresult->Response` (capital R). We've done this deliberately to remind you of this fact. Capitalization conventions are a matter of personal style.

___

Lastly, we give CURL our REST request and return the response into the variable $googleresult using the `curl_exec()` function. This returns the KML-style XML response that contains the meat of what we're interested in—the latitude and longitude, which we simply extract and echo to the screen for now. SimpleXML's node selectors make the job of accessing the data extremely trivial.

Listing 4-4 contains the output you should see when you execute this script. For convenience, you might prefer to output HTML `<br />` tags instead of newline characters (\n), so that you can see the results (without viewing the source) if you are using a browser to run the code, or you could prepend `header('content-type:text/plain;')` to the PHP file to convert the output to plaintext mode.

Listing 4-4. *Output from the Google Geocoding Script*

```
Store: "The Original" Ron Jon Surf Shop
Source Address: 901 Central Avenue,  Long Beach Island , NJ, 08008
Status: 200
Result Address: 901 Central Ave, Barnegat Light, NJ 08008, USA
   Latitude: 39.748586
   Longitude: -74.111764
Result Address: 901 Central Ave, Surf City, NJ 08008, USA
   Latitude: 39.661016
   Longitude: -74.168010
Result Address: 901 Central Ave, Ship Bottom, NJ 08008, USA
   Latitude: 39.649667
   Longitude: -74.177253

Store: "One of a Kind" Ron Jon Surf Shop
Source Address: 4151 North Atlantic Avenue, Cocoa Beach, FL, 32931
Status: 200
Result Address: 4151 N Atlantic Ave, Cocoa Beach, FL 32931, USA
```

```
Latitude: 28.356453
Longitude: -80.608170
```

```
Store: Ron Jon Surf Shop - Sunrise
Source Address: 2610 Sawgrass Mills Circle, Sunrise, FL, 33323
Status: 200
Result Address: 2610 Sawgrass Mills Cir, Sunrise, FL 33323, USA
  Latitude: 26.150899
  Longitude: -80.316233
```

```
Store: Ron Jon Surf Shop - Orlando
Source Address: 5160 International Drive, Orlando, FL, 32819
Status: 200
Result Address: 5160 International Dr, Orlando, FL 32819, USA
  Latitude: 28.469873
  Longitude: -81.450311
```

```
Store: Ron Jon Surf Shop - Key West
Source Address: 503 Front Street, Key West, FL, 33040
Status: 200
Result Address: 503 Front St, Key West, FL 33040, USA
  Latitude: 24.560287
  Longitude: -81.805817
```

```
Store: Ron Jon Surf Shop - California
Source Address: 20 City Blvd., Orange, CA, 92868
Status: 200
Result Address: 100 City Blvd E, Orange, CA 92868, USA
  Latitude: 33.782107
  Longitude: -117.889878
Result Address: 2 City Blvd W, Orange, CA 92868, USA
  Latitude: 33.779838
  Longitude: -117.893568
```

```
Store: Ron Jon Cape Caribe Resort
Source Address: 1000 Shorewood Drive, Cape Canaveral, FL, 32920
Status: 200
Result Address: 699 Shorewood Dr, Cape Canaveral, FL 32920, USA
  Latitude: 28.402944
  Longitude: -80.604093
```

There are several interesting things to discuss in this result:

"The Original" Ron Jon Surf Shop: "The Original" store listed Long Beach Island as the city. Google doesn't recognize this as a valid city and has instead used the ZIP code to determine which cities might be more appropriate. More important, each of the answers differs by at least a few tenths of a degree, and this is a significant difference (about 10 kilometers). It's up to you to decide how to handle this situation. A few suggestions might be to always use the first answer and assume that this is the one Google thinks is best. Another option would be to average the answers. Lastly, you could treat multiple `Placemark` nodes as a geocoding failure and ignore all of the data.

`Ron Jon Surf Shop - California`: For the store in California, the website lists the address as 20 City Boulevard but fails to give a direction. Google's two closest matches are 100 City Blvd E. and 2 City Blvd W. Both closest matches are returned in a separate `Placemark` node, and this is where the xAL data becomes very useful. Since each `Placemark` node is broken down in a consistent way, you can determine in which component the answer differs from your input. Doing so will allow you to write code that will make educated decisions about what to do with the answers. In this case, you probably want to assume that City Blvd is a straight line and employ some of the math in Chapters 10 and 11 to use a point approximately 20% of the way along the line between the two answers (20/(100-2) = ~20%).

`Ron Jon Cape Caribe Resort`: The Cape Caribe Resort doesn't geocode perfectly. This is probably because the resort is extremely new and the address hasn't yet been officially marked in the data that Google received. What you do in this case is again your decision, but our suggestion would be to assume that when you receive a single answer, it's the best you're going to get.

The Google JavaScript Geocoding API

Google also provides a means to geocode user input without the intervention of your server. This is a first in the realm of geocoders and enables a few things that can be cumbersome with server-side geocoding. This geocoder is built directly into the JavaScript API itself and makes Ajax calls directly to Google's servers from your visitor's computer.

The benefit is that it's quick and convenient because the API abstracts out all of the Ajax stuff, leaving you with a simple client-side JavaScript call. In addition to this, the latitude and longitude data can come back in such a way that it is trivial to use to place a point on your map using the API.

However, you need to keep in mind that while you don't have to contact *your own* server, you are talking to *a server*—Google's. So, you still need to carefully design your application to minimize the wait times your visitor sees while using your application.

Good and Bad Reasons to Use the JavaScript Geocoder

Here are some cases where it might be appropriate to use the JavaScript geocoder:

- When the visitor is inputting an address that you then plot on a map, but would never otherwise *store* for future use or display to another visitor. For example, this might be the case for a store locator that suggests locations based on proximity to a particular address.

- You are unable to create files on your web server that can be written to by your PHP scripts. This should almost never be the case, as a text file could (at the very worst) be set to world-writable (see the "Caching Lookups" section later in this chapter).

- Once Google exposes its route calculation capabilities, it may become useful for computing one endpoint of the path on the fly, but this is pure speculation.

A good reason to use this geocoder is to get a point from the user that is used *solely* for math calculations. We'll walk through an example of using the JavaScript geocoder in Chapter 10, where we show you how to add a corner to a polygon by either clicking on the map or entering an address into a text field.

It is *not* appropriate to geocode a list of points (such as the Ron Jon stores) on the fly client-side simply because it's easy. Overall, this would be a waste of bandwidth. This in turn means a longer download time for your visitor and a less-responsive map. Also, you definitely don't want to use this approach if the user is likely to be looking up the same thing over and over again.

Basically, while useful for quick-and-dirty mapping, the JavaScript geocoder isn't really useful for many professional map applications since you'll almost always have a server-side component. Thus, accessing the REST-based geocoder from your own Ajax service will allow you to integrate and consolidate the geocoding calls with the rest of your application (say, combining geocoding with looking up store hours). Another benefit of using your own server follows from Chapter 3's geocaching discussion about ensuring consistency by guaranteeing that your points are saved back to the server before showing them on a map. The same principle applies here. If you need to record any information at all back to your own server, you might as well use the REST-based geocoder to do the lookups and save yourself one Ajax call.

Client-Side Caching

Google has made a significant effort to limit the impact of lazy mappers (not you!) who will use the JavaScript geocoder just because it's easy. Aside from pleading with developers to "please cache your lookups" when it announced the geocoder, Google has integrated a client-side geocoding cache into the API. It is on by default and merely uses your visitors' RAM to store things they've previously looked up in case they look the same thing up again. You don't need to do anything special to use this cache, but there is something special you can do with it: you can seed it with information you already have. This means that you could precompute all of the addresses for your stores server-side, and then seed the client-side cache with the data. In certain applications, this could provide a huge speed boost for your map.

As of the time of publishing, the jury is still out on the best way to use some of these shiny new features. The official Google Maps API newsgroup is gushing with discussion about the best ways to do things and when to use the client-side cache and JavaScript geocoder to the best effect. We suggest that you check our website (`http://googlemapsbook.com`) and the official documentation to see what the current best practices are when you read this.

The Yahoo Geocoding API

Currently, the Yahoo Geocoding API (`http://developer.yahoo.net/maps/rest/V1/geocode.html`) is really useful only for geocoding addresses in the United States, though with competition from Google, we're sure this will change. Before Google's geocoder came along, this was the geocoder of choice for many people doing US-centric mashups using both the Google Maps API and the Yahoo Maps API. The only real limitation is that you can make only 5,000 lookup requests per day (per IP address).

■**Caution** The rate limit for Yahoo is based on a 24-hour window, not a calendar day. This window begins when you first send a request to the service and is reset 24 hours later. Also the window does not "slide" (as it does with other services), meaning that it's not a count of the requests made in the *last* 24-hours, but rather a fixed time frame. For a more thorough explanation of the rate limiting in the Yahoo Geocoding Web Service, please visit `http://developer.yahoo.net/search/rate.html`.

To use the API, you must register for a Yahoo application ID (like the Google API key you received in Chapter 2). To obtain your application ID, visit `http://api.search.yahoo.com/webservices/register_application` after logging in to your Yahoo account. If you do not have a Yahoo account, you'll need to create one before proceeding. Once you have your application ID, you'll need to include it in the requests to the service.

Like the Google geocoder, the Yahoo service is REST-based and requires you to append URL-encoded parameters onto the end of the request URL, as listed in Table 4-2.

Table 4-2. *Request Parameters to the Yahoo Geocoding API*

Parameter	Value	Description
appid	String (required)	The application ID you obtained from Yahoo.
street	String	The name and number of the street address. The number is optional but can improve accuracy.
city	String	The name of the city or town.
state	String	The name of the state, either spelled-out in full or as the two-letter abbreviation, which is more accurate.
zip	Integer	The five-digit ZIP code. This could also be a string of five digits, a dash, and the four-digit extension.
location	String	A free-form string representing an address.*
output	String	The format for the output. Possible values are xml (the default) or php. If php is requested, the results will be returned in serialized PHP format.

*The location *parameter overrides the* street, city, state, *and* zip *parameters, and allows you to enter many different common formats for addresses. Thus, you are relying on Yahoo to parse the string accurately and as you intended, much like the Google service does. Yahoo's geocoder is quite good at doing this parsing (for the same reasons as Google's geocoder), so unless you already have the data broken out into components, your best bet might be to use the single* location *parameter instead of the individual parameters.*

Yahoo Geocoder Responses

The following is an example of a request for geocoding the Apress headquarters:

```
http://api.local.yahoo.com/MapsService/V1/geocode?appid=YOUR_APPLICATION_ID&street=➥
2560+Ninth+Street&city=Berkeley&state=CA&zip=94710
```

This returns the XML shown in Listing 4-5.

Listing 4-5. *Sample Response from the Yahoo Geocoding API*

```
<?xml version="1.0" encoding="UTF-8"?>
<ResultSet xmlns:xsi="http://www.w3.org/2001/XMLSchema-instance"
           xmlns="urn:yahoo:maps" xsi:schemaLocation="urn:yahoo:maps
           http://api.local.yahoo.com/MapsService/V1/GeocodeResponse.xsd">
   <Result precision="address" warning="The exact location could not be found,➥
here is the closest match: 2560 9th St, Berkeley, CA 94710">
      <Latitude>37.859569</Latitude>
      <Longitude>-122.291673</Longitude>
      <Address>2560 9TH ST</Address>
      <City>BERKELEY</City>
      <State>CA</State>
      <Zip>94710-2500</Zip>
      <Country>US</Country>
   </Result>
</ResultSet>
```

For the purposes of this discussion, we will ignore the xmlns: and xsi: namespaces. What we care about is the Result node and the elements inside it.

■**Caution** As with the Google service, it is possible to get a ResultSet with multiple Result values. If you would like to see this, try geocoding The White House (1600 Pennsylvania Avenue, Washington DC) while leaving out the ZIP code.

The Result node has two attributes in this case:

precision: This is a string indicating how accurate Yahoo thinks the answer is. This can be one of eight values at the moment: address, street, zip+4, zip+2, zip, city, state, or country. Changes to this list and additional information can be found in Yahoo's API developer documentation (http://developer.yahoo.net/maps/rest/V1/geocode.html).

warning: In our experience, nearly all requests had an "exact location could not be found" warning. This seems to occur for valid addresses whenever the capitalization of the street name, abbreviation of the street type, or spelling in the address don't exactly match the form in the database. In the example in Listing 4-5, it happens because the word "Ninth" is spelled out in full, and the Yahoo database has it listed as "9th." Using the warning node to determine if Yahoo's answer is a good match can be tricky, so for now, let's assume that the first answer in the result set is always the *best* answer (but not necessarily the *right* answer).

Next, we have the actual result fields corresponding to latitude, longitude, address, city, state, ZIP code, and country. Most of this data probably corresponds to the information you used to make the request; however, getting back all of this information is useful in picking the "right" answer in the event of Yahoo returning multiple matches. For now, the latitude and longitude fields are the ones we're most interested in, as those will be used to plot the Ron Jon store locations on our map.

Yahoo Geocoder Requests

So now that you have a handle on what you should be expecting out of the Yahoo API, let's create some PHP code to automate this process. Listing 4-6 shows the script.

Listing 4-6. *Using the Yahoo Geocoding API to Locate the Stores*

```php
<?php
// Your Yahoo! Application id
$appid = "YOUR_YAHOO_APPLICATION_ID";

// Create a CURL object for later use
$ch = curl_init();
curl_setopt($ch, CURLOPT_HEADER, 0);
curl_setopt($ch, CURLOPT_RETURNTRANSFER, 1);

// Open the ronjons.xml file
$datafile = simplexml_load_file("ronjons.xml");
if (!$datafile) die("Unable to open input file!");

foreach ($datafile->store as $store) {
  // Construct the request string
  $url = "http://api.local.yahoo.com/MapsService/V1/geocode?appid=$appid";
  if ($store->address) $url .= "&street=".urlencode($store->address);
  if ($store->city) $url .= "&city=".urlencode($store->city);
  if ($store->state) $url .= "&state=".urlencode($store->state);
  if ($store->zip) $url .= "&zip=".$store->zip;

  echo "Store: {$store->name}\n";

  // Query Yahoo for this store's lat/long
  curl_setopt($ch, CURLOPT_URL, $url);
  $response = curl_exec($ch);

  // Use SimpleXML to parse our answer into something we can use
  $yahooresult = simplexml_load_string($response);
  if (!$yahooresult) echo "Unable to parse Yahoo response for {$store->name}!\n";
  else foreach ($yahooresult->Result as $result) {
    echo "Result Precision: {$result['precision']}\n";
    if ($result['precision'] != "address") {
      echo "Warning: {$result['warning']}\n";
      echo "Address: {$result->Address}\n";
    }
    echo "Latitude: {$result->Latitude}\n";
    echo "Longitude: {$result->Longitude}\n\n";
  } // for each Yahoo result
} // for each store
```

```
// Close the CURL file and destroy the object
curl_close($ch);
?>
```

The code in Listing 4-6 is similar to the one for the Google geocoder (Listing 4-3). In fact, this is a template we will use a few more times in this chapter, and one that will serve you well for most REST-based services that return XML. The only real difference in the Yahoo example is that we've chosen to use the individual parameters since our data file already has them split up. This means that we need to use PHP's urlencode() on any parameter that might need it (those with spaces or special characters, for example), instead of on a single mammoth string. If you used the location parameter, this example could probably be 95% identical to the one in Listing 4-3.

We also check for the presence of each option before appending it to the URL of the REST request, despite the fact that Yahoo will silently ignore blank inputs. After all, defensive programming is always good practice, no matter how trivial the task—especially for experimental code that will probably grow into production code.

Listing 4-7 gives the resulting output from Listing 4-6.

Listing 4-7. *Output from the Yahoo Geocoding Script*

```
Store: "The Original" Ron Jon Surf Shop
Result Precision: address
Latitude: 39.6351
Longitude: -74.1883

Store: "One of a Kind" Ron Jon Surf Shop
Result Precision: address
Latitude: 28.356577
Longitude: -80.608069

Store: Ron Jon Surf Shop - Sunrise
Result Precision: address
Latitude: 26.156292
Longitude: -80.316945

Store: Ron Jon Surf Shop - Orlando
Result Precision: address
Latitude: 28.469972
Longitude: -81.450143

Store: Ron Jon Surf Shop - Key West
Result Precision: address
Latitude: 24.560448
Longitude: -81.805998

Store: Ron Jon Surf Shop - California
Result Precision: address
Latitude: 33.783329
Longitude: -117.890562
```

```
Store: Ron Jon Cape Caribe Resort
Result Precision: street
Warning:
Address: [600-699] SHOREWOOD DR
Latitude: 28.40232
Longitude: -80.59554

Result Precision: street
Warning:
Address: SHOREWOOD DR
Latitude: 28.40168
Longitude: -80.59774
```

■Note You may need to view the source to see formatted output from Listing 4-7.

The only real surprise here is the last entry, `Cape Caribe Resort`, failed to geocode any more accurately than the general location of the street. This seems to corroborate Google's answer quite nicely (remember that it gave us 699 Shorewood instead of 1000 Shorewood). For now, simply remember that you'll always need to do some sort of error checking on the results or you might end up sending your customers to the wrong place. This entry also shows an example of multiple results being returned, as discussed earlier.

A possible solution to the ambiguous answer problem is to cross-reference (and average) the answers you get from one service (Google) with another (Yahoo). This is an onerous task if done for all of the data, but might be an excellent solution for your particular application if applied only to data that gives you grief.

Geocoder.us

Let's adapt our code for another US-centric geocoding service. Geocoder.us is a very popular service and was introduced well before Yahoo's and Google's services hit the market. For a long while, it was the measuring stick against which all other services were compared. The service was developed by two enterprising programmers, who took the freely available 2004 US Census Bureau's data and converted it into a web service.

■Note The developers of Geocoder.us have made the Perl code that they wrote for their service available under an open source license and a module called `Geo::Coder::US`. If this interests you, then Chapter 11 may also interest you. In Chapter 11, we dig deep into the US Census data to build our own geocoder from scratch using PHP instead of Perl.

Just as with the Google and Yahoo services, there are limitations to the Geocoder.us service. The free service cannot be used for commercial purposes, and is rate-limited to prevent abuse, though the developers haven't published exactly what the limit is. You can purchase a high-volume or commercial account that will get you four lookups per penny (20,000 lookups for $50) with no rate limiting whatsoever.

Geocoder.us offers four different ways to access its web services: an XML-RPC interface, a SOAP interface, a REST interface that returns an RDF/XML document, and a REST interface that returns a plaintext CSV result. The accuracy, methods, and return values are equivalent across all of these interfaces. It's merely a matter of taste as to which one you'll use. For our example, we'll use the REST-based service and the CSV result (for some variety).

The following is an example of a Geocoder.us request for geocoding the Apress headquarters:

```
http://geocoder.us/service/csv/geocode?address=2560+Ninth+Street,+Berkeley+CA+94710
```

This returns the CSV string `37.859524,-122.291713,2560 9th St,Albany,CA,94710`. You can see that it has mistaken Berkeley for Albany, despite the fact that the ZIP codes match. The latitude and longitude are nearly identical to the results Yahoo gave.

Let's again reuse the code from Listing 4-3 and adapt it to suit this new service. As with the Google geocoder, only one parameter is passed into this REST service, and it is called `address`. At minimum, either a city and state or a ZIP code must be contained in the `address` parameter. Listing 4-8 shows the adapted code.

■**Caution** The code in Listing 4-8 takes a while to run. We'll discuss why in a moment, but for now be patient.

Listing 4-8. *Using the Geocoder.us Service to Locate the Stores*

```php
<?php
// Create a CURL object for later use
$ch = curl_init();
curl_setopt($ch, CURLOPT_HEADER, 0);
curl_setopt($ch, CURLOPT_RETURNTRANSFER, 1);

// Open the ronjons.xml file
$datafile = simplexml_load_file("ronjons.xml");
if (!$datafile) die("Unable to open input file!");

foreach ($datafile->store as $store) {
  // Construct the request string
  $url = "http://geocoder.us/service/csv/geocode?address=";
  $address = "";
  if ($store->address) $address .= $store->address.", ";
  if ($store->city) $address .= $store->city." ";
  if ($store->state) $address .= $store->state." ";
  if ($store->zip) $address .= $store->zip;
  $url .= urlencode($address);

  echo "Store: {$store->name}\n";
```

```
    // Query Geocoder.us for this store's lat/long
    curl_setopt($ch, CURLOPT_URL, $url);
    $response = curl_exec($ch);

    // Split up the CSV result into components
    list($lat,$long,$address,$city,$state,$zip) = split(",",$response);
    echo "Latitude: $lat\n";
    echo "Longitude: $long\n\n";
} // for each store

// Close the CURL file and destroy the object
curl_close($ch);
?>
```

The only real difference here is with the CSV-style response. We've used a convention for splitting here that is common to the code snippets found on http://www.php.net, namely, using list() to get named strings instead of an array when calling the split() function. Listing 4-9 shows the output of the code in Listing 4-8.

Listing 4-9. *Output from the Geocoder.us Script*

```
Store: "The Original" Ron Jon Surf Shop
Latitude: 39.649509
Longitude: -74.177136

Store: "One of a Kind" Ron Jon Surf Shop
Latitude: 28.356433
Longitude: -80.608227

Store: Ron Jon Surf Shop - Sunrise
Latitude: 26.150513
Longitude: -80.316476

Store: Ron Jon Surf Shop - Orlando
Latitude: 28.466795
Longitude: -81.449860

Store: Ron Jon Surf Shop - Key West
Latitude: 24.560083
Longitude: -81.806069

Store: Ron Jon Surf Shop - California
Latitude: 33.781086
Longitude: -117.892520

Store: Ron Jon Cape Caribe Resort
Latitude: 2: couldn't find this address! sorry
Longitude:
```

When executing the code, the first thing you'll probably notice is that this request takes a long time to run. We believe this is a result of Geocoder.us rate limiting being based on requests per minute instead of requests per day. When testing, it took well over a minute to geocode just the seven points in the `ronjons.xml` data file.

The next thing you'll see if you look carefully is that the latitude and longitude results are the same as those from Yahoo only to three decimal places (on average). This is not a large difference and is the result of using different interpolation optimizations on the same data set, which we'll discuss in Chapter 11.

Notice that "The Original" store has given us a single answer this time, instead of multiple answers, and that the resort has given us grief yet again, except in this case, we didn't even get a best guess.

■**Note** To determine just how large a distance difference the various geocoders give you for each of the results, you'll need to use the spherical distance equations (such as the Haversine method) we provide in Chapter 10.

Geocoder.ca

Geocoder.ca is similar to the service provided by Geocoder.us, but it is specifically targeted at providing information about Canada. (This service is in no way affiliated with Geocoder.us, and it uses a completely different data set, provided by Statistics Canada.)

The people behind Geocoder.ca built it specifically for their own experiments with the Google Maps API when they had trouble finding a timely, accurate, and cost-effective solution for geocoding Canadian addresses. They obtained numerous sources of data (postal, census, and commercial) and cross-referenced everything to weed out the inevitable errors in each set. This means that the Geocoder.ca service is quite possibly the *most* accurate information for Canada so far. (However, now that Google's solution covers Canada with relatively good accuracy, we're afraid that this extremely comprehensive service will become marginalized.)

Geocoder.ca provides a lot of neat features like intersection geocoding, reverse geocoding, and a suggestion system for correcting mistyped (or renamed) street names—none of which are provided by Google's geocoder, or any other for that matter. We don't cover any of these alternative features in this chapter, but you can find more information about them at their website if you're interested.

Remember that there is still no free lunch, so as with the other services, there are also limitations on the Geocoder.ca service. The free service is limited to between 500 and 2000 lookups per day per source IP address, depending on server load (light days you get more; heavy days less). The developers are willing to extend the limits for nonprofit organizations, but everyone else will need to purchase an account for commercial uses. The cost is currently the same as Geocoder.us: 20,000 lookups for $50. Purchasing a commercial account might be an excellent way to cross-reference Google's multiple-result answers quickly, cheaply, and effectively.

An example of a query for geocoding the CN Tower in Toronto, Ontario is as follows:

```
http://geocoder.ca/?&stno=301&addresst=Front%2BStreet%2BWest&city=Toronto&prov=➥
ON&postal=M5V2T6&geoit=XML.
```

This yields the exceedingly simple XML result in Listing 4-10.

Listing 4-10. *Sample Response from Geocoder.ca*

```
<?xml version="1.0" encoding="UTF-8" ?>
<geodata>
        <latt>43.643865000</latt>
        <longt>-79.388545000</longt>
</geodata>
```

Notice that the XML response uses `latt` and `longt`. The trailing t is easy to miss when reading the raw XML.

For an example, the Ron Jon Surf Shop data will not work, since the chain has yet to open a store in Canada. Instead, we'll again use the CN Tower in Toronto, Ontario. The address for the CN Tower is 301 Front Street West, Toronto, Ontario M5V 2T6 Canada. Listing 4-11 shows a small PHP snippet for geocoding this single address, which could easily be looped and abstracted as in previous examples to do multiple addresses. Feel free to substitute your own address if you live in the Great White North or know someone who does.

Listing 4-11. *Using Geocoder.ca to Locate the CN Tower in Toronto*

```php
<?php
// Address to geocode (the CN Tower)
$street_no = "301";
$street = "Front Street West";
$city = "Toronto";
$prov = "ON";
$postal = "M5V2T6";

// Create a CURL object for later use
$ch = curl_init();
curl_setopt($ch, CURLOPT_HEADER, 0);
curl_setopt($ch, CURLOPT_RETURNTRANSFER, 1);

// Construct the request string
$url = "http://geocoder.ca/?";
$url .= "&stno=".urlencode($street_no);
$url .= "&addresst=".urlencode($street);
$url .= "&city=".urlencode($city);
$url .= "&prov=".$prov;
$url .= "&postal=".$postal;
$url .= "&geoit=XML";

// Query Geocoder.ca for the lat/long
curl_setopt($ch, CURLOPT_URL, $url);
$response = curl_exec($ch);

// Use SimpleXML to parse our answer into something we can use
$resultset = simplexml_load_string($response);
if (!$resultset) die("Unable to parse the response!");
```

```
echo "The CN tower is located here:\n";
echo "Latitude: {$resultset->latt}\n";
echo "Longitude: {$resultset->longt}\n";

// Close the CURL file and destroy the object
curl_close($ch);
?>
```

The most important lines in Listing 4-11 are highlighted in bold. The first is that the Geocoder.ca service prefers you to split out the street number from the street name. This isn't strictly necessary, but it does imply that greater accuracy can be achieved by doing so. The second is that the geoit parameter *must* be included. At this point, there is no alternative value for this parameter, but there probably will be in the future. Lastly, when parsing the results, again, remember that the XML response uses latt and longt.

Listing 4-12 shows the output from Listing 4-11.

Listing 4-12. *Output from our Geocoder.ca Script*

```
The CN tower is located here:
Latitude: 43.643865000
Longitude: -79.388545000
```

When you compare this answer with the one Google gives you (43.642411,-79.386649) by clicking on a map, as in Chapter 3, you see that Geocoder.ca has done an excellent job of finding the correct coordinates for the CN Tower given its street address.

Services for Geocoding Addresses Outside Google's Coverage

For addresses outside the set provided by Google's geocoder, the job becomes much more difficult due to the lack of good, freely available data. In Chapter 11, you'll see how to create your own service from some sources of free data for the UK and the US. Maybe some of you will be inspired to find data for your country and create a service for the rest of us.

For now, however, we're simply going to share a few of the geocoding services we've found to date for areas outside Google's coverage area. We can't guarantee the accuracy or completeness of data from these services, since we don't have any real addresses to test with or enough knowledge of the local geography to wing it. We'll try to keep an updated list of services as we hear about them on our website at http://googlemapsbook.com/geocoders. Please let us know if you find or make more!

Geonames.org

Geonames.org has quite a few web services that might fit your needs. There is a full-text search of its database of place names, landmarks, and other geopositional data at http://www.geonames.org/export/geonames-search.html. However, you can also find (partial) postal code lookups for many countries (currently over 50), as well as reverse geocoding solutions for finding the name of the country or closest named feature for a given latitude and longitude (reverse geocoding). In Appendix A, we discuss the use of complete database dumps as a possible means to acquire the data you need to build your application without using external geocoding services.

ViaMichelin.com

One interesting solution for geocoding addresses in western Europe is `http://www.viamichelin.com`. The company that runs this service is part of the same company that makes Michelin tires (remember the Michelin Man?). The service offers route calculation, geocoding, and even an alternative source of map data. ViaMichelin is in competition with Google when it comes to maps, but for European locations where Google does not yet have geocoding services, the ViaMichelin solution could mean the difference between a successful project and a failure.

Bulk Geocoders

Many bulk geocoding services out there will accept a CSV or Excel file from you, determine latitude and longitude to the best of their ability, and give you the results a few hours to a few days later. These services typically charge a per-point fee when they are successful and nothing when they are not. Many of them use the Microsoft MapPoint Web Service to do the work. The quality of the data varies (with provider, price, and country), so we suggest that you do your research before hiring one of them to geocode your points.

Caching Lookups

As programmers, we hate wasting resources, and as service providers, we hate having our resources wasted. Therefore, for many of the examples in the rest of this book, you'll be precomputing the latitude and longitude programmatically and storing that information along with the point data you want to use in your mashup. This saves your bandwidth by not requiring unnecessary CURL/API requests, and saves the bandwidth of the services you'll be using for geocoding. Best of all, it provides a much faster user experience for your map visitors, which is almost always the single largest factor in determining the success of a website or service.

■**Caution** Caching is not *always* the right answer. In some of the more novel mashups we've seen, the data is so dynamic that caching the latitude and longitude of the plotted point is actually more of a waste than not caching it. These examples are typically mashups where a single given point is plotted for only one or two visitors before it's never seen again, such as plotting the current position of a GPS device.

To cache the data for your store locator map, you'll modify the code in Listing 4-6 to create a script (Listing 4-13) that does a bulk geocoding of all of the stores and adds the latitude and longitude to the data file in Listing 4-14. In the next section, you'll use this data file to make your map, and assume that the stores already have latitude and longitude values associated with them.

Listing 4-13. *Modified Code Showing Write-Back of Cached Data*

```
<?php
// Your Yahoo! Application Code
$appid = YOUR_YAHOO_APPLICATION_ID;
```

```php
// Create a CURL object for later use
$ch = curl_init();
curl_setopt($ch, CURLOPT_HEADER, 0);
curl_setopt($ch, CURLOPT_RETURNTRANSFER, 1);

// Open the ronjons.xml file
$datafile = simplexml_load_file("ronjons.xml");

// Open a file to store our consolidated information in
$newfile = fopen("ronjons_cache.xml", "w+");
fputs($newfile,'<?xml version="1.0" encoding="UTF-8"?>'."\n");
fputs($newfile,'<stores>'."\n");

foreach ($datafile->store as $store) {
  // Construct the request string
  $url = "http://api.local.yahoo.com/MapsService/V1/geocode?appid=$appid";
  if ($store->address) $url .= "&street=".urlencode($store->address);
  if ($store->city) $url .= "&city=".urlencode($store->city);
  if ($store->state) $url .= "&state=".urlencode($store->state);
  if ($store->zip) $url .= "&zip=".trim($store->zip);

  // Query Yahoo for this store's lat/long
  curl_setopt($ch, CURLOPT_URL, $url);
  $response = curl_exec($ch);

  // Use SimpleXML to parse our answer into something we can use
  $yahooresult = simplexml_load_string($response);
  foreach ($yahooresult->Result as $result) {
    $latitude = $result->Latitude;
    $longitude = $result->Longitude;
  } // for each Yahoo Result

  // Lastly output the XML to our file
  fputs($newfile,' <store>'."\n");
  fputs($newfile,'  <name>'.trim($store->name).'</name>'."\n");
  fputs($newfile,'  <address>'.trim($store->address).'</address>'."\n");
  if ($store->address2)
    fputs($newfile,'  <address2>'.trim($store->address2).'</address2>'."\n");
  fputs($newfile,'  <city>'.trim($store->city).'</city>'."\n");
  fputs($newfile,'  <state>'.trim($store->state).'</state>'."\n");
  fputs($newfile,'  <zip>'.trim($store->zip).'</zip>'."\n");
  fputs($newfile,'  <phone>'.trim($store->phone).'</phone>'."\n");
  fputs($newfile,'  <pin>'.trim($store->pin).'</pin>'."\n");
  fputs($newfile,'  <latitude>'.trim($latitude).'</latitude>'."\n");
  fputs($newfile,'  <longitude>'.trim($longitude).'</longitude>'."\n");
  fputs($newfile,' </store>'."\n");
} // for each store
```

```
// Close the CURL file and destroy the object
curl_close($ch);

// Close the new file freeing the memory
fputs($newfile,'</stores>'."\n");
fclose($newfile);
?>
```

As you can see from the code, in our example we've elected to use the standard fopen(), fwrite(), and fclose() PHP commands to create the new file. SimpleXML doesn't provide a facility to add elements to an open XML document, and getting into a full-blown DOM example would be counterproductive.

Your modified script now creates a new file on the file system, as shown in Listing 4-14. You could have just as easily written the file on top of the existing ronjons.xml file, but if the conversion failed, you could lose all your existing data. The only trick is that you'll need to grant the web server user access to make new files in the folder you're working in, or you'll need to create a blank file and make it world-writable before executing this code.

Listing 4-14. *The New ronjons_cache.xml File with Caching (ronjons_cache.xml)*

```xml
<?xml version="1.0" encoding="UTF-8"?>
<stores>
 <store>
  <name>"The Original" Ron Jon Surf Shop</name>
  <address>901 Central Avenue</address>
  <city>Long Beach Island</city>
  <state>NJ</state>
  <zip>08008</zip>
  <phone>(609) 494-8844</phone>
  <pin>store</pin>
  <latitude>39.649652</latitude>
  <longitude>-74.177547</longitude>
 </store>
 <store>
  <name>"One of a Kind" Ron Jon Surf Shop</name>
  <address>4151 North Atlantic Avenue</address>
  <city>Cocoa Beach</city>
  <state>FL</state>
  <zip>32931</zip>
  <phone>(321) 799-8888</phone>
  <pin>store</pin>
  <latitude>28.356577</latitude>
  <longitude>-80.608069</longitude>
 </store>
 <store>
  <name>Ron Jon Surf Shop - Sunrise</name>
  <address>2610 Sawgrass Mills Circle</address>
  <address2>Suite 1415</address2>
```

```
 <city>Sunrise</city>
 <state>FL</state>
 <zip>33323</zip>
 <phone>(954) 846-1880</phone>
 <pin>store</pin>
 <latitude>26.156292</latitude>
 <longitude>-80.316945</longitude>
</store>
<store>
 <name>Ron Jon Surf Shop - Orlando</name>
 <address>5160 International Drive</address>
 <city>Orlando</city>
 <state>FL</state>
 <zip>32819</zip>
 <phone>(407) 481-2555</phone>
 <pin>store</pin>
 <latitude>28.469972</latitude>
 <longitude>-81.450143</longitude>
</store>
<store>
 <name>Ron Jon Surf Shop - Key West</name>
 <address>503 Front Street</address>
 <city>Key West</city>
 <state>FL</state>
 <zip>33040</zip>
 <phone>(305) 293-8880</phone>
 <pin>store</pin>
 <latitude>24.560448</latitude>
 <longitude>-81.805998</longitude>
</store>
<store>
 <name>Ron Jon Surf Shop - California</name>
 <address>20 City Blvd.</address>
 <address2>West Building C Suite 1</address2>
 <city>Orange</city>
 <state>CA</state>
 <zip>92868</zip>
 <phone>(714) 939-9822</phone>
 <pin>store</pin>
 <latitude>33.783329</latitude>
 <longitude>-117.890562</longitude>
</store>
<store>
 <name>Ron Jon Cape Caribe Resort</name>
 <address>1000 Shorewood Drive</address>
 <city>Cape Canaveral</city>
 <state>FL</state>
```

```
    <zip>32920</zip>
    <phone>(321) 328-2830</phone>
    <pin>resort</pin>
    <latitude>28.40168</latitude>
    <longitude>-80.59774</longitude>
  </store>
</stores>
```

■**Note** Ideally, you would be using some sort of relational database rather than a flat file on your file system for storing the points for your map. This would allow you to check each point at mapping time and look up (and cache) only those that don't have geocoded data yet. We'll begin using SQL databases in the next chapter.

The performance gain for caching just seven points is probably not noticeable on your high-speed connection. However, as your code scales to hundreds or thousands of data points, it will become critical. Also, if you are paying for each lookup, even at hundreds of lookups per dollar, the costs can add up quickly if a popular blog links to your map.

Note that the one place to avoid using caching is when your visitors are required to enter their current location so that the map can tailor itself to their situation and surroundings. This is often used in a store finder application where visitors enter their address and how far they are willing to drive to buy your product from a brick-and-mortar store.

Building a Store Location Map

Now that you have your stores and their latitude and longitude coordinates, you're ready to make your map. This will be a very basic map, but it serves our demonstration nicely. You'll customize the marker GIcon using the Ron Jon Surf Shop logo, and use the info window to display the store's address and phone number to visitors when they click the marker.

To make things a little easier, you can begin by taking the map you created in Chapter 2, with the addition of the icon creation from Chapter 3, and use the map_data.php file to convert your XML file of cached locations into the data structure from the map_data.php file in Listing 2-6. Listings 4-15, 4-16, and 4-17 show the modified map_data.php file, its output, and the map_functions.js file, respectively.

Listing 4-15. *PHP Generation of the JavaScript (JSON) Data File in map_data.php*

```php
<?php
// Open the ronjons_cache.xml file and load the data for the pins
$datafile = simplexml_load_file("ronjons_cache.xml");
echo "var markers = [\n";
foreach ($datafile->store as $store) {
  $description = "{$store->address}<br />";
  if ($store->address2) $description .= "{$store->address2}<br/>";
  $description .= "{$store->city}, {$store->state}<br/>";
  $description .= "{$store->zip}<br/>";
  $description .= "Phone: {$store->phone}<br/>";
```

```
  echo "{
    'latitude': {$store->latitude},
    'longitude': {$store->longitude},
    'name': '{$store->name}',
    'description': '$description'
  },\n";
}

echo "];\n";
?>
```

Listing 4-16. *Generated JSON Data Structure in map_data.php*

```
var markers = [
{
  'latitude': 39.649652,
  'longitude': -74.177547,
  'name': '"The Original" Ron Jon Surf Shop',
  'description': '901 Central Avenue<br />Long Beach Island,➥
 NJ<br/>08008<br/>Phone: (609) 494-8844<br/>'
}, {
  'latitude': 28.356577,
  'longitude': -80.608069,
  'name': '"One of a Kind" Ron Jon Surf Shop',
  'description': '4151 North Atlantic Avenue<br />Cocoa Beach,➥
 FL<br/>32931<br/>Phone: (321) 799-8888<br/>'
}, {
  'latitude': 26.156292,
  'longitude': -80.316945,
  'name': 'Ron Jon Surf Shop - Sunrise',
  'description': '2610 Sawgrass Mills Circle<br />Suite 1415<br/>Sunrise,➥
 FL<br/>33323<br/>Phone: (954) 846-1880<br/>'
}, {
  'latitude': 28.469972,
  'longitude': -81.450143,
  'name': 'Ron Jon Surf Shop - Orlando',
  'description': '5160 International Drive<br />Orlando,➥
 FL<br/>32819<br/>Phone: (407) 481-2555<br/>'
}, {
  'latitude': 24.560448,
  'longitude': -81.805998,
  'name': 'Ron Jon Surf Shop - Key West',
  'description': '503 Front Street<br />Key West,➥
 FL<br/>33040<br/>Phone: (305) 293-8880<br/>'
}, {
  'latitude': 33.783329,
  'longitude': -117.890562,
  'name': 'Ron Jon Surf Shop - California',
```

```
  'description': '20 City Blvd.<br />West Building C Suite 1<br/>Orange,➡
 CA<br/>92868<br/>Phone: (714) 939-9822<br/>'
}, {
  'latitude': 28.40168,
  'longitude': -80.59774,
  'name': 'Ron Jon Cape Caribe Resort',
  'description': '1000 Shorewood Drive<br />Cape Canaveral,➡
 FL<br/>32920<br/>Phone: (321) 328-2830<br/>'
},
];
```

Listing 4-17. *map_functions.js from Chapter 2 Modified to Add Customized Icons and Info Windows*

```
var centerLatitude = 40.6897;
var centerLongitude = -95.0446;
var startZoom = 3;

var map;

var RonJonLogo = new GIcon();
RonJonLogo.image = 'ronjonsurfshoplogo.png';
RonJonLogo.iconSize = new GSize(48, 24);
RonJonLogo.iconAnchor = new GPoint(24, 14);
RonJonLogo.infoWindowAnchor = new GPoint(24, 24);

function addMarker(latitude , longitude, description) {
    var marker = new GMarker(new GLatLng(latitude, longitude), RonJonLogo);
    GEvent.addListener(marker, 'click',
        function() {
            marker.openInfoWindowHtml(description);
        }
    );

    map.addOverlay(marker);
}

function init() {
    map = new GMap2(document.getElementById("map"));
    map.addControl(new GSmallMapControl());
    map.setCenter(new GLatLng(centerLatitude, centerLongitude), startZoom);

    for(id in markers) {
        addMarker(markers[id].latitude , markers[id].longitude,
        markers[id].description);
    }
}

window.onload = init;
```

Figure 4-1 shows the completed map.

Figure 4-1. *The completed map of the Ron Jon Surf Shop US locations*

There you have it. The best bits of all of our examples so far combined into a map application. Data is geocoded, automatically cached for speed, and plotted quickly based on a JSON representation of our XML data file.

Summary

This chapter covered using geocoding services with your maps. It's safe to assume that you'll be able to adapt the general ideas and examples here to use almost any web-based geocoding service that comes along in the future. From here on, we'll assume that you know how to use these services (or ones like them) to geocode and cache your information efficiently.

This ends the first part of the book. In the next part, we'll move on to working with third-party data sets that have hundreds of thousands of points. Our examples will use the FCC's antenna structures database that currently numbers well over a hundred thousand points.

PART 2

■ ■ ■

Beyond the Basics

CHAPTER 5

Manipulating Third-Party Data

In this chapter, we're going to cover two of the most popular ways of obtaining third-party data for use on your map: downloadable character-delimited text files and screen scraping. To demonstrate manipulating data, we'll use a single example in this and the next two chapters (the FCC Antenna Structures Database). In the end, you'll have an understanding of the data that will be used for the sample maps, as well as how the examples might be generalized to fit your own sources of raw information.

In Appendix A, you'll find a list of other sources of free information that you could harvest and combine to make maps. You might want to thumb to this appendix to see some other neat things you could do in your own experiments and try applying the tips and tricks presented in this chapter to some other source of data. The scripts in this chapter should give you a great toolbox for harvesting nearly any data source, and the ideas in the next two chapters will help you make an awesome map, no matter how much data there is.

In this chapter, you'll learn how to do the following:

- Split up and store the information from character-delimited text files in a convenient way for later use.

- Use SQL as a server-side information storage system instead of the file-system-based text files (XML, CSV, and so on) you've been using so far.

- Optimize your SQL queries to extract the information you want quickly and easily.

- Parse the visible HTML from a website and extract the parts that you care about—a process called *screen scraping*.

Using Downloadable Text Files

For the next three chapters, we're going to be working with the US Federal Communications Commission (FCC) Antenna Structure Registration (ASR) database. This database will help us highlight many of the more challenging aspects of building a professional map mashup.

So why the FCC ASR database? There are several reasons:

- The data is free to use, easy to obtain, and well documented. This avoids copyright and licensing issues for you while you play with the data.

- There is a lot of data, allowing us to discuss issues of memory consumption and interface speed. At the time of publication, there were more than 120,000 records.

- The latitudes and longitudes are already recorded in the database, removing the need to cover something we've already discussed in depth.

- None of the preceding items are likely to have changed since this book was published, serving as a future-proof example that should still be relevant as you read this.

- The maps you can make with this data look extremely cool (Figure 5-1)!

Figure 5-1. *Example of a map built with FCC ASR data (which you will build in Chapter 7)*

Downloading the Database

The first thing you need to do is obtain the FCC ASR database. It's available from `http://wireless.fcc.gov/uls/data/complete/r_tower.zip`. This file is approximately 65MB to 70MB when compressed.

After you've downloaded the file, unpack it and transfer `RA.dat`, `EN.dat`, and `CO.dat` into your working folder. You won't need the rest of the files for this experiment, although they do contain interesting data. If you're interested in the official documentation, feel free to visit `http://wireless.fcc.gov/cgi-bin/wtb-datadump.pl`.

Tables 5-1 through 5-3 outline the contents of the `RA.dat`, `EN.dat`, and `CO.dat` files. `RA.dat` (Table 5-1) is the key file, and the one you will use to bind the three together. It lists the unique identification numbers for each structure, as well as the physical properties, like size and street address. `EN.dat` (Table 5-2) outlines the ownership of each structure, and `CO.dat` (Table 5-3) outlines the coordinates for the structure in latitude and longitude notation. The Used in Our Example? column in each table indicates the data you will be using.

Table 5-1. *RA.dat: Registrations and Applications*

Column	Data Element	Content Definition	Used in Our Example?
0	Record Type	char(2)	
1	Content Indicator	char(3)	
2	File Number	char(8)	
3	Registration Number	char(7)	Yes
4	Unique System Identifier	numeric(9)	Yes
5	Application Purpose	char(2)	
6	Previous Purpose	char(2)	
7	Input Source Code	char(1)	
8	Status Code	char(1)	
9	Date Entered	mm/dd/yyyy	
10	Date Received	mm/dd/yyyy	
11	Date Issued	mm/dd/yyyy	
12	Date Constructed	mm/dd/yyyy	Yes
13	Date Dismantled	mm/dd/yyyy	Yes
14	Date Action	mm/dd/yyyy	
15	Archive Flag Code	char(1)	
16	Version	integer	
17	Signature First Name	varchar(20)	
18	Signature Middle Initial	char(1)	
19	Signature Last Name	varchar(20)	
20	Signature Suffix	varchar(3)	
21	Signature Title	varchar(40)	
22	Invalid Signature	char(1)	
23	Structure_Street Address	varchar(80)	Yes
24	Structure_City	varchar(20)	Yes
25	Structure_State Code	char(2)	Yes
26	Height of Structure	numeric(5,1)	Yes
27	Ground Elevation	numeric(6,1)	Yes
28	Overall Height Above Ground	numeric(6,1)	Yes
29	Overall Height AMSL	numeric(6,1)	Yes
30	Structure Type	char(6)	Yes
31	Date FAA Determination Issued	mm/dd/yyyy	
32	FAA Study Number	varchar(20)	
33	FAA Circular Number	varchar(10)	
34	Specification Option	Integer	
35	Painting and Lighting	varchar(100)	
36	FAA EMI Flag	char(1)	
37	NEPA Flag	char(1)	

Table 5-2. *EN.dat: Ownership Entity*

Column	Data Element	Content Definition	Used in Our Example?
0	Record Type	char(2)	
1	Content Indicator	char(3)	
2	File Number	char(8)	
3	Registration Number	char(7)	Yes
4	Unique System Identifier	numeric(9,0)	Yes
5	Entity Type	char(1)	
6	Licensee ID	char(9)	
7	Entity Name	varchar(200)	Yes
8	First Name	varchar(20)	
9	MI	char(1)	
10	Last Name	varchar(20)	
11	Suffix	char(3)	
12	Phone	char(10)	
13	Internet Address	varchar(50)	
14	Street Address	varchar(35)	Yes
15	PO Box	varchar(20)	
16	City	varchar(20)	Yes
17	State	char(2)	Yes
18	Zip Code	char(9)	Yes
19	Attention	varchar(35)	

■**Note** In the Entity Name column of the EN.dat file, there is often an equal sign (=). If you are going to build a map that has ownership search features (say for cellular carriers), you might want to import only the part after the equal sign, so that you can more accurately display results to your users.

Table 5-3. *CO.dat: Physical Location Coordinates*

Column	Data Element	Content Definition	Used in Our Example?
0	Record Type	char(2)	
1	Content Indicator	char(3)	
2	File Number	char(8)	
3	Registration Number	char(7)	Yes
4	Unique System Identifier	numeric(9)	Yes
5	Coordinate Type	char(1)	
6	Latitude Degrees	integer	Yes

Column	Data Element	Content Definition	Used in Our Example?
7	Latitude Minutes	integer	Yes
8	Latitude Seconds	numeric(4,1)	Yes
9	Latitude Direction	char(1)	Yes
10	Latitude_Total_Seconds	numeric(8,1)	
11	Longitude Degrees	integer	Yes
12	Longitude Minutes	integer	Yes
13	Longitude Seconds	numeric(4,1)	Yes
14	Longitude Direction	char(1)	Yes
15	Longitude_Total_Seconds	numeric(8,1)	

As you can see, we're not concerned with most of the data that is available in this database. Our main interest is the location and physical properties of each structure.

Parsing CSV Data

Now that you know what you want to use from the massive amount of data provided by the FCC, you need to break out those bits into something useful. For this task, you're going to use some simple PHP. We'll start with the standard fopen()/fgets() example from http://www.php.net/fgets and add in the code to convert each line into an array. The code in Listing 5-1 shows this process.

Listing 5-1. *Parsing a Pipe (|) Delimited File*

```php
<?php
// Open the Registrations and Applications Data file
$handle = @fopen("RA.dat","r");

// Parse and output the first 50 USI numbers.
$i = 0;
if ($handle) {
    while (!feof($handle)) {
        $buffer = fgets($handle, 1024);
        $row = explode("|",$buffer);
        echo "USI#: ".$row[4]."<br />\n";
        if ($i == 50) break; else $i++;
    }
    fclose($handle);
}
?>
```

The code in Listing 5-1 doesn't do much other than fill your screen with useless information. We've separated it from the data import into SQL data structures (shown later in Listing 5-3 in the next section) because it's a recipe that you'll use repeatedly if you're working with most third-party data, and thus we felt it warranted its own section.

■**Note** In Listing 5-1, we've limited our script to output only the first 50 lines to prevent abuse and save you time. However, it also serves as a good lesson: you should protect your own (long-running) import/parsing scripts from being unintentionally (or intentionally) executed by general web surfers, or you may find yourself the victim of a denial-of-service (DoS) attack.

Optimizing the Import

Leaving all of this data in the flat files won't be very efficient for creating a map from the data, since it will take minutes each time to parse the files and will likely flood all the memory buffers on your server and your visitors' machines. Therefore, you'll import the data points into a SQL data structure so that you can selectively plot the information based on your visitors' interests (as described in the next two chapters).

■**Caution** We assume you are already familiar with MySQL and have an administration tool for your database that you are skilled at using. If you're not familiar with MySQL, we recommend *Beginning PHP and MySQL 5: From Novice to Professional, Second Edition*, by W. Jason Gilmore (http://www.apress.com/book/bookDisplay.html?bID=10017).

You'll be storing the information from each of your data files in its own table. While the data you are interested in has a 1:1:1 relationship among the three files, the reason for doing this is threefold:

- Reading in the contents of each file into a gigantic array and then inserting the data into a single unified table one record at a time would consume hundreds of megabytes of memory. Since the default PHP per-script memory limit is 8MB, and most web hosts don't increase this limit, this isn't a workable solution in general. We also assume you do not have sufficient permissions at your web host to increase your own memory limits. If you do control your own server, feel free to use this method if you prefer, as there are no real drawbacks other than the one-time memory consumption issue.

- Opening the three files simultaneously and sequentially reassembling the corresponding records would require that the files be sorted first. (The FCC explicitly states that it will never sort the files before you download them.) Doing this in PHP would again exceed the memory limits, and using the Unix sort file system utility requires the use of PHP's exec(), which is also a protected function on many web hosts.

- Using a SQL INSERT statement for the data in the RA.dat file, then using an UPDATE statement to fill in the blanks when you later read in EN.dat and CO.dat. would require heavy use of the MySQL UPDATE feature, which is an order of magnitude (ten times) slower than using INSERT. We tried this method, and it took more than eight hours to import all of the data. Listing 5-3 only takes a few minutes.

The structure we've chosen for the three-table design is in Listing 5-2. Copy these statements into your administration tool and execute them.

Listing 5-2. *The MySQL Table Creation Statements for the Example*

```
CREATE TABLE fcc_location (
  loc_id int(10) unsigned NOT NULL auto_increment,
  unique_si_loc bigint(20) NOT NULL default '0',
  lat_deg int(11) default '0',
  lat_min int(11) default '0',
  lat_sec float default '0',
  lat_dir char(1) default NULL,
  latitude double default '0',
  long_deg int(11) default '0',
  long_min int(11) default '0',
  long_sec float default '0',
  long_dir char(1) default NULL,
  longitude double default '0',
  PRIMARY KEY  (loc_id),
  KEY unique_si (unique_si_loc)
) ENGINE=MyISAM  ;

CREATE TABLE fcc_owner (
  owner_id int(10) unsigned NOT NULL auto_increment,
  unique_si_own bigint(20) NOT NULL default '0',
  owner_name varchar(200) default NULL,
  owner_address varchar(35) default NULL,
  owner_city varchar(20) default NULL,
  owner_state char(2) default NULL,
  owner_zip varchar(10) default NULL,
  PRIMARY KEY  (owner_id),
  KEY unique_si (unique_si_own)
) ENGINE=MyISAM ;

CREATE TABLE fcc_structure (
  struc_id int(10) unsigned NOT NULL auto_increment,
  unique_si bigint(20) NOT NULL default '0',
  date_constr date default '0000-00-00',
  date_removed date default '0000-00-00',
  struc_address varchar(80) default NULL,
  struc_city varchar(20) default NULL,
  struc_state char(2) default NULL,
  struc_height double default '0',
  struc_elevation double NOT NULL default '0',
  struc_ohag double NOT NULL default '0',
  struc_ohamsl double default '0',
  struc_type varchar(6) default NULL,
  PRIMARY KEY  (struc_id),
```

```
    KEY unique_si (unique_si),
    KEY struc_state (struc_state)
) ENGINE=MyISAM;
```

After you create the tables, run Listing 5-3 from either a browser or the command line to import the data. Importing the data could take up to ten minutes, so be patient.

Listing 5-3. *FCC ASR Conversion to SQL Data Structures*

```php
<?php
set_time_limit(0); // this could take a while

// Connect to the database
require($_SERVER['DOCUMENT_ROOT'] . '/db_credentials.php');
$conn = mysql_connect("localhost", $db_name, $db_pass);
mysql_select_db("googlemapsbook", $conn);

// Open the Physical Location Coordinates file
$handle = @fopen("RA.dat","r");

if ($handle) {
    while (!feof($handle)) {
        $buffer = fgets($handle, 4096);
        $row = explode("|",$buffer);
        if ($row[3] > 0) {
            // Modify things before we insert them
            $row[12] = date("Y-m-d",strtotime($row[12]));
            $row[13] = date("Y-m-d",strtotime($row[13]));
            $row[23] = addslashes($row[23]);
            $row[24] = addslashes($row[24]);
            $row[30] = addslashes($row[30]);

            // Formulate our query
            $query = "INSERT INTO fcc_structure (unique_si, date_constr,
                date_removed, struc_address, struc_city, struc_state, struc_height,
                struc_elevation, struc_ohag, struc_ohamsl, struc_type)
                VALUES ({$row[4]}, '{$row[12]}', '{$row[13]}', '{$row[23]}',
                '{$row[24]}', '{$row[25]}', '{$row[26]}', '{$row[27]}', '{$row[28]}',
                '{$row[29]}', '{$row[30]}')";

            // Execute our query
            $result = @mysql_query($query);
            if (!$result) echo("ERROR: Duplicate structure info #{$row[4]} <br>\n");
        }
    }
    fclose($handle);
```

```php
}
echo "Done Structures. <br>\n";

// Open the Ownership Data file
$handle = @fopen("EN.dat","r");

if ($handle) {
    while (!feof($handle)) {
        $buffer = fgets($handle, 4096);
        $row = explode("|",$buffer);
        if ($row[3] > 0) {
            $row[7] = addslashes($row[7]);
            $row[14] = addslashes($row[14]);
            $row[16] = addslashes($row[16]);

            $query = "INSERT INTO fcc_owner (unique_si_own, owner_name,
                owner_address, owner_city, owner_state, owner_zip) VALUES ({$row[4]},
                 '{$row[7]}', '{$row[14]}','{$row[16]}', '{$row[17]}', '{$row[18]}')";

            $result = @mysql_query($query);
            if (!$result) {
                // Newer information later in the file: UPDATE instead
                $query = "UPDATE fcc_owner SET owner_name='{$row[7]}',
                        owner_address='{$row[14]}', owner_city='{$row[16]}',
                        owner_state='{$row[17]}', owner_zip='{$row[18]}'
                        WHERE unique_si_own={$row[4]}";
                $result = @mysql_query($query);
                if (!$result)
                    echo "Failure to import ownership for struc. #{$row[4]}<br>\n";
                else
                    echo "Updated ownership for struc. #{$row[4]} <br>\n";
            }
        }
    }
    fclose($handle);
}
echo "Done Ownership. <br>\n";

// Open the Physical Locations file
$handle = @fopen("CO.dat","r");

if ($handle) {
    while (!feof($handle)) {
        $buffer = fgets($handle, 4096);
        $row = explode("|",$buffer);
        if ($row[3] > 0) {
```

```
        if ($row[9] == "S") $sign = -1; else $sign = 1;
        $dec_lat = $sign*($row[6]+$row[7]/60+$row[8]/3600);
        if ($row[14] == "W") $sign = -1; else $sign = 1;
        $dec_long = $sign*($row[11]+$row[12]/60+$row[13]/3600);

        $query = "INSERT INTO fcc_location (unique_si_loc, lat_deg, lat_min,
                lat_sec, lat_dir, latitude, long_deg, long_min, long_sec,
                long_dir, longitude) VALUES ({$row[4]},'{$row[6]}', '{$row[7]}',
                '{$row[8]}', '{$row[9]}', '$dec_lat','{$row[11]}', '{$row[12]}',
                '{$row[13]}', '{$row[14]}', '$dec_long')";

        $result = @mysql_query($query);
        if (!$result) {
            // Newer information later in the file: UPDATE instead
            $query = "UPDATE fcc_location SET lat_deg='{$row[6]}',
                    lat_min='{$row[7]}', lat_deg='{$row[8]}', lat_dir='{$row[9]}',
                    latitude='$dec_lat', long_deg='{$row[11]}', long_min='{$row[12]}',
                    long_sec='{$row[13]}', long_dir='{$row[14]}', longitude='$dec_long'
                        WHERE unique_si_loc='{$row[4]}'";
            $result = @mysql_query($query);
            if (!$result)
                echo "Failure to import location for struc. #{$row[4]} <br>\n";
            else
                echo "Updated location for struc. #{$row[4]} <br>\n";
        }
    }
}

    fclose($handle);
}
echo "Done Locations. <br>\n";
?>
```

Using Your New Database Schema

You could retrieve and combine data from this database in three ways:

- Use PHP to query each table and reassemble it into an array by joining the results based on the Unique Structure Id field.

- Use a multitable SELECT query and have SQL do the recombination for you.

- If your version of SQL supports views, create a view (a virtual table) and use PHP to select directly from that instead.

Each method has various drawbacks and benefits, as explained in the following sections.

Reconstruction Using PHP's Memory Space

Using PHP to put the data back together isn't really practical in a production environment. It's an obvious method if your SQL skills are still new; however, it only works if you're going to be using a *very* small set of information. We cover it here to show you how it would work in case you find a valid use for it, but we do so with hesitation. This is neither a sane nor scalable method, and the SQL-based solutions presented in a moment are much more robust. The code in Listing 5-4 locates all of the towers in Hawaii and consumes a huge amount of memory to do so.

Listing 5-4. *Using PHP to Determine the List of Structures in Hawaii*

```php
<?php
// Connect to the database
require($_SERVER['DOCUMENT_ROOT'] . '/db_credentials.php');
$conn = mysql_connect("localhost", $db_name, $db_pass);
mysql_select_db("googlemapsbook", $conn);

// Create our temporary holding arrays
$hawaiian_towers = array();
$usi_list = array();

// Get a list of the structures in Hawaii
$structures = mysql_query("SELECT * FROM fcc_structure WHERE struc_state='HI'");
for($i=0; $i<mysql_num_rows($structures); $i++) {
    $row = mysql_fetch_array($structures, MYSQL_ASSOC);
    $hawaiian_towers[$row['unique_si']] = $row;
    $usi_list[] = $row['unique_si'];
}
unset($structures);

// Get all of the owners for the above structures
$owners = mysql_query("SELECT * FROM fcc_owner
            WHERE unique_si_own IN (".implode(",",$usi_list).")");
for($i=0; $i<mysql_num_rows($owners); $i++) {
    $row = mysql_fetch_array($owners, MYSQL_ASSOC);
    $hawaiian_towers[$row['unique_si_own']] =
        array_merge($hawaiian_towers[$row['unique_si_own']],$row);
}
unset($owners);

// Figure out the location of each of the above structures
$locations = mysql_query("SELECT * FROM fcc_location
            WHERE unique_si_loc IN (".implode(",",$usi_list).")");
for($i=0; $i<mysql_num_rows($locations); $i++) {
    $row = mysql_fetch_array($locations,MYSQL_ASSOC);
    $hawaiian_towers[$row['unique_si_loc']] =
```

```
            array_merge($hawaiian_towers[$row['unique_si_loc']],$row);
}
unset($locations);

echo memory_get_usage();
?>
```

You can see that the only thing this script outputs to the screen is the total memory usage in bytes. For our data set, this is approximately 780KB. This illustrates the fact that this method is very memory-intensive, consuming one-eighth of the average allotment simply for data retrieval. As a result, this method is probably one of the worst ways you could go about reassembling your data. However, this code does introduce the use of the SQL IN clause. IN simply takes a list of things (in this case integers) and selects all of the rows where one of the values in the list is in the column unique_si. It's still better to use joins to take advantage of the SQL engine's internal optimizations, but IN can be quite handy at times. You can use PHP's implode() function and a temporary array to create the list to pass to IN quickly and easily. For more information about the array_merge() function, check out http://ca.php.net/manual/en/function.array-merge.php.

The Multitable SELECT Query

Next, you'll formulate a single query to the database that allows you to retrieve all the data for a single structure as a single row. This means that you could iterate over the entire database doing something with each record as you go, without having a single point in time where you're consuming a lot of memory for temporary storage. Working from the example we had at the end of Chapter 2, we're going to replace the static data file with one that is generated with PHP and uses our SQL database of the FCC structures. Due to the volume of data we'll be limiting the points plotted to only those that are owned and operated in Hawaii. For more data management techniques see Chapter 7. Listing 5-5 shows the new map_data.php file. You will either need to zoom in on Hawaii or change your centering in the map_functions.js file, too. In Chapter 6, you will work on the user interface for the map, so right now, you will just plot all of the points.

■**Note** In reality, this approach is primarily shifting the location where you consume the vast amounts of memory. We're pushing the problem off the web server and onto the database server. However, in general, the database server is more capable of handling the load and is optimized explicitly for this purpose.

Listing 5-5. *map_data.php: Using a Single SQL Query to Determine the List of Structures*

```php
<?php

// Connect to the database
require($_SERVER['DOCUMENT_ROOT'] . '/db_credentials.php');
$conn = mysql_connect("localhost", $db_name, $db_pass);
mysql_select_db("googlemapsbook", $conn);
```

```php
$query = "SELECT * FROM fcc_structure, fcc_owner, fcc_location
    WHERE struc_state='HI' AND owner_state='HI'
    AND unique_si=unique_si_own AND unique_si=unique_si_loc";

$result = mysql_query($query, $conn);
$joiner = '';
$count = 0;
?>

var markers = [
<?php while($row = mysql_fetch_assoc($result)): ?>
    <?= $joiner ?>
    {
        'latitude': <?= $row['latitude'] ?>,
        'longitude': <?= $row['longitude'] ?>,
        'name': '<?= addslashes($row['struc_address']) ?>'
    }
    <?
        $joiner = ',';
        $count++;
    ?>
<?php endwhile; ?>
];

/* Memory used at the end of the script: <? echo memory_get_usage(); ?> */
/* Output <?= $count ?> points */
```

You can see that this approach uses a much more compact and easily maintained query, as well as much less memory. In fact, the memory consumption reported by memory_get_usage() this time is merely the memory used by the last fetch operation, instead of all of the fetch operations combined.

The tricky part is the order of the WHERE clauses themselves. The basic idea is to list the WHERE clauses in such an order that the largest amounts of information are eliminated from consideration first. Therefore, having the struc_state='HI' be the first clause removes more than 99.8% of all the data in the fcc_structure table from consideration. The remaining clauses simply tack on the information from the other two tables that correlates with the 0.2% of remaining information.

Using this map_data.php script in the general map template from Chapter 2 gives you a map like the one shown in Figure 5-2. Chapter 6 will expand on this example and help you design and build a good user interface for your map.

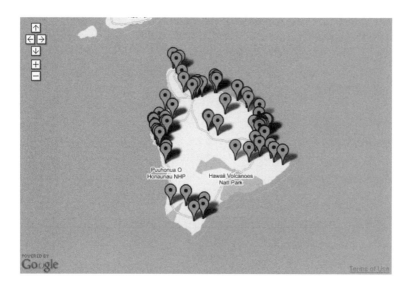

Figure 5-2. *The FCC structures in Hawaii*

■**Note** Most database engines are smart enough to reorder the WHERE clauses to minimize their workload if they can, and in this case, MySQL would probably do a pretty good job. However, in general, it's good practice to help the database optimization engine and use a human brain to think about a sane order for the WHERE clauses whenever possible.

A SQL View

The other approach you could take is to create a SQL view on the data and use PHP to select directly from that. A *view* is a temporary table that is primarily (in our case, exclusively) used for retrieving data from a SQL database. A view is basically the cached result of a query like the one in Listing 5-5, without the state-specific data limitation. You can select from a view in the same way that you can select from an ordinary table, but the actual data is stored across many different tables. Updating is done on the underlying tables instead of the view itself.

■**Note** Using a SQL view in this way is possible only with MySQL 5.0.1 and later, PostgreSQL 7.1.x and later, and some commercial SQL databases. If you're using MySQL 3.x or 4.x and would like to use the new view feature, consider upgrading.

Listing 5-6 shows the MySQL 5.*x* statements needed to create the view.

Listing 5-6. *MySQL Statement to Create a View on the Three Tables*

```
CREATE VIEW fcc_towers
    AS SELECT * FROM fcc_structure, fcc_owner, fcc_location
        WHERE unique_si=unique_si_own AND unique_si=unique_si_loc
            ORDER BY struc_state, struc_type
```

After the view is created, you can replace the query in Listing 5-5 with the insanely simple `$query = "SELECT * FROM fcc_towers WHERE struc_state='HI' AND owner_state='HI'";` and you're finished.

So why is a view better than the multitable `SELECT`? Basically, it precomputes all of the correlations between the various tables and stores the answer for later use by *multiple future queries*. Therefore, when you need to select some chunk of information for use in your script, the correlation work has already been done, and the query executes much faster. However, please realize that creating a view for a single-run script doesn't make much sense, since the value is realized in a time/computation savings *over time*.

For the next two chapters, we'll assume that you were successful in creating the `fcc_towers` view. If your web host doesn't have a view-compatible SQL installation for you to use, then simply replace our queries in the next two chapters with the larger one from Listing 5-5 and make any necessary adjustments, or find a different way to create a single combined table from all of the data.

Tip For more information on the creation of views in MySQL, visit `http://dev.mysql.com/doc/refman/5.0/en/create-view.html`. To see the limitations on using views, visit `http://dev.mysql.com/doc/refman/5.0/en/view-restrictions.html`. For more information on views in PostgreSQL, visit `http://www.postgresql.org/docs/8.1/static/sql-createview.html`.

KEEPING YOUR DATABASE CURRENT

So now that you have this database full of data, how do you keep it up-to-date? The FCC adds or changes the data for more than a dozen structures each day, so it doesn't take long for your information to become outdated.

To keep current, you can use the daily transaction files that the FCC has made available for this specific purpose, which are located at `http://wireless.fcc.gov/cgi-bin/wtb-transactions.pl#tow`. These are available each night and represent all of the structures added to the system in the previous day.

To automate this task, you need access to three things on your web-host account:

- The ability to schedule your update program to run periodically

- A shell-scripting language in which to write your update tool

- A program for retrieving the transaction files using your shiny new tool

In our example here, we're going to use the Unix cron daemon to schedule our program to run each night, the command-line version of PHP (known as PHP-CGI or PHP-CLI in most Linux distributions), and wget to retrieve the transaction files from the FCC. If you have a different combination, the general idea presented here should be adaptable to most combinations.

The basic idea is that you'll write a script that runs each night after midnight and retrieves the zipped file for the previous day into a temporary folder. You'll unpack the file, and then extract and insert the information into your database exactly as you did in Listing 5-3. In fact, the following code is simply a wrapper around the code from Listing 5-3.

You'll be making extensive use of PHP's exec() function, which simply runs an external program. This is sometimes a banned function on shared-server web hosts, and in that case, this function call will cause an error, so you'll need to find another way to do the same thing. If you have access to Perl from the command line, you could easily write this in Perl and call your code from Listing 5-3 as an external program instead of a code include.

```php
<?php
// Remove any temporary files (left over from last night).
exec("rm r_tow_$day.zip CO.dat EN.dat RA.dat");

// Decide which day it is we're interested in
$day = strtolower(date("D",strtotime("yesterday")));

// Formulate the URL we want wget to retrieve
$url = "http://wireless.fcc.gov/uls/data/daily/r_tow_$day.zip";

// Get the zipped file
exec("/usr/bin/wget -q $url");

// Unpack the parts of the zipped file we care about
exec("/usr/bin/unzip -qq r_tow_$day.zip CO.dat EN.dat RA.dat");

// Import data into our database using Listing 5-3. You may need to change paths.
require_once("../03/index.php");

// Remove our temporary files (prepare for tomorrow night).
exec("rm r_tow_$day.zip CO.dat EN.dat RA.dat");
?>
```

As you can see, the wrapper code around Listing 5-3 is fairly simple. The tricky part (if you've never done this before) comes in setting up the cron job itself, which you'll do now.

The first thing you need to do is open your personal cron schedule. In your shell, you can do this by running the command crontab -e. Your default command-line text editor should open to your current list of scheduled jobs (quite likely an empty file).

You'll need to enter the following two lines into the file that opens when you type crontab -e.

```
MAILTO = youremailaddress
0 2 * * *    cd $HOME/public_html/path_to_your_script/; php fcc_update.php
```

The first line simply tells cron where to send all of the output. If there is no output, it won't send an e-mail message, but if you want to output diagnostics using echo (as we have), then you'll get an e-mail message showing you the details of the update each night.

The second line is a single instruction telling cron what to do. The first number tells cron which minute of the hour to run (0 through 59). In this case, it will run on the hour at zero minutes. The second number is which hour(s) to run on (0 through 23), which is 2 a.m. in this example. The three asterisk symbols are wildcards telling cron to run each day of the month (1 through 31), each month of the year (1 through 12), on each day of the week (0 through 6, where Sunday is 0). Therefore, our script will update the database at 2 a.m. 365 days a year. The second half of the line merely tells cron what you would like it to do on your behalf.

Save the file, and you're finished. Your database should now stay in sync. If you want to debug your `crontab`, simply change the hours and minutes to be a few minutes in the future and wait for your e-mail.

Screen Scraping

Sometimes the data you want to use just isn't available in a nice, neat little package or service. In these cases, you can try searching the Web for the data you want, and you might find part or all of it on someone else's website. If it's not available for download, as a web service, or for purchase, you might consider parsing the visible HTML and extracting the parts that you care about. This process is called *screen scraping*, because you are writing a program that pretends to be a normal, legitimate visitor but is really harvesting the data and usually storing it in your own database.

Accomplishing this is different for every single source of data, but we'll try to give you the basic tools you'll need to be successful. The basic idea is to download the pages (maybe using CURL or wget) in sequence, then using loops and regular expressions or string mangling to find and extract the interesting bits. Most scrapers also store the data they find in a local data store to avoid going back to the source of the information each time it's needed.

COPYRIGHT AND LEGAL ISSUES

There are legal and ethical concerns to consider when scraping, and neither the authors of this book nor Apress condone information or intellectual property theft or copyright infringement in any form. Please always ask for permission from site owners before scraping their sites. Sometimes owners would prefer to provide you with the data in a less bandwidth-intensive (and more convenient for you) way, or have other terms and conditions for using their data (like reciprocal links or copyright attributions).

There are many legitimate reasons to use screen scraping to obtain data. Among other reasons, site owners may not have the resources or the skills to create a web service or an API for their data. Therefore, they might say you're welcome to take any data you want, but they can't help you get it into a more convenient format.

Regardless of the reason for scraping, you should always get written permission. Simply because the data is available without fee on a website does not mean that you are free to take it and republish it at your whim, *even if you do not charge any sort of fee*. Consult a lawyer if you can't get permission; otherwise, you might find that your hobby map turns into a crushing lawsuit against you.

A Scraping Example

As an example, you'll be taking a list of latitudes and longitudes for the capital cities of many countries in the world. The page that you'll scrape is located at http://googlemapsbook.com/chapter5/scrape_me.html. It's not the most challenging scraping example, but it will serve our purposes.

The first thing you need to do is use wget to retrieve a local copy of the page. From the shell, run the following command while in your working directory for this example:

```
wget http://googlemapsbook.com/chapter5/scrape_me.html
```

■**Tip** If you would prefer to snag this page live from the Web directly from within your code, then grab a snippet of the CURL code from Chapter 4's geocoding web services examples. The only trick should be splitting up the result on the newlines to form an array of lines, instead of using fgets() to read each line in sequence.

Next, you need to do some analysis of the HTML of this page to decide what you can do with it. Listing 5-7 shows the important bits for our discussion.

Listing 5-7. *Snippets of HTML from the Sample Scraping Page*

```
(After about 10 lines of header HTML you'll find this...)
<!-- Content Body -->
<table border="1" width="100%">
<tr>
<td >Country</td>
<td >Capital City</td>
<td >Latitude</td>
<td >Longitude</td></tr>

<tr><td class="latlongtable">Afghanistan</td>
<td class="latlongtable">Kabul</td>
<td class="latlongtable">34.28N</td>
<td class="latlongtable">69.11E</td></tr>

<tr><td class="latlongtable">Albania</td>
<td class="latlongtable">Tirane</td>
<td class="latlongtable">41.18N</td>
<td class="latlongtable">19.49E</td></tr>

<tr><td class="latlongtable">Algeria</td>
<td class="latlongtable">Algiers</td>
<td class="latlongtable">36.42N</td>
<td class="latlongtable">03.08E</td></tr>

(and 190 countries later...)
```

```
<tr><td class="latlongtable">Zambia</td>
<td class="latlongtable">Lusaka</td>
<td class="latlongtable">15.28S</td>
<td class="latlongtable">28.16E</td></tr>

<tr><td class="latlongtable">Zimbabwe</td>
<td class="latlongtable">Harare</td>
<td class="latlongtable">17.43S</td>
<td class="latlongtable">31.02E</td>
</tr>
</table>
<!-- Content Body End -->
```

So how do you extract the information that you care about? The first thing is to find the patterns that you can exploit. In our case, we're going to ignore all of the data that comes before the HTML comment `<!-- Content Body -->` and after the closing comment `<!-- Content Body End -->`. In between, we'll care about only the lines where `class="latlongtable"` appears. We're lucky that the data we care about is surrounded entirely by HTML and that PHP has a handy function to remove it: `strip_tags()`. The largest string mangling we need to do is determining the sign of the latitude and longitude measurements based on the N/S E/W labels. You can see the required code in Listing 5-8.

Listing 5-8. *Screen Scraping Example*

```php
<?php
// Open the file and the database
$handle = @fopen("scrape_me.html","r");
$conn = mysql_connect("localhost","username","password");
mysql_select_db("geocoding_experiment",$conn);

// Status flags and temporary variables
$in_main_table = false;
$count = 0;

if ($handle) {
   while (!feof($handle)) {
     $buffer = fgets($handle, 4096);

     // Look for "<!-- Content Body -->"
     if (trim($buffer) == "<!-- Content Body -->") {
       $in_main_table = true;
       continue;
      }

     // For each line that has "latlongtable" in it trim
      if ($in_main_table && strstr($buffer,'class="latlongtable"') !== false) {
        // Dig out the part we care about
        $interesting_data = trim(strip_tags($buffer));
```

```
        switch($count % 4) {
            case 0:
              // Country Info
              $city = array(); // reset
              $city[0] = addslashes($interesting_data);
              break;
            case 1:
              // Capital City Info
              $city[1] = addslashes($interesting_data);
              break;
            case 2:
              // Latitude Information (determine sign)
              $latitude = substr($interesting_data,0,strlen($interesting_data)-1);
              if (substr($interesting_data,-1,1) == 'S') $sign = "-";
              else $sign = "";
              $city[2] = $sign.$latitude;
              break;
            case 3:
              //Longitude Information (determine sign)
              $longitude = substr($interesting_data,0,strlen($interesting_data)-1);
              if (substr($interesting_data,-1,1) == 'W') $sign = "-";
              else $sign = "";
              $city[3] = $sign.$longitude;

              echo implode(" ",$city)."<br />";

              // Write to the database
              $result = mysql_query("INSERT INTO capital_cities
                      (country,capital,lat,lng) VALUES ('".implode("','",$city)."')");

              break;
          } // switch

          // Increment our counter
          $count++;

          // Stop when we find "<!-- Content Body End -->"
          if ($buffer == "<!-- Content Body End -->") break;
        } // if
    } // while
} // if

fclose($handle);
?>
```

You can store this information using a database table like the one in Listing 5-9.

Listing 5-9. *SQL Database Structure for the Screen Scraping Example*

```
CREATE TABLE capital_cities (
  uid int(11) NOT NULL auto_increment,
  country text NOT NULL,
  capital text NOT NULL,
  lat float NOT NULL default '0',
  lng float NOT NULL default '0',
  PRIMARY KEY  (uid),
  KEY lat (lat,lng)
) ENGINE=MyISAM;
```

Note We hereby explicitly grant permission to any person who has purchased this book to use the information contained in the body table of `scrape_me.html` for any purpose (commercial or otherwise), provided it is in conjunction with a map built on the Google Maps API and conforms to Google's terms of service. We make no warranties about the accuracy of the information (in fact, there is one deliberate error) or its suitability for any purpose.

Screen Scraping Considerations

You need to consider a few things when doing screen scraping:

- If you intend to scrape a dynamic source on a schedule or repeatedly over the course of time, you'll need to build in a lot of error checking. For example, our code would completely break if we made a change as simple as the name of the CSS class or the words in the HTML comments.

- Rarely will the data be this cleanly laid out. If the problem is at all challenging, you should look into using the PHP regular expression extensions. Many tutorials and books are available that can help you with regular expressions. Some simple searching will do the trick. Regular expressions are very, very powerful. Used properly with some status flags, they can extract just about anything from an HTML page.

- Not all sources of data are going to be 100% accurate. For example, we've deliberately made a mistake for Ottawa, Canada, changing the sign from N to S, thereby flipping it below the equator. This causes our import script to treat the latitude as negative instead of positive. These kinds of mistakes are likely to happen with *any* data source you use, and in most cases, they will need to be corrected manually after the import.

- Sometimes the data is static or from a single source, and writing a program to do the work doesn't make sense. If the problem looks simple, you might try using your code editor's built-in search and replace functions. They certainly would have worked well as an alternative for our example in Listing 5-9.

Summary

As you can see, there are a lot of ways to get the information you need to create a successful map. We encourage you to look at Appendix A, where we've collected a wide variety of different sources of information for common (and not so common) mapping applications. You'll find things like political boundaries and the locations of airports, schools, and churches, as well as data on lakes and rivers.

In the next chapter, we'll continue with the example from Listing 5-5 and build a proper user interface. We'll show you how to do some fancy things with CSS and DOM manipulation. In Chapter 7, we'll round out this example with a thorough discussion of ways to handle such vast amounts of data on a map simultaneously and reminisce about the days when Google Maps API version 1 gave us a practical limit of 50 to 75 pins and a crash-the-browser limit of just a couple hundred. Progress is wonderful.

CHAPTER 6

Improving the User Interface

In this chapter, you'll use the FCC ASR data you collected in Chapter 5 and create a mashup that really shines. What kind of interface surrounds a helpful map? What tricks can you do with a little more CSS and JavaScript? What kinds of things besides markers can you put on a map to increase its usefulness? You'll find some suggestions in this chapter.

This chapter begins where the middle of Chapter 5 left off, but if you're starting here, it's easy to catch up. As a basis, we're using the code from Chapter 2, which plots points listed in a file called `map_data.php`. We've replaced that flat data file, however, with a PHP script that queries the database and dynamically serves up a list of points corresponding to FCC broadcast structures in Hawaii.

In this chapter, you'll learn how to use CSS and JavaScript to enhance your maps as follows:

- Have your map adjust its size to fill any browser.

- Add a toolbar that hovers over the map.

- Create side panels for your map.

- Display a loading message to alert users when the map is processing or initializing.

- Allow users to selectively view or hide groups of data points.

CSS: A Touch of Style

CSS is the modern method of choice for controlling the visual appearance of an XML document. Just as we've kept the HTML structure separate from JavaScript behavior and JavaScript data, we're also going to keep the CSS separate.

In your `index.php` file, you'll need to add a reference to an external style sheet, as shown in Listing 6-1. Since its appearance will momentarily be controlled by this CSS file, it's also possible to remove the explicit size from the `map` div.

Listing 6-1. *Index.php with External Style Sheet Reference*

```
<!DOCTYPE html PUBLIC "-//W3C//DTD XHTML 1.0 Strict//EN"➥
"http://www.w3.org/TR/xhtml1/DTD/xhtml1-strict.dtd">
<html xmlns="http://www.w3.org/1999/xhtml">
<head>
```

```
    <script src="http://maps.google.com/maps?file=api&v=2&key=API_KEY"➥
type="text/javascript"></script>
    <script src="map_data.php" type="text/javascript"></script>
    <script src="map_functions.js" type="text/javascript"></script>
    <link href="style.css" rel="stylesheet" type="text/css" />
</head>
<body>
    <div id="map"></div>
</body>
</html>
```

Without the style attribute, the map div collapses to nothing, and thus, no map appears. Clearly, you need to actually *create* the style sheet and reapply the size declarations that were removed. Listing 6-2 shows the style.css file that you should create and save in the same directory as everything else.

Listing 6-2. *Style.css to Give the Map Dimensions*

```
#map {
    width: 500px;
    height: 400px;
}
```

With the style sheet from Listing 6-2 in place, all should be as it was when we set out at the beginning of the chapter. Now that you have a central styling mechanism, read on for some of the interesting things you can put there.

Maximizing Your Map

A surprising number of Google Maps projects seem to use fixed-size maps. But why lock the users into particular dimensions when their screen may be significantly smaller or larger than yours? It's time to meet the map that fills up your browser, regardless of its screen size. Try swapping out your style.css file for Listing 6-3.

Listing 6-3. *Style.css for a Maximized Map*

```
html, body {
    margin: 0;
    padding: 0;
    height: 100%;
}

#map {
    position: absolute;
    top: 0;
    left: 0;
    width: 100%;
    height: 100%;
}
```

As you can see in Figure 6-1, the map is now completely flexible and fills any size of browser screen.

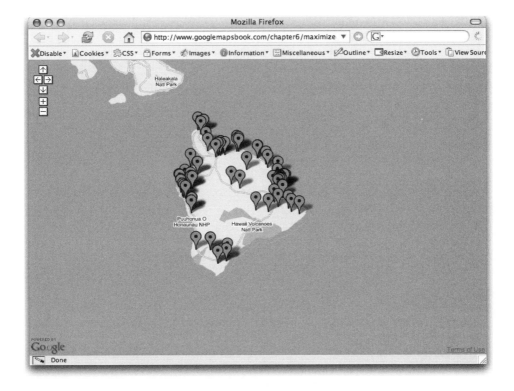

Figure 6-1. *Our map fills up the browser at 800×600.*

This method is particularly ideal for situations where a map is being used as part of a slide show or on a kiosk. However, it also works in the web-page context, especially when combined with the trick described in the next section.

■**Tip** Once you have the map maximized, you might notice how Internet Explorer 6 likes to show a disabled vertical scrollbar on our perfectly fitted page. Under most circumstances, this is actually desired behavior, since it means that centered sites are consistent with both short and long content. In our case, however, you really don't want it there. Fortunately, banishment is achieved with a pretty straightforward rule: html { overflow: hidden; }.

Adding Hovering Toolbars

The introduction of CSS brought the concept of *layering* to web page layout. Prior to CSS, the only way to stack up any content was by nesting table tags, and then placing different images in the backgrounds of the successive table cells. However, using the CSS declaration for position, it's possible to pile up anything you like, including text, images, and even things like Flash movies and scrolling `div` elements.

For the map, this means you can make content of various kinds hover on top of the map that the API generates. For comparison, Windows Live Local uses a full-screen map with translucent control widgets; check it out at `http://local.live.com/`.

Continuing the example from Listing 6-3, change the `index.php` file to include some markup for a toolbar, as shown in Listing 6-4.

Listing 6-4. *Index.php with Added Markup for a Toolbar*

```
<!DOCTYPE html PUBLIC "-//W3C//DTD XHTML 1.0 Strict//EN"➥
"http://www.w3.org/TR/xhtml1/DTD/xhtml1-strict.dtd">
<html xmlns="http://www.w3.org/1999/xhtml">
<head>
    <script src="http://maps.google.com/maps?file=api&v=2&key=API_KEY"➥
type="text/javascript"></script>
    <script src="map_data.php" type="text/javascript"></script>
    <script src="map_functions.js" type="text/javascript"></script>
    <link href="style.css" rel="stylesheet" type="text/css" />
</head>
<body>
    <div id="map"></div>
    <div id="toolbar">
        <h1>Cell-Tower Locations</h1>
        <ul id="options">
            <li><a href="#">Towers</a></li>
            <li><a href="#">Poles</a></li>
            <li><a href="#">Masts</a></li>
            <li><a href="#">Other</a></li>
        </ul>
    </div>
</body>
</html>
```

And now, some CSS magic to take that markup and pull the toolbar up on top of the map. Add the styles in Listing 6-5 to your `style.css` file.

Listing 6-5. *Styles for a Floating Toolbar*

```
#toolbar {
    position: absolute;
    top: 20px;
    left: 60px;
    width: 400px;
    padding: 5px;
    background: white;
    border: 1px solid black;
}
```

You can see in Figure 6-2 that we've added a few more styles to make the toolbar's menu and titles prettier, but they're not critical to the layout example here. The important thing to note is the `position: absolute` bit. A block-level element such as a `div` naturally expands to fill all of the width it has available, but once you position it as absolute or float it, it no longer exhibits that behavior. So, unless you want it shrink-wrapping its longest line of text, you'll need to specify a width as either a fixed amount or some percentage of the window width.

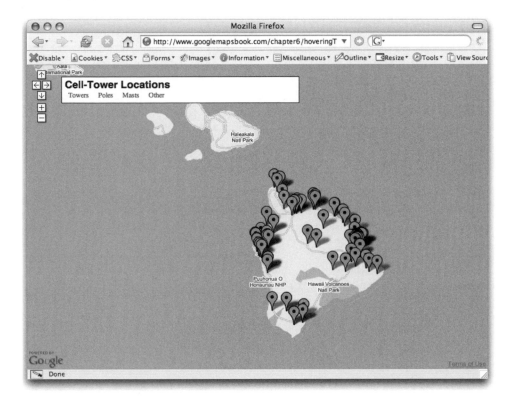

Figure 6-2. *Some styles for the toolbar*

■Note If you're curious how to make a floating toolbar actually draggable, a number of resources and libraries out there can help you achieve this. Unfortunately, several seem to exhibit frustrating bad practices or are simply way overengineered. This one is a good starting point, though: `http://tool-man.org/examples/dragging.html`.

WHAT ABOUT A FULL-WIDTH TOOLBAR?

Shouldn't it be possible to create a bar that's some fixed amount *less* than 100% of the available width? What about a floating toolbar that starts exactly 60 pixels from the left edge and then goes to exactly 40 pixels from the right edge?

It's possible, in two different ways. In a few pages, you'll see how to accomplish sizing maneuvers like this using JavaScript. However, you can also create a full-width toolbar using just CSS. It's a little hairy, but there's certainly convenience (and possibly some pride, too) in keeping the solution all CSS.

The gist of the approach is that you need to "push in" the width of the absolutely positioned toolbar, so that when it has a declared width of 100%, the 100% is 100% of the exact width you want it to have, rather than 100% of the browser's entire client area.

The toolbar `div` will need an extra wrapper around it, to do the "pushing-in." So start by changing your markup:

```
<div id="toolbar-wrapper">
    <div id="toolbar">
    ...
    </div>
</div>
```

Now add the following styles to the `style.css` file:

```
#toolbar-wrapper {
    margin-right: 100px;
    position: relative;
}

#toolbar {
    width: 100%;
    ...
}
```

The right margin on the toolbar wrapper causes the toolbar itself to lose that horizontal space, even though the toolbar is ultimately being sucked out of the main document flow with `position: absolute`.

Creating Collapsible Side Panels

A common feature on many Google Maps mashups is some kind of side panel that provides supplementary information, such as a list of the pins being displayed. You can implement this simple feature in a number of ways. Here, we'll show you one that uses a little CSS and JavaScript to make a simple, collapsible panel.

First, the new side panel will need some markup. Modify the body section of Listing 6-4 to look like Listing 6-6.

Listing 6-6. *Index Body with Added Markup for a Side Panel*

```
<body class="sidebar-right">
    <div id="map-wrapper">
```

```
        <div id="map"></div>
    </div>
    <div id="toolbar">
        ...
    </div>
    <div id="sidebar">
        <p>Lorem ipsum dolor sit amet, consectetuer adipiscing elit. Proin
        accumsan condimentum dolor. Vestibulum ante fabicum...</p>
    </div>
</body>
```

And now, to style this, you use almost the same trick as you used for the floating toolbar. This time, that wrapper has a margin that pushes the map div out of the way, so the elements appear beside each other, rather than overlapping. Listing 6-7 shows the CSS to add to style.css.

Listing 6-7. *New Styles for the Side Panel*

```
#map-wrapper {
    position: relative;
    height: 100%;
}

#sidebar {
    position: absolute;
    top: 0;
    width: 300px;
    height: 100%;
    overflow: auto;
}

body.sidebar-right #map-wrapper { margin-right: 300px; }
body.sidebar-right #sidebar { right: 0; }

body.sidebar-off #map-wrapper { margin: 0; }
body.sidebar-off #sidebar { display: none; }
```

If you fill up the side panel with some more content, you can see how the overflow declaration causes it to scroll. It behaves just like a 1997-era frame, but without all the hassle of broken back buttons and negative frame stigma.

■**Note** Listing 6-7 provides only the simplest styles for this side panel. You'll find when you try to apply a right-side padding to #sidebar that it pushes in not just the content, but the scrollbar, too, an undesirable effect. Fortunately, it's an easy fix: just nest a sidebar contents div inside the main sidebar, and then put your styles on that. Alternatively, you can use the CSS selector #sidebar p to give special margins to all paragraphs residing inside.

So, what about those classes on the body element? In Figure 6-3, we used the Firefox DOM Inspector to change the body element's class attribute, and suddenly the side panel vanished. It may seem insignificant now, since there are just the two styles that change, but picture a future where you're making more significant user interface changes dependent on the presence or absence of the side panel. The technique of hooking major layout rules to a body class is well worth adopting for its flexibility and scalability.

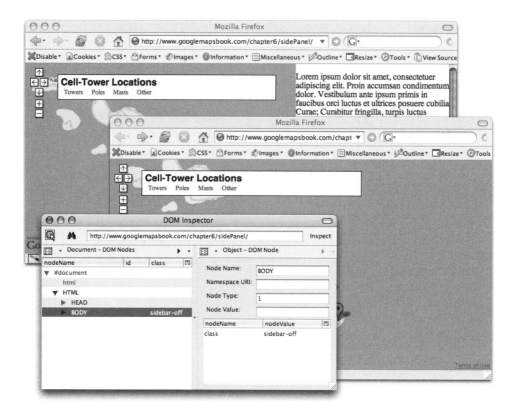

Figure 6-3. *The side panel obeys the body's class.*

Scripted Style

With the examples of the previous section in mind, we'll now examine a few ways to augment those CSS tricks with a little JavaScript.

Switching Up the Body Classes

The class attribute of a markup tag is not limited to a single value. You can actually have as many classes as you like, separated by spaces. For example, on the popular mezzoblue.com site, Dave Shea uses the following body element:

```
<body class="nosidebarplease articles entry">
```

In a single location, he is stating several important characteristics of the page in question. The ability to mix and match the various designations (article, blog entry, and so on) offers an extraordinary amount of control and precision in styling the various pages. This flexibility is what makes controlling page layout with the body class so appealing.

However, when it comes to accessing it via JavaScript, this means that you can't just get and set, as you can with most other attributes. You need to use find and replace operations on the whole className text string. Add the general-purpose function shown in Listing 6-8 to your map_functions.js file.

Listing 6-8. *Function to Swap a Class in the Document's Body Element*

```
function changeBodyClass(from, to) {
    document.body.className = document.body.className.replace(from, to);
    return false;
}
```

All that remains now is to call that function from a link somewhere. How you do that may be partially dependent on your level of JavaScript snobbery, with respect to separating markup from script. Some would consider the following markup perfectly adequate:

```
<a href="#" onclick="changeBodyClass('sidebar-right', 'sidebar-off');➥
return false;">Hide</a>
<a href="#" onclick="changeBodyClass('sidebar-off', 'sidebar-right');➥
return false;">Show</a>
```

A JavaScript purist, however, might advocate a more elaborate solution, such as the one in Listing 6-9.

Listing 6-9. *Markup for the Side Panel Toggle Buttons*

```
<div id="toolbar">
    ...
    <ul id="sidebar-controls">
        <li><a href="#" id="button-sidebar-hide">Hide</a></li>
        <li><a href="#" id="button-sidebar-show">Show</a></li>
    </ul>
</div>
```

▓Note We joke about JavaScript purists, but it's only because we like the methods they advocate. See http://www.digital-web.com/articles/separating_behavior_and_structure_2/ for Peter-Paul Koch's article, "Separating behavior and structure."

Accompanying that markup, you'll need to hook on the event handlers in the map_functions.js initialization function:

```
document.getElementById('button-sidebar-hide').onclick = function() {➥
return changeBodyClass('sidebar-right', 'sidebar-off'); };
document.getElementById('button-sidebar-show').onclick = function() {➥
return changeBodyClass('sidebar-off', 'sidebar-right'); };
```

Finally, you can add some styles to spruce up the buttons a little. Using CSS, it's trivial to hide (or otherwise restyle) whichever button corresponds to the mode you're already in:

```
body.sidebar-right a#button-sidebar-show { display: none; }
body.sidebar-off a#button-sidebar-hide { display: none; }
```

Using these style makes the two buttons appear to be the same one, as you can see in Figure 6-4.

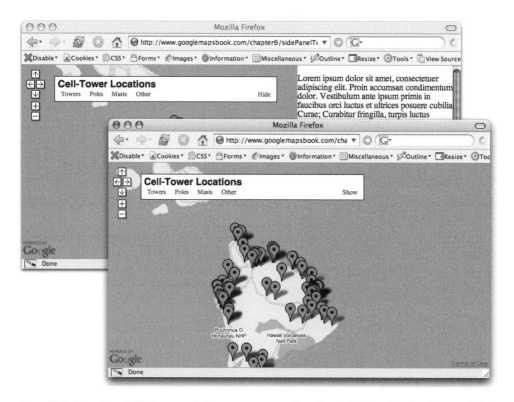

Figure 6-4. *The show/hide buttons behave as one, toggling the visibility of each other and of the side panel.*

We like the second method with the cleaner markup, but bear in mind that its normal advantages of fallback capabilities mean absolutely nothing here. The application centers around a JavaScript-powered map created with the Google Maps API. Without JavaScript turned on in their browser, users won't care whether or not they can hide the side panel.

■Tip If you're ever facing a situation involving a lot of complex event handlers being hooked onto various markup elements, you could consider taking advantage of the brilliant Behaviour library, which allows you to specify event handlers using the same selectors you already use to specify CSS rules. Check it out here: `http://bennolan.com/behaviour/`.

Resizing with the Power of JavaScript

As you saw earlier, CSS gives you a significant amount of control over a page's horizontal layout. However, control over the vertical spacing is very much lacking. With only a style sheet, you can make a map the entire height of the window, or some percentage of that height, but you *cannot* make it be "from here to the bottom," or "100% minus 90 pixels." With JavaScript, however, this is very much possible.

JavaScript is an event-driven programming language. You don't need to be checking for things to have happened all the time; you simply "hook" functionality onto various events triggered by the web browser.

With that in mind, all of the examples so far have already made use of the event `window.onload` to initialize the API and plot points on its map. What you're going to do next is hook some resizing functionality onto the event `window.onresize`. This code will execute when the window changes shape and resize the map to fit it.

Unfortunately, as is very obvious in the `windowHeight()` function of Listing 6-10, it has taken browser makers a long time to agree on how to expose the height of the client area to JavaScript. The method we've used here is the product of some exceptional research by Peter-Paul Koch (see `http://www.quirksmode.org/viewport/compatibility.html`). Incidentally, it's almost identical to the one Google itself uses to control the height of the Google Maps site's main map and side panel.

Pull up your `map_functions.js` file and add the code shown in Listing 6-10 to it.

Listing 6-10. *Filling Vertical Space with the onresize Event*

```
function windowHeight() {
    // Standard browsers (Mozilla, Safari, etc.)
    if (self.innerHeight)
        return self.innerHeight;
    // IE 6
    if (document.documentElement && document.documentElement.clientHeight)
        return y = document.documentElement.clientHeight;
    // IE 5
    if (document.body)
        return document.body.clientHeight;
    // Just in case.
    return 0;
}

function handleResize() {
    var height = windowHeight();
    height -= document.getElementById('toolbar').offsetHeight - 30;
    document.getElementById('map').style.height = height + 'px';
    document.getElementById('sidebar').style.height = height + 'px';
}

function init() {
    ...
```

```
        handleResize();
}

window.onresize = handleResize;
```

The handleResize()function itself is actually pretty straightforward. The offsetHeight and offsetWidth properties are provided by the browser, and return—in pixels—the dimensions of their element, including any padding. Finding the correct height for the map and side panel is simply a matter of subtracting that from the overall client window height, and then also removing the 30 pixels of padding that appear in three 10-pixel gaps between the top, the toolbar, the content area, and the bottom.

■**Note** It's awkward to be individually assigning heights to the map and side panel. It would be cleaner if we could just assign the calculated height to a single wrapper, and then set the children to each be permanently height: 100%. Indeed, such an approach works splendidly with Firefox. Unfortunately, Internet Explorer isn't able to get it quite right, so we're forced to use the slightly less optimal method of Listing 6-10.

Back in Listing 6-4, we placed the toolbar markup *after* the map div itself. This was partly arbitrary and partly because it's a convention to put the layers that are closer to the user later in the document. Now, however, the layering is to be removed in favor of a tiled approach, closer to what the Google Maps site itself uses. It's natural, then, to move the toolbar markup to before the map.

Also, we've added that content wrapper around the map and side panel. This is technically superfluous, but having a bit of extra markup to work with really helps to keep the style sheet sane. It's nearly always better to add wrappers to your template than to fill your CSS with ugly browser-specific hacks. (Some might disagree with us on this, but remember that wrappers are future-proof, while hacks can break with each new browser release.)

You can view the complete CSS changes that accompany Listing 6-11 on this book's website, but it's not a dramatic departure from the styles of Listing 6-7. The changes are mostly aesthetic, now that the handleResize() method lets us do things like put a nice 10-pixel margin between the key elements.

Listing 6-11. *Index Body with Markup Changes for Paneled Layout*

```
<body class="sidebar-right">
    <div id="toolbar">
        ...
    </div>
    <div id="content">
        <div id="map-wrapper">
            <div id="map"></div>
        </div>
        <div id="sidebar">
          ...
        </div>
    </div>
</body>
```

You can see how this example looks in Figure 6-5.

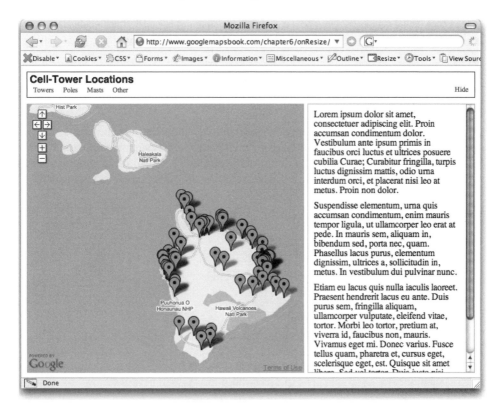

Figure 6-5. *The map area is divided into three elegant panels, one of which is collapsible.*

Populating the Side Panel

With our fancy side panel up and running, it would be good to get some actual content in there. A typical side panel use would be to present a list of all the markers plotted. This is particularly helpful when the markers are distributed in clusters. For example, a user could be zoomed in on an urban area to view a number of points bunched together, but she would be made aware that points exist elsewhere because that additional display has them listed.

For the markup in this case, you just need to edit the sidebar section of the main HTML file, as shown in Listing 6-12.

Listing 6-12. *Adding Markup for a Sidebar List*

```
<div id="content">
    ...
    <div id="sidebar">
        <ul id="sidebar-list">
        </ul>
    </div>
</div>
```

■**Note** It's incorrect HTML to have a `ul` element that doesn't contain any children. In our case, however, we know that as soon as the map loads, there will be elements added to this list, so it's another standards gray area. If having it empty troubles you, you could put in a dummy `li` node, and then start your JavaScript out by removing this node. But, of course, there would still be a moment in time where the `ul` is empty, which is why doing anything more than what we've got here feels a little silly.

Obviously, the current iteration of `map_data.php` provides only latitude, longitude, and a text label. The side panel will be much more useful if it can display *supplementary* information, rather than just the same thing with different formatting. Let's arbitrarily pick a handful more fields from the `fcc_towers` view and add them to the output, as shown in Listing 6-13.

Listing 6-13. *An Updated map_data.php Output Section*

```
var markers = [
<?php while($row = mysql_fetch_assoc($result)): ?>
    <?= $joiner ?>
    {
        'latitude': <?= $row['latitude'] ?>,
        'longitude': <?= $row['longitude'] ?>,
        'address': '<?= addslashes($row['struc_address']) ?>',
        'city': '<?= addslashes($row['struc_city']) ?>',
        'state': '<?= addslashes($row['struc_state']) ?>',
        'height': '<?= addslashes($row['struc_height']) ?>',
        'elevation': '<?= addslashes($row['struc_elevation']) ?>',
        'type': '<?= addslashes($row['struc_type']) ?>',
        'owner': '<?= addslashes($row['owner_name']) ?>'
    }
    <?
        $joiner = ',';
        $count++;
    ?>
<?php endwhile; ?>
];
```

Now we're ready to step back in JavaScript.

Regarding how to actually add these items to the side panel list, there are a number of different schools of thought. The strictest camps would argue for using only XML DOM methods. This would mean creating each tag—ahem, *element*—with `createElement`, putting text inside it using `createTextNode`, and then adding it to the list with `appendChild`. To use this method is to respect the sanctity of the HTML document tree as an abstract XML data structure in memory. In contrast, using the `innerHTML` property lets us inject blobs of already marked-up content—unvalidated content, which may or may not keep the document correct.

Our method, shown in Listing 6-14, is a hybrid approach. We create and attach the list items using DOM methods, but each list item's content is created as a text string and assigned using `innerHTML`.

Listing 6-14. *The createMarker Function Reimagined As initializePoint*

```
function initializePoint(pointData) {
    var point = new GLatLng(pointData.latitude, pointData.longitude);
    var marker = new GMarker(point);
    var listItem = document.createElement('li');
    var listItemLink = listItem.appendChild(document.createElement('a'));
    listItemLink.href = "#";
    listItemLink.innerHTML = '<strong>' + pointData.address + ' </strong><span>' +➥
pointData.city + ', ' + pointData.state + ' (' + pointData.height + 'm)</span>';

    var focusPoint = function() {
        marker.openInfoWindowHtml(pointData.address);
        map.panTo(point);
        return false;
    }

    GEvent.addListener(marker, 'click', focusPoint);
    listItemLink.onclick = focusPoint;

    document.getElementById('sidebar-list').appendChild(listItem);

    map.addOverlay(marker);
}

...

function init() {
    ...

    for(id in markers) {
        initializePoint(markers[id]);
    }

    handleResize();
}
```

Here, we greatly expanded the role of the function that used to just create a marker. Now, it creates a marker and a sidebar list item, as well as a common event-handler function that fires when *either* of them is clicked. We added some styles to it, and you can see the results in Figure 6-6.

■Note There might be a case here for isolating the generate-sidebar code from the generate-marker code, but the lure of a common focusPoint function is simply too great. Indeed, keeping the two tightly knit offers us more opportunities for crossover functionality, as you'll see shortly.

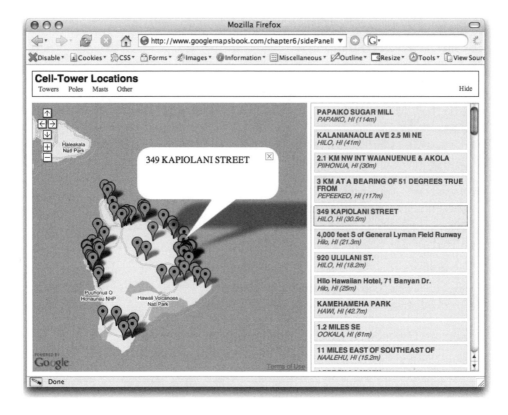

Figure 6-6. *The side panel populated with marker details*

Getting Side Panel Feedback

In the code as of Listing 6-14, the users can interact with both the side panel item *and* the marker itself. However, they're receiving feedback through only the map marker—its info window pops up. It would be ideal if we could enhance this behavior by also highlighting the current point in the side panel list.

Up until now, we've managed to avoid manipulating the classes of elements other than body. Indeed, with a static navigation system, using body classes is a highly robust way to respond to feedback. However, the side panel is full of dynamic content, generated within the browser; as possible as it is, it would be absurd to be dynamically modifying the style rules to accommodate an unknown number of items.

The real key to this problem, though, is that the *first* click means "highlight me," but every subsequent click means "highlight me and unhighlight the previous selection." Previously, the API handled this transparently, by providing only a single info window. Now, you need to do it yourself.

The method will be a global variable, called deselectCurrent, which always stores a function for unselecting the current selection. Whenever something new is selected, the handler can simply run the current function, select itself, and then reassign the variable to a new function that will unselect *itself*. Perhaps it will make more sense in code, as shown in Listing 6-15.

Listing 6-15. *A Function to Deselect the Current List Item*

```
var deselectCurrent = function() {}; // Empty function

function initializePoint(pointData) {
    var point = new new GLatLng(pointData.latitude, pointData.longitude);
    var marker = new GMarker(point);

    var listItem = document.createElement('li');
    var listItemLink = listItem.appendChild(document.createElement('a'));

    listItemLink.href = "#";
    listItemLink.innerHTML = '<strong>' + pointData.address + ' </strong><span>' +➥
pointData.city + ', ' + pointData.state + ' (' + pointData.height + 'm)</span>';

    var focusPoint = function() {
        deselectCurrent();
        listItem.className = 'current';
        deselectCurrent = function() { listItem.className = ''; }
        marker.openInfoWindowHtml(pointData.address);
        map.panTo(point);
        return false;
    }

    GEvent.addListener(marker, 'click', focusPoint);
    listItemLink.onclick = focusPoint;

    document.getElementById('sidebar-list').appendChild(listItem);

    map.addOverlay(marker);
}
```

And once again, with a few styles thrown in, you can see the results in Figure 6-7. Although other sections have done so already, this code is one of the most explicit examples we've had so far of using a *closure*. In the code in Listing 6-15, every time a new copy of focusPoint is created (one per pin, right?), the JavaScript interpreter makes a copy of the environment *in which it was created*. So even though the initializePoint() function has long finished by the time focusPoint runs, each instance of focusPoint has access to the particular listItem object that was in existence at the time.

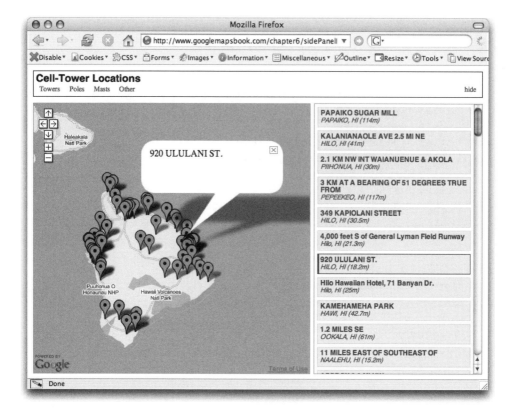

Figure 6-7. *The selected item in the side panel is highlighted.*

This, of course, applies to the deselectCurrent() function as well. Although there's only one of them at any particular time, whatever one is in existence is maintaining access to the listItem object that the focusPoint function that spawned it was carrying.

Doesn't make sense? Don't worry too much. Closures are just one of those computer science topics that will become clearer after you encounter them a few times.

Warning, Now Loading

As you create map projects of increasing complexity, users will begin to experience a noticeable lag while the browser gets everything set up. One courtesy that can be added is a message to alert your users when the map is processing or initializing.

You're going to use almost the exact same trick as was used for the hovering toolbar, except this time, you're hovering a temporary message rather than a persistent user control. Modify the body of your markup file to add some structure for a loading message as shown in Listing 6-16.

Listing 6-16. *Markup to Add a Loading Message to the Map*

```
<body class="sidebar-right loading">
    <div id="toolbar">
        ...
```

```
            </div>
        <div id="content">

                <div id="map-wrapper">
                    <div id="map"></div>
                </div>
                <div id="sidebar">
                    ...
                </div>
                <div id="alert">
                        <p>Loading data ...</p>
                </div>
        </div>
</body>
```

If you wanted, you could add a fancy spinning GIF animation, but this is adequate for a start. You'll need some similar additions to the CSS to pull this message in front of the map and center it, as shown in Listing 6-17.

Listing 6-17. *Styles to Position the Loading Message in Front of the Map*

```
#alert {
    position: absolute;
    top: 50%;
    left: 0;
    width: 100%;
    text-align: center;
    display: none;
}

#alert p {
    width: 150px;
    margin: 0 auto 0 auto;
    padding: 10px;
    background: white;
    border: 1px solid #aaa;
}

body.loading #alert { display: block; }
```

This uses the same strategy as we used in Listing 6-7 to show and hide the side panel. By hooking the visibility of the alert on the body's class, you can centralize control of it on that one spot, and yet still be free later on to move it around and not need to change any JavaScript. Moreover, you avoid the hassle of having to keep track of specific elements to hide and unhide, as in Listing 6-15. Figure 6-8 shows the new loading notice.

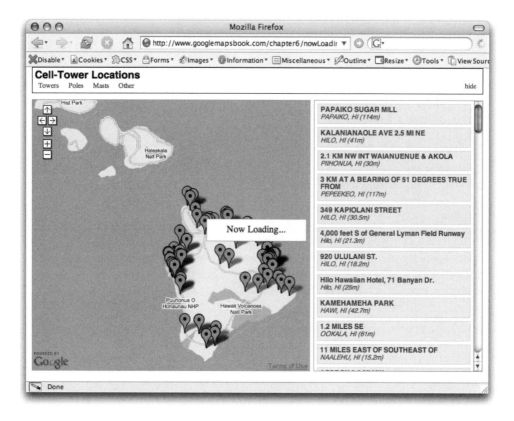

Figure 6-8. *A loading notice on the map*

Here's how to banish the loading message after the map is set up. Tack the line shown in Listing 6-18 to the end of the init()function.

Listing 6-18. *JavaScript to Hide the Loading Notice After Map Loading Is Completed*

```
function init() {
    ...
    changeBodyClass('loading', 'standby');
}
```

■**Tip** It may seem weird to replace "loading" with "standby," rather than just deleting it outright. This way, however, makes it more straightforward to revert back to loading status again at a later point. For example, if the user interacts with the map in such a way that it needs to download another big block of data, it becomes trivial to pop up that message again and let the user know you're working on it.

Data Point Filtering

Just one more area of the application still shows dummy content. With the data just begging to be broken down by category, why not use that menu bar as a mechanism for selectively displaying groups of points?

In this final example of the chapter, we'll show you how to filter points into rudimentary groups.

■**Note** Typically, when you want to display a bunch of things, and then display a bunch of different things, you think of dashing back to the server to grab the next block of information. While this is important to be able to do, we're not actually making an Ajax call here. We're just selectively limiting what is displayed. When the entire data set for Hawaii is less than 40KB, what would be the point of breaking it up into multiple server calls? When you grab it in one big lump, it makes for a more seamless user interface, since there's no waiting around for network latency on a 5KB file.

Flipping through the database view, it seems there are a handful of different structures shown in the `type` field. Most of the Hawaii data seems to fall under either "Tower" or "Pole," but there are a few maverick types. Why bother hard-coding in the types of structures, when the program could just figure them out at runtime?

Let's go with pretty much the same starting markup for the toolbar list as we did for the side panel list, as shown in Listing 6-19.

Listing 6-19. *Markup for a Dynamic Filter Bar*

```
<div id="toolbar">
    <h1>Cell-Tower Locations</h1>
    <ul id="filters">
    </ul>
    <ul id="sidebar-controls">
        <li><a href="#" id="button-sidebar-hide">hide</a></li>
        <li><a href="#" id="button-sidebar-show">show</a></li>
    </ul>
</div>
```

From here, you have three main tasks:

- Use an efficient mechanism for showing and hiding particular points.

- Figure out which groups exist in the given data.

- Create a function that can cycle through and hide all points not belonging to a particular group.

Showing and Hiding Points

The current implementation of initializePoint() (as of Listing 6-15) doesn't provide any
obvious mechanism for toggling the points on and off—it's a one-way operation. This isn't
hard to fix, though. All you need to do is create a pair of functions for each point: one to show
and the other to hide. As for where to store these functions, what better place than inside the
original markers array itself? Listing 6-20 shows how we added the new functions.

Listing 6-20. *Adding Methods to the markers Array Members*

```
function initializePoint(pointData) {
    var visible = false;

    ...

    GEvent.addListener(marker, 'click', focusPoint);
    listItemLink.onclick = focusPoint;

    pointData.show = function() {
        if (!visible) {
            document.getElementById('sidebar-list').appendChild(listItem);
            map.addOverlay(marker);
            visible = true;
        }
    }
    pointData.hide = function() {
        if (visible) {
            document.getElementById('sidebar-list').removeChild(listItem);
            map.removeOverlay(marker);
            visible = false;
        }
    }

    pointData.show();
}
```

Isn't that clever? Now along with latitude and longitude data members, each of those
markers array items has a pair of on-board functions for controlling their visibility.

Discovering Groupings

Figuring out all the unique values appearing in the type field is just a matter of iterating over
all the markers. Inside the init() function, we've added a single line to the existing loop that
runs over each record already, to call initializePoint() on it. This is shown in Listing 6-21.

Listing 6-21. *Augmented Initialization Function to Check for Different Structure Types*

```
function init() {
    var type;
    var allTypes = { 'All':[] };

    ...

    for(id in markers) {
        initializePoint(markers[id]);
        allTypes[markers[id].type] = true;
    }

    for(type in allTypes)
    {
        initializeSortTab(type);
    }

    handleResize();
    changeBodyClass('loading', 'standby');
}
```

For each element of the markers array, initializePoint() is called, and then the point's
type value is assigned as a key to the allTypes object. The nature of an object is that the keys
are unique, so by the end, allTypes has as its keys the different marker types. From there, you
can simply loop through *that* object and create a button and handler for each of the discovered types.

Creating Filter Buttons

The last section, shown in Listing 6-22, is just implementing the initializeSortTab() function
called in Listing 6-21. Creating the button is identical to how you created sidebar links in
initializePoint(). The primary "gotcha" to pay attention to here is the special case for the All
button. And, of course, you'll want to use the spiffy loading message.

Listing 6-22. *Adding Filter Buttons to Show and Hide Groups of Markers*

```
function initializeSortTab(type) {
    var listItem = document.createElement('li');
    var listItemLink = listItem.appendChild(document.createElement('a'));

    listItemLink.href = "#";
    listItemLink.innerHTML = type;
    listItemLink.onclick = function() {
        changeBodyClass('standby', 'loading');
```

```
        for(id in markers) {
            if (markers[id].type == type || 'All' == type) {
                markers[id].show();
            } else {
                markers[id].hide();
            }
        }

        changeBodyClass('loading', 'standby');
        return false;
    }
    document.getElementById('filters').appendChild(listItem);
}
```

And there it is. It's simple code, but there's a lot of really classy functionality here. Given almost any set of points, these techniques can be applied to create a useful, high-quality presentation. The final result is shown in Figure 6-9.

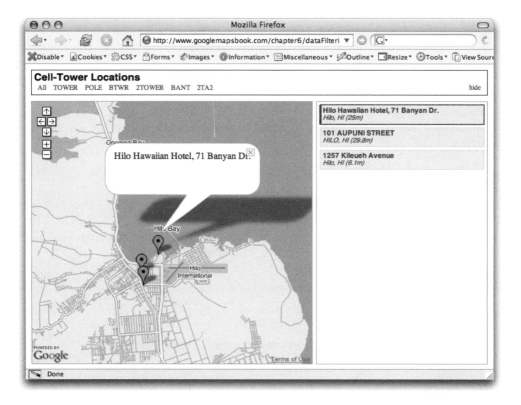

Figure 6-9. *Marker filters in action*

Summary

In this chapter, we took a look at a number of cross-browser layout tricks involving JavaScript and CSS, as well as a handful of other methods to make your maps more visually and functionally interesting. Together, we can stop the proliferation of boring, fixed-size, single-pane mashups!

In Chapter 7, you'll continue to develop this code, focusing on how to deal with the vastness of the full US-wide database.

CHAPTER 7

■■■

Optimizing and Scaling for Large Data Sets

So far in the book, we've looked at the basics of the Google Maps API and shown how it's possible to retrieve and store data for your map. You've probably come up with some great ideas for your own map applications and started to assemble the information for your markers. And you may have found that your data set is overwhelmingly large—far larger than the simple examples you've been experimenting with so far.

In the previous chapters, you've been experimenting with the US FCC data in the Antenna Structure Registration (ASR) database. As you've probably noticed, the FCC tower information is a rather large data set, containing more than 115,000 points across the United States. If you tried to map the towers using one GMarker per point, the map, or even the user's computer, would simply crawl to a halt.

When your data grows from a dozen to a few thousand points, or even hundreds of thousands of points, you need to select the best way to present your information without confusing or frustrating your users. This chapter presents a variety of methods for working with larger data sets such as the FCC tower data. The methods you'll learn will provide your users with an interactive experience while maintaining a sensible overhead in your web application.

When dealing with large data sets, you need to focus on three areas of your application: the communication between the server and browser, the server side, and the client side. In this chapter, you'll learn techniques for each of these areas as follows:

- Streamline the data flowing between your server and client's web browser.

- Optimize your server-side script and data storage.

- Improve the users' experience with the client-side JavaScript and web browser.

Understanding the Limitations

Before we discuss how to overcome any limitations that arise from dealing with large data sets, you should probably familiarize yourself with what those limitations are. When we refer to the "limits of the API," we don't mean to imply that Google is somehow disabling features of the map and preventing you from doing something. What we're referring to are the *ambiguous* limits that apply to any web-based software, such as the software's ability to run in the client's web browser.

If you're developing your map application on a cluster of supercomputers, the limitations of your computer are going to be different than those of someone who is browsing on an old 486 laptop with just a few megabytes of RAM. You'll never know for sure what type of computer your users are going to have, so remember that not everyone is going to experience a map in the same way. For this chapter, we'll focus on the limitations related to plotting larger than normal data sets on an average home computer. These issues are mainly performance-related and occur when there are too many GOverlay objects on the map at one time.

Overlays are objects that build on the API's GOverlay class and include any items added to the map using the GMap2.addOverlay() method. In the Google Maps API, Google uses overlays for GMarker objects, GPolyline objects, and info windows, all of which you've probably been playing with a lot as you've progressed through this book. In each case, the overlay is built into the JavaScript class, and in some cases, may include shadows or translucent images. Along with the API overlays, the map may also contain custom overlays that you've built yourself. You can implement your own overlays, using the API's GOverlay object, to display all sorts of information. In fact, one of the methods you'll explore in this chapter uses a custom overlay to display detailed information using a transparent GIF.

Here is a summary of the relevant limits:

GMarker *limits*: If you're going to display only markers on your map, the *maximum* number to try for the average user is around 100; however, performance will be slow on anything but the latest computer hardware. Loading markers and moving them around with JavaScript is an expensive operation, so for better performance and reliability, try to keep the number to around 50 to 75 GMarker objects on the map at one time—even fewer if you're combining them with GPolyline objects.

GPolyline *limits*: Too many GPolyline objects will slow the map in the same way as do too many markers. The difference with polylines is in the number of points in the lines, not the number of lines. One really long line with a bunch of points will slow the map down just as much as a few little lines. Load a maximum of 100 to 150 points, but keep in mind that using around 50 to 75 will make your application run a lot smoother. If your application requires a large, complicated set of polygons with hundreds of points, check out the server-side overlay and tile solutions described in this chapter. The examples demonstrate generating your own overlays and tiles, but the embedded images don't need to be limited to just markers—you could draw complicated images, lines, and shapes as well.

Info window limits: As you saw in Chapter 3, there's only one instance of an info window on the map at any given time, so there are no direct limits on the info window with regard to performance. However, remember that the info window adds more complexity to the map, so if you try to slide the map around while the window is open, the map may begin to slow down.

Streamlining Server-Client Communications

Throughout the book, we've mentioned that providing an interactive experience to your users is a key characteristic of your mapping application's success. Adding interactivity often means creating more requests back and forth between the client's web browser and the server. More requests means more traffic and accordingly, a slower response, unless you invest in additional resources such as hardware to handle the load. To avoid making these investments yet still improve response time, you should always streamline any process or data that you'll be using to communicate with the client.

As you've probably figured out by now, Ajax doesn't really need to talk in XML. You can send and receive any information you want, including both HTML and JavaScript code. Initially, many web developers make the mistake of bloating their server responses with full, and often verbose, JavaScript. Bloating the response with JavaScript is easy on you as a developer, but becomes a burden on both the server and the client. For example, the response from the server could add ten markers to your map by sending:

```
map.addOverlay(new GMarker(new GLatLng(39.49,-75.07)));
map.addOverlay(new GMarker(new GLatLng(39.49,-76.24)));
map.addOverlay(new GMarker(new GLatLng(39.64,-74.29)));
map.addOverlay(new GMarker(new GLatLng(40.76,-73.00)));
map.addOverlay(new GMarker(new GLatLng(40.83,-74.47)));
map.addOverlay(new GMarker(new GLatLng(40.83,-74.05)));
map.addOverlay(new GMarker(new GLatLng(40.83,-72.60)));
map.addOverlay(new GMarker(new GLatLng(40.83,-76.64)));
map.addOverlay(new GMarker(new GLatLng(41.17,-71.56)));
map.addOverlay(new GMarker(new GLatLng(41.26,-70.06)));
```

The problem with sending all this code in your response becomes apparent as your data set scales to larger and larger requests. The only unique information for each point is the latitude and longitude, so that's all you really need to send. The response would be better trimmed and rewritten using the JSON objects introduced in Chapter 2, such as the following:

```
var points = {
    {lat:39.49,lng:-75.07},
    {lat:39.49,lng:-76.24},
    {lat:39.64,lng:-74.29},
    {lat:40.76,lng:-73.00},
    {lat:40.83,lng:-74.47},
    {lat:40.83,lng:-74.05},
    {lat:40.83,lng:-72.60},
    {lat:40.83,lng:-76.64},
    {lat:41.17,lng:-71.56},
    {lat:41.26,lng:-70.06},
}
```

By sending only what's necessary, you decrease every line from about 55 characters to just 23, an overall reduction of 32 characters per line and a savings of about 9KB for a single request with 300 locations! Trimming your response and generating the markers from the data in the response will also give your client-side JavaScript much more control over what to do with the response. If you're sending a larger data set of 1000 points, you can easily see how you could save megabytes in bandwidth and download time, plus, considering the number of requests your application could receive, that will add up to a big savings over time.

Reducing data bloat is a fairly easy concept and requires little, if any, extra work. Though you may shrug it off as obvious, remember to think about it the next time you build your web application. Less bloat will make your application run faster! Plus, it will also make your code much easier to maintain, as JavaScript operations will be contained in one place rather than spread around in the server response.

Optimizing Server-Side Processing

When building a map with a large and complex set of data, you'll most likely be interacting with the server to retrieve only a small subset of the available information. The trick, as you will soon see, is in how you request the information combined with how it's processed and displayed. You could retrieve everything from the server and then display everything in your client's web browser but, as we mentioned earlier in the chapter, the client will slow to a crawl, and in many cases, just quit. To avoid slowing the map and annoying your users, it's important to optimize the method of your requests.

How you store your information on your server is up to you, but whichever way you choose, you'll need to ensure the data is easily accessible and searchable. Processing a large flat file for each request will just slow down the server and waste valuable resources, while at the same time searching multiple XML files can get a bit tricky. For optimum speed and efficiency, you'll probably want to use a database to store your information. We've already discussed databases and how to create them throughout the book, so in this chapter we'll just focus on targeting the information you need from your database for each request.

To easily search, filter, and categorize the information displayed on the map, make sure your database has the appropriate data types for each of the fields in your database table. For example, if you have a lat and a lng column, make sure they're floats with the appropriate precision for your data. Using the proper data types will allow the database to better optimize the storage and retrieval of your information, making it a lot quicker to process each request. Additionally, if your database supports it, be sure to use indexing on frequently requested columns or other database-specific optimizations on your data.

Once your database is flush with information, your requests and queries will most likely be retrieving information about points within a particular latitude and longitude boundary. You'll also need to consider how much information you *want* to display versus how much information it is actually *possible* to display. After you've decided on an appropriate balance of wants versus needs, you'll need to pick the solution that best fits your data. Here, we'll explore five possible solutions:

- Server-side boundary method

- Server-side common point method

- Server-side clustering

- Custom detail overlay method

- Custom tile method

These approaches have varying degrees of effectiveness, depending on your database of information and the context of the map. We'll describe each method and then point out its advantages and disadvantages.

Server-Side Boundary Method

The boundary method involves requesting only the points within a specific boundary, defined using some relevant reference such as the viewport of the visible map. The success of the boundary method relies on highly dispersed data at a given zoom level.

If you have a large data set and the information is relatively dispersed over the globe, you can use the GLatLngBounds of the GMap2 object as a boundary for your query. This essentially restricts the data in your response to those points that are within the on-screen viewable area of the map. For globally dispersed data at zoom level 1, where the map covers the entire globe, you'll see the whole world at once, so plotting the data set using markers is still is going to go beyond the suggested 100 marker limit and cause problems, as shown in Figure 7-1. At closer zoom levels, say 5 or higher, you'll have a smaller portion of the markers on the map at one time, and this method will work great, as shown in Figure 7-2. The same would apply for localized data dispersed across a smaller area or large, less dispersed data, but you'll need to zoom in much closer to have success.

Figure 7-1. *Server-side boundary method with the entire world at zoom level 1*

Figure 7-2. *Server-side boundary method at a closer zoom level*

To experiment with a smaller, globally dispersed data set, suppose you want to create a map of capital cities around the world. There are 192 countries, so that would mean 192 markers to display. Capital cities are an appropriate data set for the boundary method because there are relatively few points and they are dispersed throughout the globe. If you adjust the zoom of the map to something around 5, you'll have only a small portion of those points on the map at the same time.

Tip The boundary method is usually used in combination with one of the other solutions. You'll notice that in many of the server-based methods, the first SQL query still uses the boundary method to initially limit the data set to a particular area, and then additional optimizations are performed.

Listings 7-1 and 7-2 contain a working example of the server-side boundary method (http://googlemapsbook.com/chapter7/ServerBounds/) using the SQL database of capital city locations you created in Chapter 5 (in the screen scraping example). If you haven't created the database from Chapter 5, you can quickly do so using the Chapter 7 capital_cities_seed.sql file in the supplemental code for the book.

Listing 7-1. *Client-Side JavaScript for the Server-Side Boundary Method*

```
var map;
var centerLatitude = 49.224773;
var centerLongitude = -122.991943;
var startZoom = 4;
```

```
function init() {
    map = new GMap2(document.getElementById("map"));
    map.addControl(new GSmallMapControl());
    map.setCenter(new GLatLng(centerLatitude, centerLongitude), startZoom);

    updateMarkers();

    GEvent.addListener(map,'zoomend',function() {
        updateMarkers();
    });

    GEvent.addListener(map,'moveend',function() {
        updateMarkers();
    });
}

function updateMarkers() {

    //remove the existing points
    map.clearOverlays();

    //create the boundary for the data
    var bounds = map.getBounds();
    var southWest = bounds.getSouthWest();
    var northEast = bounds.getNorthEast();
    var getVars = 'ne=' + northEast.toUrlValue()
    + '&sw=' + southWest.toUrlValue()

    //log the URL for testing
    GLog.writeUrl('server.php?'+getVars);

    //retrieve the points using Ajax
    var request = GXmlHttp.create();
    request.open('GET', 'server.php?'+getVars, true);
    request.onreadystatechange = function() {
        if (request.readyState == 4) {
            var jscript = request.responseText;
            var points;
            eval(jscript);

            //create each point from the list
            for (i in points) {
                var point = new GLatLng(points[i].lat,points[i].lng);
                var marker = createMarker(point,points[i].city);
                map.addOverlay(marker);
            }
        }
    }
```

```
    request.send(null);
}

function createMarker(point, html) {
    var marker = new GMarker(point);
    GEvent.addListener(marker, 'click', function() {
        var markerHTML = html;
        marker.openInfoWindowHtml(markerHTML);
    });
    return marker;
}

window.onload = init;
```

Listing 7-2. *PHP Server-Side Script for the Server-Side Boundary Method*

```
<?php

//retrieve the variables from the GET vars
list($nelat,$nelng) = explode(',',$_GET['ne']);
list($swlat,$swlng) = explode(',',$_GET['sw']);

//clean the data
$nelng=(float)$nelng;
$swlng=(float)$swlng;
$nelat=(float)$nelat;
$swlat=(float)$swlat;

//connect to the database
require($_SERVER['DOCUMENT_ROOT'] . '/db_credentials.php');
$conn = mysql_connect("localhost", $db_name, $db_pass);
mysql_select_db("googlemapsbook", $conn);

if($nelng > $swlng) {

    //retrieve all points in the southwest/northeast boundary
    $result = mysql_query(
        "SELECT
            lat,lng,capital,country
        FROM
            capital_cities
        WHERE
            (lng > $swlng AND lng < $nelng)
            AND (lat <= $nelat AND lat >= $swlat)
        ORDER BY
            lat"
        , $conn);
```

```
    } else {

        //retrieve all points in the southwest/northeast boundary
        //split over the meridian
        $result = mysql_query(
            "SELECT
                lat,lng,capital,country
            FROM
                capital_cities
            WHERE
                (lng >= $swlng OR lng <= $nelng)
                AND (lat <= $nelat AND lat >= $swlat)
            ORDER BY
                lat"
            , $conn);
    }

$list = array();
$i=0;
$row = mysql_fetch_assoc($result);

while($row)
{
    $i++;
    extract($row);
    $city = addcslashes($capital.', '.$country,"'");
    $list[] = "p{$i}:{lat:{$lat},lng:{$lng},city:'{$city}'}";
    $row = mysql_fetch_assoc($result);
}

//echo back the JavaScript object nicely formatted
header('content-type:text/plain;');
echo "var points = {\n\t".join(",\n\t",$list)."\n}";
?>
```

This method has two key parts. The first is the request to the server in Listing 7-1, which includes the bounds of the map by sending the southwest and northeast corners:

```
//create the boundary for the data
var bounds = map.getBounds();
var southWest = bounds.getSouthWest();
var northEast = bounds.getNorthEast();
var getVars = 'ne=' + northEast.toUrlValue()
+ '&sw=' + southWest.toUrlValue()
```

The second is the SQL query to the database in Listing 7-2, which limits the points to the boundary defined by the southwest and northeast corners:

```
if($nelng > $swlng) {

    //retrieve all points in the southwest/northeast boundary
    $result = mysql_query(
        "SELECT
            lat,lng,capital,country
        FROM
            capital_cities
        WHERE
            (lng > $swlng AND lng < $nelng)
            AND (lat <= $nelat AND lat >= $swlat)
        ORDER BY
            lat"
        , $conn);

} else {

    //retrieve all points in the southwest/northeast boundary
    //split over the meridian
    $result = mysql_query(
        "SELECT
            lat,lng,capital,country
        FROM
            capital_cities
        WHERE
            (lng >= $swlng OR lng <= $nelng)
            AND (lat <= $nelat AND lat >= $swlat)
        ORDER BY
            lat"
        , $conn);
}
```

■**Caution** You may have noticed the SQL is wrapped in an `if` statement and two different queries are performed depending on the relationship of the longitudes. This is due to the meridian in the Mercator projection of the map. The map is displayed using a Mercator projection where the meridian of the earth is at the left and right edges. When you slide to the left or right, the map will wrap as you move past the meridian at +/– 180 degrees. In that case, the bounds are partially split across the left and right edges of the map and the northeast corner is actually positioned at a point that is greater than 180 degrees. The Google Maps API (and probably your data) automatically adjusts the longitude values to fit between –180 and + 180 degrees, so you need to request two portions of the map from your database covering the left and right sides.

When you move the map around or change the zoom level, a new request is created by the moveend and zoomend events in Listing 7-1. The request to the server retrieves a new JSON object, which is then processed by the JavaScript to create the necessary markers.

As you would expect, there are both pros and cons to using the boundary method. The advantages are as follows:

- This technique uses the standard existing Google Maps API methods to create the markers on the map.

- It doesn't drastically change your code from the simple examples presented earlier in the book.

- The PHP requires little server-side processing and little overhead.

The following are the boundary method's disadvantages:

- It works for only dispersed data or higher zoom levels.

- It may not work for lower zoom levels, as too many markers will be shown at once.

- The client's web browser makes a new request for markers after each map movement, which could increase server traffic.

Server-Side Common Point Method

Unlike the server-side boundary method, the server-side common point method relies on a *known point*, one around which you can centralize your data, and retrieves the maximum number of points relative to that known point. This method is useful for location-based applications where you are asking your users to search for things relative to other things, or possibly even relative to themselves. It works for any zoom level and any data set, whether it's a few hundred points or thousands of points, but larger data sets may require more time to process the relative distance to each point.

For example, suppose you want to create a map of all the FCC towers relative to someone's position so he can determine which towers are within range of his location. Simply browsing the map using the server-side boundary method won't be useful because the data is fairly dense and you would need to maintain a very close zoom. What you really want is to find towers relative to the person's street address or geographic location. You could have him enter an address on your map, and then you could create the central point by geocoding the address using the methods you learned in Chapter 4.

The difficulty with the common point method is calculating the distance between the central point and all the other points. The calculation itself is fairly simple and can be done using kilometers, miles, or nautical miles, as shown in the PHP surfaceDistance() function in Listing 7-3.

Listing 7-3. *Surface Distance Calculation Function in PHP*

```php
<?php

function surfaceDistance($lat1,$lng1,$lat2,$lng2,$type='km'){
    $a1 =  deg2rad($lat1); //lat 1 in radians
    $a2 = deg2rad($lat2); //lat 2 in radians
    $b1 =  deg2rad($lng1); //lng 1 in radians
    $b2 = deg2rad($lng2); //lng 2 in radians
```

```
    //earth radius = 6378.8 kilometers or 3963 miles
    switch(strtolower($type)) {
        case 'km': $r = 6378.8; break; //kilometers
        case 'm': $r = 3963; break; //miles
        case 'n': $r = 3443.9; break; //nautical
    }
    return acos(cos($a1)*cos($b1)*cos($a2)*cos($b2) +
        cos($a1)*sin($b1)*cos($a2)*sin($b2) +
        sin($a1)*sin($a2)) * $r;
}

?>
```

The problem arises when you need to calculate the distance to every point in your database. Looping through each point is fine for a relatively small database, but when you are dealing with hundreds of thousands of points, you should first reduce your data set using other methods. For example, you could limit the search to a certain range from the central point and construct a latitude/longitude boundary, as you did with the server-side boundary method in Listing 7-2. This would limit the surface distance calculation to each point in the boundary rather than the entire database. You could also look up the city or state when you geocode the address and filter your SQL query to points only in that city or state. Either way, it's best to provide some level of additional search criteria so you don't waste resources by calculating distances to points on the other side of the world.

If you choose to use this method, also be aware that user interface problems may arise if you don't design your interface correctly. The problem may not be obvious at first, but what happens when you slide the map away from the common central point? Using strictly this method means no additional markers are shown outside those closest to the common point. Your users could be dragging the map around looking for the other markers that they know are there, but aren't shown due to the restrictions of the central point location, as shown in Figure 7-3.

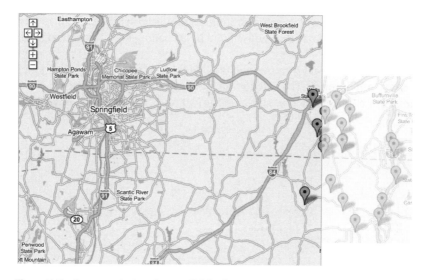

Figure 7-3. *A map missing the available data outside the viewable area*

Some maps we've seen use "closest to the center" of the map to filter points. This imposes the same ambiguity, as the map actually contains much more information but it's simply ignored. When using the server-side common point method, be sure to indicate to the users that the information on the map is filtered relative to the known point. That way, they are aware they must perform an additional search to retrieve more information.

Listings 7-4 and 7-5 show a working example of the common point method (http://googlemapsbook.com/chapter7/ServerClosest/). To provide a simpler example, we've made the map clickable. The latitude and longitude of the clicked point is sent back to the server as the known point. Then, using the FCC tower database, the map will plot the closest 20 towers to the click. You could easily modify the example to send an address in the request and use a server-side geocoding application to encode the address into latitude and longitude coordinates, or you could use the API's GClientGeocoder object to geocode an address.

Listing 7-4. *Client-Side JavaScript for the Closest to Common Point Method*

```
var map;
var centerLatitude = 42;
var centerLongitude = -72;
var startZoom = 10;

function init() {
    map = new GMap2(document.getElementById("map"));
    map.addControl(new GSmallMapControl());
    map.setCenter(new GLatLng(centerLatitude, centerLongitude), startZoom);

    //pass in an initial point for the center
    updateMarkers(new GLatLng(centerLatitude, centerLongitude));

    GEvent.addListener(map,'click',function(overlay,point) {
        //pass in the point for the center
        updateMarkers(point);
    });

}

function updateMarkers(point) {

    //remove the existing points
    map.clearOverlays();

    //create the boundary for the data to provide
    //initial filtering
    var bounds = map.getBounds();
    var southWest = bounds.getSouthWest();
    var northEast = bounds.getNorthEast();
    var getVars = 'ne=' + northEast.toUrlValue()
    + '&sw=' + southWest.toUrlValue()
    + '&known=' + point.toUrlValue();
```

```
        //log the URL for testing
        GLog.writeUrl('server.php?'+getVars);

        //retrieve the points
        var request = GXmlHttp.create();
        request.open('GET', 'server.php?'+getVars, true);
        request.onreadystatechange = function() {
            if (request.readyState == 4) {
                var jscript = request.responseText;
                var points;
                GLog.write(jscript);
                eval(jscript);

                //create each point from the list
                for (i in points) {
                    var point = new GLatLng(points[i].lat,points[i].lng);
                    var marker = createMarker(point);
                    map.addOverlay(marker);
                }
            }
        }
        request.send(null);
}

function createMarker(point) {
    var marker = new GMarker(point);
    return marker;
}

window.onload = init;
```

Listing 7-5. *Server-Side PHP for the Closest to Common Point Method*

```php
<?php

//surface distance calculation from Listing 7-3
function surfaceDistance($lat1,$lng1,$lat2,$lng2,$type='km'){
    $a1 =  deg2rad($lat1); //lat 1 in radians
    $a2 = deg2rad($lat2); //lat 2 in radians
    $b1 =  deg2rad($lng1); //lng 1 in radians
    $b2 = deg2rad($lng2); //lng 2 in radians

    //earth radius = 6378.8 kilometers or 3963 miles
    switch(strtolower($type)) {
        case 'km': $r = 6378.8; break; //kilometers
        case 'm': $r = 3963; break; //miles
        case 'n': $r = 3443.9; break; //nautical
    }
```

```php
        return acos(cos($a1)*cos($b1)*cos($a2)*cos($b2)
            + cos($a1)*sin($b1)*cos($a2)*sin($b2)
            + sin($a1)*sin($a2)) * $r;
}


//retrieve the variables from the GET vars
list($knownLat,$knownLng) = explode(',',$_GET['known']);
list($nelat,$nelng) = explode(',',$_GET['ne']);
list($swlat,$swlng) = explode(',',$_GET['sw']);

//clean the data
$knownLat=(float)$knownLat;
$knownLng=(float)$knownLng;
$nelng=(float)$nelng;
$swlng=(float)$swlng;
$nelat=(float)$nelat;
$swlat=(float)$swlat;

//connect to the database
require($_SERVER['DOCUMENT_ROOT'] . '/db_credentials.php');
$conn = mysql_connect("localhost", $db_name, $db_pass);
mysql_select_db("googlemapsbook", $conn);

/*
 * Retrieve the points within the boundary of the map.
 * For the FCC data, all the points are within the US so we
 * don't need to worry about the meridian problem.
 */
$result = mysql_query(
    "SELECT
        longitude as lng,latitude as lat
    FROM
        fcc_towers
    WHERE
        (longitude > $swlng AND longitude < $nelng)
        AND (latitude <= $nelat AND latitude >= $swlat)
    ORDER BY
        lat");

$list = $distanceList = array();
$i=0;
$row = mysql_fetch_assoc($result);
while($row)
{
    $i++;
    extract($row);
```

```
      $list[$i] = "p{$i}:{lat:{$lat},lng:{$lng}}";
      $distanceList[$i] = surfaceDistance($lat,$lng,$knownLat,$knownLng,'km');
      $row = mysql_fetch_assoc($result);
}

//sort the arrays by distance
array_multisort($distanceList,$list);

//free the distance list
unset($distanceList);

//slice the array to the desired number of points
//20 in this case
$list = array_slice($list,0,20);

//echo back the JavaScript object
header('content-type:text/plain;');
echo "var points = {\n\t".join(",\n\t",$list)."\n}";

?>
```

You may notice the GET variables for the request in Listing 7-4 contain the bounds of the viewable area along with the clicked point:

```
var getVars = 'ne=' + northEast.toUrlValue()
 + '&sw=' + southWest.toUrlValue()
 + '&known=' + point.toUrlValue();
```

As mentioned earlier, sending the bounds allows you to filter the points to the viewable area first, reducing the number of distance calculations. In Listing 7-5, the script simply records all the distances into the distanceList array, and then sorts and slices the array by distance to the known point before returning the request.

The closest to common point method offers the following advantages:

- It works at any zoom level.

- It works for any sized data provided you add additional filtering.

- This method is great for relative location-based searches.

Its disadvantages are as follows:

- Each request must be calculated and can't be easily cached.

- Not all available data points appear on the map.

- It requires a relative location.

- It may require server resources for larger/dense data sets.

Server-Side Clustering

The server-side clustering solution involves using the server to further analyze your requests, and it works well for high-density data sets. In this case, the server analyzes the locations you've requested along with their proximity, and then *clusters* markers to provide the maximum amount of information from the fewest number of markers. A cluster is just a normal GMarker, but it represents more than one marker within a close distance and therefore usually has a different icon.

If your data has a very high density and markers are often overlapping, you can reduce the number of markers on the map simply by combining near markers into one single cluster marker. When you zoom the map for a closer look, the cluster marker will expand into several individual markers, or more cluster markers, until the zoom is close enough that no clusters are needed. For data sets of around 1000 points, clustering can be accomplished through JavaScript on the client side, which we'll discuss in the "Client-Side Clustering" section later in the chapter. Here, you'll see how to cluster data on the server side when you have hundreds of thousands of points.

To initially filter your data for the request, you can use either the server-side boundary method or the server-side closest to common point method. For this example, we've chosen to request all the points within the viewable area of the map (the boundary method), and then we've applied clustering to the remaining points, as shown in Figure 7-4.

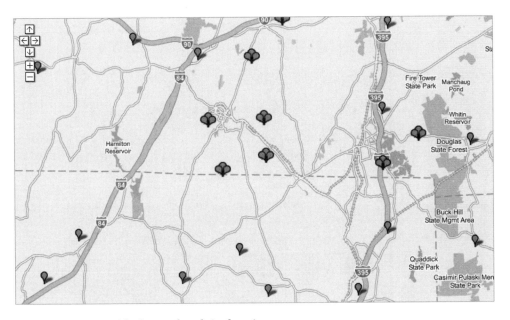

Figure 7-4. *A map with clustered and single points*

Combining clustering with either of the previous two methods can overcome some of their limitations. The drawback of the server-side boundary method was its limitation to a "closer to earth" zoom level. Zooming out meant that there would be too many points to display at one time on the map. By clustering the points, you can zoom out and still view the map within the marker limit, but some markers will be combined until you zoom in closer.

To cluster data into common groups, you need to determine which points lay relatively close to each other, and then figure out how much clustering to apply to achieve the correct number of points. There are a variety of ways you can go about this, some simple and others much more complex. For the example here, we've chosen a simple method that we like to call the "grid" method.

To cluster using a grid, you take the outer boundary of the data set (for example the viewport), divide the area into equally sized grid cells, and then allocate each of your points to a cell. The size of the grid cells will determine how detailed the map data is. If you use a grid cell that is 100 pixels wide, then all markers within the 100-by-100 block will be combined into one marker. Listing 7-6 uses an incremental grid size starting with one-thirtieth of the longitude resolution:

```
$gridSize+=($nelng-$swlng)/30;
```

which increases if the total is still too large at the end of the loop:

```
if(count($clustered)>$limit) continue;
```

By incrementing the size of the cell, you can achieve the best resolution of data for the number of points available. Figure 7-5 shows an example map with grid cells and map areas outlined.

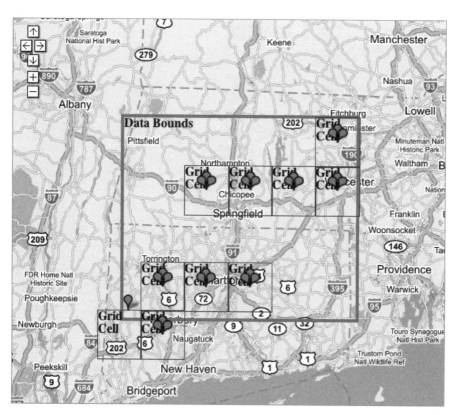

Figure 7-5. *A map showing the marked grid cells used for clustering*

Listings 7-6 and 7-7 (http://googlemapsbook.com/chapter7/ServerCluster/) are modified versions of the server-side boundary method.

Listing 7-6. *Cluster Icon Additions to Improve the Server-Side Boundary Method JavaScript*

```
var map;
var centerLatitude = 42;
var centerLongitude = -72;
var startZoom = 10;

//create an icon for the clusters
var iconCluster = new GIcon();
iconCluster.image = "http://googlemapsbook.com/chapter7/icons/cluster.png";
iconCluster.shadow = "http://googlemapsbook.com/chapter7/icons/cluster_shadow.png";
iconCluster.iconSize = new GSize(26, 25);
iconCluster.shadowSize = new GSize(22, 20);
iconCluster.iconAnchor = new GPoint(13, 25);
iconCluster.infoWindowAnchor = new GPoint(13, 1);
iconCluster.infoShadowAnchor = new GPoint(26, 13);

//create an icon for the pins
var iconSingle = new GIcon();
iconSingle.image = "http://googlemapsbook.com/chapter7/icons/single.png";
iconSingle.shadow = "http://googlemapsbook.com/chapter7/icons/single_shadow.png";
iconSingle.iconSize = new GSize(12, 20);
iconSingle.shadowSize = new GSize(22, 20);
iconSingle.iconAnchor = new GPoint(6, 20);
iconSingle.infoWindowAnchor = new GPoint(6, 1);
iconSingle.infoShadowAnchor = new GPoint(13, 13);


function init() {
    map = new GMap2(document.getElementById("map"));
    map.addControl(new GSmallMapControl());
    map.setCenter(new GLatLng(centerLatitude, centerLongitude), startZoom);

    updateMarkers();

    GEvent.addListener(map,'zoomend',function() {
        updateMarkers();
    });
    GEvent.addListener(map,'moveend',function() {
        updateMarkers();
    });
}

function updateMarkers() {
```

```
        //remove the existing points
        map.clearOverlays();
        //create the boundary for the data to provide
        //initial filtering
        var bounds = map.getBounds();
        var southWest = bounds.getSouthWest();
        var northEast = bounds.getNorthEast();
        var getVars = 'ne=' + northEast.toUrlValue()
        + '&sw=' + southWest.toUrlValue()

        //log the URL for testing
        GLog.writeUrl('server.php?'+getVars);

        //retrieve the points
        var request = GXmlHttp.create();
        request.open('GET', 'server.php?'+getVars, true);
        request.onreadystatechange = function() {
            if (request.readyState == 4) {
                var jscript = request.responseText;
                var points;
                eval(jscript);

                //create each point from the list
                for (i in points) {
                    var point = new GLatLng(points[i].lat,points[i].lng);
                    var marker = createMarker(point,points[i].type);
                    map.addOverlay(marker);
                }
            }
        }
        request.send(null);
}

function createMarker(point, type) {
    //create the marker with the appropriate icon
    if(type=='c') {
        var marker = new GMarker(point,iconCluster,true);
    } else {
        var marker = new GMarker(point,iconSingle,true);
    }
    return marker;
}

window.onload = init;
```

Listing 7-7. *Cluster Additions to Improve the Server-Side Boundary Method PHP Script*

```php
<?php

//This script may require additional memory
ini_set('memory_limit',8388608 * 10);

//retrieve the variables from the GET vars
list($nelat,$nelng) = explode(',',$_GET['ne']);
list($swlat,$swlng) = explode(',',$_GET['sw']);

//clean the data
$nelng = (float)$nelng;
$swlng = (float)$swlng;
$nelat = (float)$nelat;
$swlat = (float)$swlat;

//connect to the database
require($_SERVER['DOCUMENT_ROOT'] . '/db_credentials.php');
$conn = mysql_connect("localhost", $db_name, $db_pass);
mysql_select_db("googlemapsbook", $conn);

/*
 * Retrieve the points within the boundary of the map.
 * For the FCC data, all the points are within the US so we
 * don't need to worry about the meridian problem.
 */
$result = mysql_query(
    "SELECT
        longitude as lng,latitude as lat,struc_height,struc_elevation
    FROM
        fcc_towers
    WHERE
        (longitude > $swlng AND longitude < $nelng)
        AND (latitude <= $nelat AND latitude >= $swlat)
    ORDER BY
        lat");

//extract all the points from the result into an array
$list = array();
$row = mysql_fetch_assoc($result);
while($row)
{
    //use 'm' to indicate this is a regular (m)arker
    $list[] = array($row['lat'],$row['lng'],'m');
    $row = mysql_fetch_assoc($result);
}
```

```php
//close the SQL connection
mysql_close($conn);

//limit to 30 markers
$limit = 30;

$gridSize = 0;
$listRemove = array();

while(count($list)>$limit) {

    //grid size in pixels. if the first pass fails to reduce the
    //number of markers below the limit, the grid will increase
    //again and redo the loop.
    $gridSize += ($nelng-$swlng)/30;

    $clustered = array();
    reset($list);

    //loop through the $list and put each one in a grid square
    while(list($k,$v) = each($list)) {
        //calculate the y position based on the latitude: $v[0]
        $y = floor(($v[0]-$swlat)/$gridSize);
        //calculate the x position based on the longitude: $v[1]
        $x = floor(($v[1]-$swlng)/$gridSize);
        //use the x and y values as the key for the array and append
        //the points key to the clustered array
        $clustered["{$x},{$y}"][] = $k;
    }

    //check if we're below the limit and if not loop again
    if(count($clustered)>$limit) continue;

    //reformat the list array
    $listRemove = array();
    while(list($k,$v) = each($clustered)) {

        //only merge if there is more than one marker in a cell
        if(count($v)>1) {

            //create a list of the merged markers
            $listRemove = array_merge($listRemove,$v);

            //add a cluster marker to the list
            $clusterLat = $list[$v[0]][0];
            $clusterLng = $list[$v[0]][1];
```

```
            //use 'c' to indicate this is a (c)luster marker
            $list[] = array($clusterLat,$clusterLng,'c');


        }
    }

    //unset all the merged pins
    //reverse to start with highest key
    rsort($listRemove);
    while(list($k,$v) = each($listRemove)) {
        unset($list[$v]);
    }

    //we're done!
    break;

}

reset($list);
$json = array();
while(list($key,$values) = each($list)) {
    $i++;
    $json[] = "p{$i}:{lat:{$values[0]},lng:{$values[1]},type:'{$values[2]}'}";
}

//echo back the JavaScript object
header('content-type:text/plain;');
echo "var points = {\n\t".join(",\n\t",$json)."\n}";

?>
```

These are good starting points for your clustering script. To make it even better, you could make some improvements. For example, you could calculate an average position of the markers within one grid cell so that the cluster marker better represents the actual location of the points in that cell. You could also develop an algorithm that would allow you to cluster based on relative positions, so only dense groups would cluster rather than the entire page.

The advantages of the cluster method are that it isn't restricted to zoom levels and it works for any sized data set. Its disadvantage is that the data is clustered over possibly large areas, so you will still need to zoom in for more detail.

Custom Detail Overlay Method

So far, all the solutions we've presented use the GMarker to represent the data points on the map. With the release of Google Maps API version 2, Google has exposed additional classes in the API for building your own custom overlays.

An overlay, as we mentioned earlier, is anything that you add to the map, such as a GMarker, GPolyline, or an info window. In version 1 of the API, you were limited to the Google-provided overlays. Now you can implement your own overlays using the GOverlay class. This opens up a realm of possibilities for creating overlays such as simple shapes or even your own info window object. Here, we present the possibility of including a detail overlay for a specified area of the map.

The custom overlay you create can contain any information you want. For example, the Google Maps API documentation gives the example of a `Rectangle` overlay, as listed in Listing 7-8 (from `http://www.google.com/apis/maps/documentation/#Custom_Overlays`).

Listing 7-8. *Google's Example Rectangle Overlay*

```
// A Rectangle is a simple overlay that outlines a lat/lng bounds on the
// map. It has a border of the given weight and color and can optionally
// have a semi-transparent background color.
function Rectangle(bounds, opt_weight, opt_color) {
  this.bounds_ = bounds;
  this.weight_ = opt_weight || 2;
  this.color_ = opt_color || "#888888";
}
Rectangle.prototype = new GOverlay();

// Creates the DIV representing this rectangle.
Rectangle.prototype.initialize = function(map) {
  // Create the DIV representing our rectangle
  var div = document.createElement("div");
  div.style.border = this.weight_ + "px solid " + this.color_;
  div.style.position = "absolute";

  // Our rectangle is flat against the map, so we add our selves to the
  // MAP_PANE pane, which is at the same z-index as the map itself (i.e.,
  // below the marker shadows)
  map.getPane(G_MAP_MAP_PANE).appendChild(div);

  this.map_ = map;
  this.div_ = div;
}

// Remove the main DIV from the map pane
Rectangle.prototype.remove = function() {
  this.div_.parentNode.removeChild(this.div_);
}

// Copy our data to a new Rectangle
Rectangle.prototype.copy = function() {
  return new Rectangle(this.bounds_, this.weight_, this.color_,
                       this.backgroundColor_, this.opacity_);
}

// Redraw the rectangle based on the current projection and zoom level
Rectangle.prototype.redraw = function(force) {
```

```
    // We only need to redraw if the coordinate system has changed
    if (!force) return;

    // Calculate the DIV coordinates of two opposite corners of our bounds to
    // get the size and position of our rectangle
    var c1 = this.map_.fromLatLngToDivPixel(this.bounds_.getSouthWest());
    var c2 = this.map_.fromLatLngToDivPixel(this.bounds_.getNorthEast());

    // Now position our DIV based on the DIV coordinates of our bounds
    this.div_.style.width = Math.abs(c2.x - c1.x) + "px";
    this.div_.style.height = Math.abs(c2.y - c1.y) + "px";
    this.div_.style.left = (Math.min(c2.x, c1.x) - this.weight_) + "px";
    this.div_.style.top = (Math.min(c2.y, c1.y) - this.weight_) + "px";
}

function load() {
  if (GBrowserIsCompatible()) {
        var map = new GMap2(document.getElementById("map"));
        map.addControl(new GSmallMapControl());
        map.addControl(new GMapTypeControl());
        map.setCenter(new GLatLng(37.4419, -122.1419), 13);

        // Display a rectangle in the center of the map at about a quarter of
        // the size of the main map
        var bounds = map.getBounds();
        var southWest = bounds.getSouthWest();
        var northEast = bounds.getNorthEast();
        var lngDelta = (northEast.lng() - southWest.lng()) / 4;
        var latDelta = (northEast.lat() - southWest.lat()) / 4;
        var rectBounds = new GLatLngBounds(
        new GLatLng(southWest.lat() + latDelta,
            southWest.lng() + lngDelta),
        new GLatLng(northEast.lat() - latDelta,
            northEast.lng() - lngDelta));
        map.addOverlay(new Rectangle(rectBounds));
    }
}

window.onload = load;
```

The Rectangle overlay simply creates a div object on the map and applies a border to it. To create a detail overlay, you can use the Rectangle object in Listing 7-8, but add one additional property to the div: a background image. The background image can contain any information you want, from pictures and icons to lines and shapes, and can be created on the fly using a server-side script. The new custom detail overlay can then be placed on the map in the appropriate area on top of the existing Google Maps tiles.

Using an overlay is best for data sets that are high density but cover a relatively small portion of the map. If your data set contains hundreds of millions of points, creating the overlay is going to take some time, and your application will still feel sluggish. If you have massive data sets spread across the world, you'll need to use custom tiles, which we'll discuss in the next section.

For the custom detail overlay example, suppose you want to mark all the FCC tower locations in Hawaii, as you did in Chapter 6. There are about 286 towers—too many for one map using just the GMarker object. Using a custom overlay, you can simply create a transparent GIF or PNG that covers all of Hawaii and mark each of the locations in whatever way you like. You can even add text, shapes, or photos. What you include in your image is up to you.

Listing 7-9 shows the client-side JavaScript for the custom overlay method.

Listing 7-9. *Client-Side JavaScript for the Custom Overlay Method*

```
var map;
var centerLatitude = 19.9;
var centerLongitude = -156;
var startZoom = 7;

//create the Detail overlay object
function Detail(bounds, opt_weight, opt_color) {
    this.bounds_ = bounds;
    this.weight_ = opt_weight || 2;
    this.color_ = opt_color || "#000";
}
Detail.prototype = new GOverlay();

Detail.prototype.initialize = function(map) {
    //create the div representing the Detail
    var div = document.createElement("div");
    div.style.border = this.weight_ + "px dotted " + this.color_;
    div.style.position = "absolute";

    //the Detail is flat against the map, so we add it to the
    //MAP_PANE pane, which is at the same z-index as the map itself (i.e.,
    //below the marker shadows)
    map.getPane(G_MAP_MAP_PANE).appendChild(div);

    this.map_ = map;
    this.div_ = div;

    //load the background image
    this.loadBackground();
}

Detail.prototype.remove = function() {
    this.div_.parentNode.removeChild(this.div_);
}

Detail.prototype.copy = function() {
    return new Detail(this.bounds_, this.weight_, this.color_,
```

```
        this.backgroundColor_, this.opacity_);
}

Detail.prototype.redraw = function(force) {
    if (!force) return;

    this.bounds_ = this.map_.getBounds();

    var c1 = this.map_.fromLatLngToDivPixel(this.bounds_.getSouthWest());
    var c2 = this.map_.fromLatLngToDivPixel(this.bounds_.getNorthEast());

    this.div_.style.width = Math.abs(c2.x - c1.x) + "px";
    this.div_.style.height = Math.abs(c2.y - c1.y) + "px";
    this.div_.style.left = (Math.min(c2.x, c1.x) - this.weight_) + "px";
    this.div_.style.top = (Math.min(c2.y, c1.y) - this.weight_) + "px";

    //the position or zoom has changed so reload the background image
    this.loadBackground();
}

Detail.prototype.loadBackground = function() {

    //retrieve the bounds of the detail area
    var southWest = this.bounds_.getSouthWest();
    var northEast = this.bounds_.getNorthEast();

    //determine the pixel position of the corners
    var swPixels = this.map_.fromLatLngToDivPixel(this.bounds_.getSouthWest());
    var nePixels = this.map_.fromLatLngToDivPixel(this.bounds_.getNorthEast());

    //send the lat/lng as well as x/y and zoom to the server
    var getVars = 'ne=' + northEast.toUrlValue()
        + '&sw=' + southWest.toUrlValue()
        + '&nePixels=' + nePixels.x + ',' + nePixels.y
        + '&swPixels=' + swPixels.x + ',' + swPixels.y
        + '&z=' + this.map_.getZoom()
        + '';

    //log the URL for testing
    GLog.writeUrl('server.php?'+getVars);

    //set the background image of the div
    this.div_.style.background='transparent url(server.php?'+getVars+')';
}


function init() {
    map = new GMap2(document.getElementById("map"));
```

```
map.addControl(new GSmallMapControl());
map.setCenter(new GLatLng(centerLatitude, centerLongitude), startZoom);

var bounds = map.getBounds();

map.addOverlay(new Detail(bounds));

}

window.onload = init;
```

Tip For examples of the mathematical formulas for different maps such as the Mercator projection maps, visit MathWorld at http://mathworld.wolfram.com/MercatorProjection.html.

Looking at Listing 7-9, you can see the Rectangle object renamed to Detail and the addition of a loadBackground method, which modifies the background style property of the Detail object:

```
Detail.prototype.loadBackground = function() {
    //retrieve the bounds of the detail area
    var southWest = this.bounds_.getSouthWest();
    var northEast = this.bounds_.getNorthEast();

    //determine the pixel position of the corners
    var swPixels = this.map_.fromLatLngToDivPixel(this.bounds_.getSouthWest());
    var nePixels = this.map_.fromLatLngToDivPixel(this.bounds_.getNorthEast());

    var getVars = 'ne=' + northEast.toUrlValue()
        + '&sw=' + southWest.toUrlValue()
        + '&nePixels=' + nePixels.x + ',' + nePixels.y
        + '&swPixels=' + swPixels.x + ',' + swPixels.y
        + '&z=' + this.map_.getZoom()
        + '';

    this.div_.style.background='transparent url(server.php?'+getVars+')';
}
```

When loading your background image, you'll need to include several variables for your server-side script, including the northeast and southwest corners in latitude and longitude, as well as the northeast and southwest corners in pixel values. You also need to pass the current zoom level for the map. This will allow you to perform the necessary calculations on the server side and also allow you to modify your image, depending on how far your users have zoomed in on the map. You can then use the server-side script in Listing 7-10 to create the appropriately sized image with the appropriate information for the boundary. For the example in Listing 7-10 (http://googlemapsbook.com/chapter7/ServerCustomOverlay/), we've chosen to create a GIF with a small circle marking each tower location within the northeast and southwest boundary.

Listing 7-10. *Server-Side PHP for the Custom Overlay Method*

```php
<?php

//retrieve the variables from the GET vars
list($nelat,$nelng) = explode(',',$_GET['ne']);
list($swlat,$swlng) = explode(',',$_GET['sw']);
list($neX,$neY) = explode(',',$_GET['nePixels']);
list($swX,$swY) = explode(',',$_GET['swPixels']);

//clean the data
$nelng = (float)$nelng;
$swlng = (float)$swlng;
$nelat = (float)$nelat;
$swlat = (float)$swlat;
$w = (int)abs($neX - $swX);
$h = (int)abs($neY - $swY);


$z = (int)$_GET['z'];

//connect to the database
require($_SERVER['DOCUMENT_ROOT'] . '/db_credentials.php');
$conn = mysql_connect("localhost", $db_name, $db_pass);
mysql_select_db("googlemapsbook", $conn);

/*
 * Retrieve the points within the boundary of the map.
 * For the FCC data, all the points are within the US so we
 * don't need to worry about the meridian.
 */
$result = mysql_query(
    "SELECT
        longitude as lng,latitude as lat,struc_height,struc_elevation
    FROM
        fcc_towers
    WHERE
        (longitude > $swlng AND longitude < $nelng)
        AND (latitude <= $nelat AND latitude >= $swlat)
    ORDER BY
        lat");
$count = mysql_num_rows($result);

//calculate the Mercator coordinate position of the top
//latitude and normalize from 0-1
$mercTop = 0.5-(asinh(tan(deg2rad($nelat))) / M_PI / 2);
```

```php
//calculate the scale and y position on the Google Map
$scale = (1 << ($z)) * 256;
$yTop = $mercTop * $scale;

//calculate the pixels per degree of longitude
$lngSpan = $nelng-$swlng;
$pixelsPerDegLng = abs($w/$lngSpan);

//create the image
$im = imagecreate($w,$h);
$trans = imagecolorallocate($im,0,0,255);
$black = imagecolorallocate($im,0,0,0);
$white = imagecolorallocate($im,255,255,255);
imagefill($im,0,0,$trans);
imagecolortransparent($im, $trans);

//label the number of points for testing
imagestring($im,1,0,0,$count.' points in this area:',$black);

$row = mysql_fetch_assoc($result);
while($row)
{
    extract($row);

    $lng = $row['lng'];
    $lat = $row['lat'];
    $x = ceil(abs($lng-$swlng)*$pixelsPerDegLng);

    //calculate the mercator cordinate position of this point
    //latitude and normalize from 0-1
    $yMerc = 0.5-(asinh(tan(deg2rad($lat))) / M_PI / 2);
    //calculate the y position on the Google Map
    $yMap = $yMerc * $scale;

    //calculate the y position in the overlay
    $y = $yMap-$yTop;

    //draw the marker, a dot in this case
    imagefilledellipse($im, $x, $y, $z+1, $z+1, $black );
    imageellipse($im, $x, $y, $z+1, $z+1, $white );

    $row = mysql_fetch_assoc($result);
}

//echo a GIF
header('content-type:image/gif;');
imagegif($im);

?>
```

Looking at Listing 7-9 again, you'll notice that your background image for the overlay is based on the viewable area of the map. You can imagine, when you zoom in very close, the image covering all of Hawaii would be exponentially larger at each zoom increment. Limiting the image to cover only the viewable area decreases the number of points that need to be drawn and decreases the size of the image.

■**Tip** Another advantage of the custom overlay method as well as the custom tile method, described next, is the ability to circumvent the same origin security policy built into most browsers. The policy doesn't apply to images, so your map can be hosted on one domain and you can request your background images or tiles from a different domain without any problems.

Once the overlay is loaded onto the map, you should have the towers for Hawaii marked something like Figure 7-6. Again, you could use any image for the markers simply by copying it onto the image in PHP using the appropriate PHP GD functions.

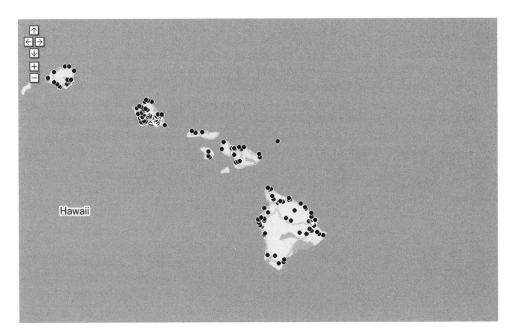

Figure 7-6. *A map showing the custom detail overlay for FCC towers in Hawaii*

The pros of using the custom overlay method are as follows:

- It overcomes API limitations on the number of markers and polylines.

- You can use the same method to display objects, shapes, photos, and more.

- It works for any sized data set and at any zoom level.

The following are its disadvantages:

- It creates a new image after each map movement or zoom change.

- Extremely large data sets could be slow to render.

Custom Tile Method

The custom tile method is the most elegant solution to display the maximum amount of information on the map with the least overhead. You could use custom tiles to display a single point or millions of points.

To add your own custom tiles to the map, version 2 of the Google Maps API exposes the GTile and GProjection objects. This means you can now use the API to show your own tiles on the map. What's even better is that you can also layer transparent or translucent tiles on top of each other to create a multilayered map. By layering tiles on top of one another, you have no limit to what information you can display. For example, you could create tiles with your own driving directions, outline buildings and environmental features, or even display your information using an old antique map rather than Google's default or satellite map types.

To demonstrate this method, let's create a map of all the available FCC towers in the United States. That's an excessively large amount of dense data (about 115,000 points as mentioned earlier), and it covers a fairly large area of the earth. You could use the custom overlay method discussed in the previous section, but the map would be very sluggish as it continually redrew the image when looking at anything larger than a single city in a dense area. Your best option would be to create transparent tiles containing all your information, and match them to Google's tiles so you can overlay them on top of each of the different map types. By slicing your data into smaller tiles, each image is relatively small (256 by 256 pixels) and both the client web browser and the server can cache them to reduce redundant processing. Figure 7-7 shows each of the tiles outlined on the sample Google map.

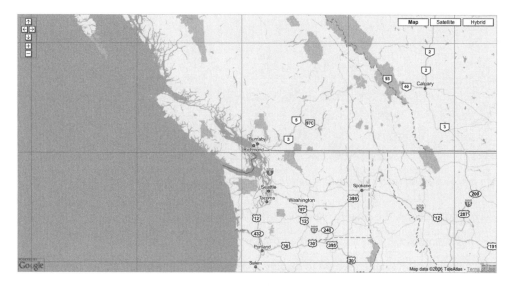

Figure 7-7. *Tiles outlined on a Google map*

To layer your data using the same tile structure as the Google Maps API, you'll need to create each of your tiles to match the existing Google tiles. Along with the sample code for the book, we've included a PHP GoogleMapsUtility class in Listing 7-11, which has a variety of useful methods to help you create your tiles. The tile script for the custom tile method (shown later in Listing 7-13) uses the methods of the GoogleMapsUtility class to calculate the various locations of each point on the tile. The calculations in the utility class are based on the Mercator projection, which we'll discuss further in Chapter 9, when we talk about types of map projections.

Listing 7-11. *The GoogleMapUtility Class Methods for Tile Construction*

```php
<?php

class GoogleMapUtility {
    //The Google Maps all use tiles 256x256
    const TILE_SIZE = 256;
    /**
     * Convert from a pixel location to a geographical location.
     **/
    public static function fromXYToLatLng($point,$zoom) {
        $mapWidth = (1 << ($zoom)) * GoogleMapUtility::TILE_SIZE;

        return new Point(
            (int)($normalised->x * $mapWidth),
            (int)($normalised->y * $mapWidth)
        );
    }


    /**
     * Calculate the pixel offset within a specific tile
     * for the given latitude and longitude.
     **/
    public static function getPixelOffsetInTile($lat,$lng,$zoom) {
        $pixelCoords = GoogleMapUtility::toZoomedPixelCoords(
            $lat, $lng, $zoom
        );
        return new Point(
            $pixelCoords->x % GoogleMapUtility::TILE_SIZE,
            $pixelCoords->y % GoogleMapUtility::TILE_SIZE
        );
    }


    /**
     * Determine the geographical bounding box for the specified tile index
     * and zoom level.
     **/
    public static function getTileRect($x,$y,$zoom) {
        $tilesAtThisZoom = 1 << $zoom;
```

```
        $lngWidth = 360.0 / $tilesAtThisZoom;
        $lng = -180 + ($x * $lngWidth);


        $latHeightMerc = 1.0 / $tilesAtThisZoom;
        $topLatMerc = $y * $latHeightMerc;
        $bottomLatMerc = $topLatMerc + $latHeightMerc;


        $bottomLat = (180 / M_PI) * ((2 * atan(exp(M_PI *
            (1 - (2 * $bottomLatMerc))))) - (M_PI / 2));
        $topLat = (180 / M_PI) * ((2 * atan(exp(M_PI *
            (1 - (2 * $topLatMerc))))) - (M_PI / 2));


        $latHeight = $topLat - $bottomLat;


        return new Boundary($lng, $bottomLat, $lngWidth, $latHeight);
    }


    /**
     * Convert from latitude and longitude to Mercator coordinates.
     **/
    public static function toMercatorCoords($lat, $lng) {
        if ($lng > 180) {
            $lng -= 360;
        }


        $lng /= 360;
        $lat = asinh(tan(deg2rad($lat)))/M_PI/2;
        return new Point($lng, $lat);
    }


    /**
     * Normalize the Mercator coordinates.
     **/
    public static function toNormalisedMercatorCoords($point) {
        $point->x += 0.5;
        $point->y = abs($point->y-0.5);
        return $point;
    }


    /**
     * Calculate the pixel location of a latitude and longitude point
     * on the overall map at a specified zoom level.
     **/
    public static function toZoomedPixelCoords($lat, $lng, $zoom) {
        $normalised = GoogleMapUtility::toNormalisedMercatorCoords(
            GoogleMapUtility::toMercatorCoords($lat, $lng)
        );
```

```php
        $scale = (1 << ($zoom)) * GoogleMapUtility::TILE_SIZE;
        return new Point(
            (int) ($normalised->x * $scale),
            (int)($normalised->y * $scale)
        );
    }
}


/**
* Object to represent a coordinate point (x,y).
**/
class Point {
    public $x,$y;
    function __construct($x,$y) {
        $this->x = $x;
        $this->y = $y;
    }

    function __toString() {
        return "({$this->x},{$this->y})";
    }
}


/**
* Object to represent a boundary point (x,y) and (width,height)
**/
class Boundary {
    public $x,$y,$width,$height;
    function __construct($x,$y,$width,$height) {
        $this->x = $x;
        $this->y = $y;
        $this->width = $width;
        $this->height = $height;
    }
    function __toString() {
        return "({$this->x},{$this->y},{$this->width},{$this->height})";
    }
}

?>
```

Using the `GoogleMapsUtility` class, you can determine what information you need to include in each tile. For example, in the client-side JavaScript for the custom tile method in Listing 7-12 (which you'll see soon), each tile request:

```
var tileURL = "server.php?x="+tile.x+"&y="+tile.y+"&zoom="+zoom;
```

contains three bits of information: an X position, a Y position, and the zoom level. These three bits of information can be used to calculate the latitude and longitude boundary of a specific Google tile using the `GoogleMapsUtility::getTileRect` method, as demonstrated in the server-side PHP script for the custom tiles in Listing 7-13 (also coming up soon). The X and Y positions represent the tile number of the map relative to the top-left corner, where positive X and Y are east and south, respectively, starting at 1 and increasing as illustrated in Figure 7-8. You can also see that the first column in Figure 7-8 contains tile (7,1) because the map has wrapped beyond the meridian, so the first column is actually the rightmost edge of the map and the second column is the leftmost edge.

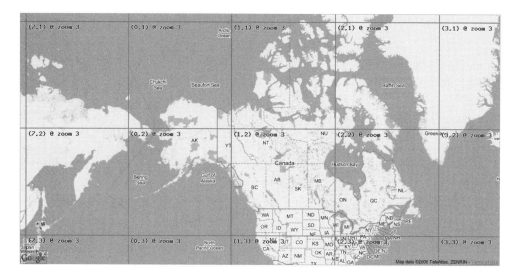

Figure 7-8. *Google tile numbering scheme*

The zoom level is also required so that the calculations can determine the latitude and longitude resolution of the current map. For now, play with the example in Listings 7-12 and 7-13 (http://googlemapsbook.com/chapter7/ServerCustomTiles/). In Chapter 9, you'll get into the math required to calculate the proper position of latitude and longitude on the Mercator projection, as well as a few other projections.

For the sample tiles, we've drawn a colored circle outlined in white with each color representing the height of the tower, as shown in Figure 7-9.

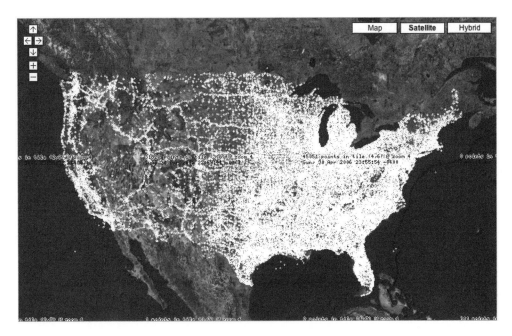

Figure 7-9. *The finalized custom tile map in satellite mode*

For testing purposes, each tile is also labeled with the date/time tile number and the number of points in that tile. If you look at the online example, you'll notice that the tiles render very quickly. Once drawn, the tiles are cached on the server side so when requested again, the tiles are automatically served up by the server. Originally, when the tiles were created for zoom level 1, some took up to 15 seconds to render, as there were almost 50,000 points per tiles in the United States. If the data on your map is continually changing, you may want to consider running a script to create all the tiles before publishing your map to the Web so your first visitors don't experience a lag when the tiles are first created.

Listing 7-12. *Client-Side JavaScript for the Custom Tile Method*

```
var map;
var centerLatitude = 49.224773;
var centerLongitude = -122.991943;
var startZoom = 6;

//create the tile layer object
var detailLayer = new GTileLayer(new GCopyrightCollection(''));

//method to retrieve the URL of the tile
detailLayer.getTileUrl = function(tile, zoom){
    //pass the x and y position as well as the zoom
    var tileURL = "server.php?x="+tile.x+"&y="+tile.y+"&zoom="+zoom;
    return tileURL;
};
```

```
detailLayer.isPng = function() {
    //the example uses GIFs
    return false;
}

//add your tiles to the normal map projection
detailMapLayers = G_NORMAL_MAP.getTileLayers();
detailMapLayers.push(detailLayer);

//add your tiles to the satellite map projection
detailMapLayers = G_SATELLITE_MAP.getTileLayers();
detailMapLayers.push(detailLayer);

function init() {
    map = new GMap2(document.getElementById("map"));
    map.addControl(new GSmallMapControl());
    map.addControl(new GMapTypeControl());

    map.setCenter(new GLatLng(centerLatitude, centerLongitude), startZoom);

}

window.onload = init;
```

Listing 7-13. *Server-Side PHP for the Custom Tile Method*

```php
<?php

//include the helper calculations
require('GoogleMapUtility.php');


//this script may require additional memory and time
set_time_limit(0);
ini_set('memory_limit',8388608*10);

//create an array of the size for each marker at each zoom level
$markerSizes = array(1,1,1,1,2,2,3,3,4,4,5,5,6,6,7,7,8,8,9,9,10,10,11,11,12,12);

//get the lat/lng bounds of this tile from the utility function
//return a bounds object with width,height,x,y
$rect = GoogleMapUtility::getTileRect(
    (int)$_GET['x'],
    (int)$_GET['y'],
    (int)$_GET['zoom']
);
```

```php
//create a unique file name for this tile
$file = 'tiles/c'.md5(
    serialize($markerSizes).
    serialize($rect).'|'.
    $_GET['x'].'|'.
    $_GET['y'].'|'.
    $_GET['zoom']).
    '.gif';

//check if the file already exists
if(!file_exists($file)) {

    //create a new image
    $im = imagecreate(GoogleMapUtility::TILE_SIZE,GoogleMapUtility::TILE_SIZE);
    $trans = imagecolorallocate($im,0,0,255);
    imagefill($im,0,0,$trans);
    imagecolortransparent($im, $trans);
    $black = imagecolorallocate($im,0,0,0);
    $white = imagecolorallocate($im,255,255,255);

    //set up some colors for the markers.
    //each marker will have a color based on the height of the tower
    $darkRed = imagecolorallocate($im,150,0,0);
    $red = imagecolorallocate($im,250,0,0);
    $darkGreen = imagecolorallocate($im,0,150,0);
    $green = imagecolorallocate($im,0,250,0);
    $darkBlue = imagecolorallocate($im,0,0,150);
    $blue = imagecolorallocate($im,0,0,250);
    $orange = imagecolorallocate($im,250,150,0);

    //init some vars
    $extend = 0;
    $z = (int)$_GET['zoom'];
    $swlat=$rect->y + $extend;
    $swlng=$rect->x+ $extend;
    $nelat=$swlat+$rect->height + $extend;
    $nelng=$swlng+$rect->width + $extend;

    //connect to the database
    require($_SERVER['DOCUMENT_ROOT'] . '/db_credentials.php');
    $conn = mysql_connect("localhost", $db_name, $db_pass);
    mysql_select_db("googlemapsbook", $conn);

     /*
     * Retrieve the points within the boundary of the map.
     * For the FCC data, all the points are within the US so we
     * don't need to worry about the meridian problem.
     */
```

```php
$result = mysql_query(
    "SELECT
        longitude as lng,latitude as lat,struc_height,struc_elevation
    FROM
        fcc_towers
    WHERE
        (longitude > $swlng AND longitude < $nelng)
        AND (latitude <= $nelat AND latitude >= $swlat)
    ORDER BY
        lat"
    , $conn);

//get the number of points in this tile
$count = mysql_num_rows($result);


$filled=array();
$row = mysql_fetch_assoc($result);
while($row)
{
    //get the x,y coordinate of the marker in the tile
    $point = GoogleMapUtility::getPixelOffsetInTile($row['lat'],$row['lng'],$z);

    //check if the marker was already drawn there
    if($filled["{$point->x},{$point->y}"]<2) {

        //pick a color based on the structure's height
        if($row['struc_height']<=20) $c = $darkRed;
        elseif($row['struc_height']<=40) $c = $red;
        elseif($row['struc_height']<=80) $c = $darkGreen;
        elseif($row['struc_height']<=120) $c = $green;
        elseif($row['struc_height']<=200) $c = $darkBlue;
        else $c = $blue;

        //if there is aready a point there, make it orange
        if($filled["{$point->x},{$point->y}"]==1) $c=$orange;

        //get the size
        $size = $markerSizes[$z];

        //draw the marker
        if($z<2) imagesetpixel($im, $point->x, $point->y, $c );
        elseif($z<12) {
            imagefilledellipse($im, $point->x, $point->y, $size, $size, $c );
            imageellipse($im, $point->x, $point->y, $size, $size, $white );
        } else {
            imageellipse($im, $point->x, $point->y, $size-1, $size-1, $c );
            imageellipse($im, $point->x, $point->y, $size-2, $size-2, $c );
```

```
                    imageellipse($im, $point->x, $point->y, $size+1, $size+1, $black );
                    imageellipse($im, $point->x, $point->y, $size, $size, $white );
            }

            //record that we drew the marker
            $filled["{$point->x},{$point->y}"]++;
        }

        $row = mysql_fetch_assoc($result);
    }

    //write some info about the tile to the image for testing
    imagestring($im,1,-1,0,
        "$count points in tile ({$_GET['x']},{$_GET['y']}) @ zoom $z ",$white);
    imagestring($im,1,0,1,
        "$count points in tile ({$_GET['x']},{$_GET['y']}) @ zoom $z ",$white);
    imagestring($im,1,0,-1,
        "$count points in tile ({$_GET['x']},{$_GET['y']}) @ zoom $z ",$white);
    imagestring($im,1,1,0,
        "$count points in tile ({$_GET['x']},{$_GET['y']}) @ zoom $z ",$white);
    imagestring($im,1,0,0,
        "$count points in tile ({$_GET['x']},{$_GET['y']}) @ zoom $z ",$black);
    imagestring($im,1,0,9,date('r'),$black);

    //output the new image to the file system and then send it to the browser
    header('content-type:image/gif;');
    imagegif($im,$file);
    echo file_get_contents($file);

} else {

    //output the existing image to the browser
    header('content-type:image/gif;');
    echo file_get_contents($file);

}

?>
```

■Tip Another benefit of using the tile layer is that it bypasses the cross-domain scripting restrictions on the browser. Each tile is actually an image and nothing more. The GET parameters specify which tile the browser is requesting, and the browser can load any image from any site, as it is not considered malicious—it's just an image.

BUT WHAT ABOUT INFO WINDOWS?

Using tiles to display your "markers" is relatively easy, and you can simulate most of the features of the `GMarker` object, with the exception of info windows. You can't attach an info window to the pretend markers in your tile, but you can fake it.

Back in Chapter 3, you created an info window when you clicked on the map by using `GMap2.openInfoWindow`. You could do the same here, and then use an Ajax request to ask for the content of the info window using something like this:

```
GEvent.addListener(map, "click", function(marker, point) {
    GDownloadUrl(
        "your_server_side_script.php?"
        + "lat=" + point.lat()
        + "&lng=" + point.lng()
        + "&z=" + map.getZoom(),
        function(data, responseCode) {
            map.openInfoWindow(point,document.createTextNode(data));
        });
});
```

The trick is figuring out what was actually clicked. When your users click your map, you'll need to send the location's latitude and longitude back to the server and have it determine what information is relative to that point. If something was clicked, you can then send the appropriate information back across the Ajax request and create an info window directly on the map. From the client's point of view, it will look identical to an info window attached to a marker, except that it will be slightly slower to appear, as your server needs to process the request to see what was clicked.

Optimizing the Client-Side User Experience

If your data set is just a little too big for the map—somewhere between 100 to 300 points— you don't necessarily need to make new requests to retrieve your information. You can achieve good results using solutions similar to those we've outlined for the server side, but store the data set in the browser's memory using a JavaScript object. This way, you can achieve the same effect but not require an excessive number of requests to the server.

The three methods we'll discuss are pretty much the same as the corresponding server-side methods, except that the processing is all done on the client side using the methods of the API rather than calculating everything on the server side:

- Client-side boundary method
- Client-side closest to a common point method
- Client-side clustering

After we look at these solutions using client-side JavaScript and data objects, we'll recommend a couple other optimizations to improve your users' experience.

Client-Side Boundary Method

With the server-side boundary method, you used the server to check if a point was inside the boundary of the map. Doing so on the server side required that you write the calculation manually into your script. Using the Google Maps API provides a much simpler solution, as you can use the contains() method of the GLatLngBounds object to ask the API if your GLatLng point is within the specified boundary. The contains() methods returns true if the supplied point is within the geographical coordinates defined by the rectangular boundary.

Listing 7-14 (http://googlemapsbook.com/chapter7/ClientBounds/) shows the working example of the boundary method implemented in JavaScript.

Listing 7-14. *JavaScript for the Client-Side Boundary Method*

```
var map;
var centerLatitude = 49.224773;
var centerLongitude = -122.991943;
var startZoom = 4;

function init() {
    map = new GMap2(document.getElementById("map"));
    map.addControl(new GSmallMapControl());
    map.setCenter(new GLatLng(centerLatitude, centerLongitude), startZoom);

    updateMarkers();

    GEvent.addListener(map,'zoomend',function() {
        updateMarkers();
    });
    GEvent.addListener(map,'moveend',function() {
        updateMarkers();
    });
}

function updateMarkers() {
    map.clearOverlays();
    var mapBounds = map.getBounds();

    //loop through each of the points from the global points object
    for (k in points) {
        var latlng = new GLatLng(points[k].lat,points[k].lng);
        if(!mapBounds.contains(latlng)) continue;
        var marker = createMarker(latlng);
        map.addOverlay(marker);
    }
}
```

```
function createMarker(point) {
    var marker = new GMarker(point);
    return marker;
}
```

```
window.onload = init;
```

When you move or zoom the map, the updateMarkers() function loops through a points object to create the necessary markers for the boundary of the viewable area. The points JSON object resembles the object discussed earlier in the chapter:

```
var points = {
    p1:{lat:-53,lng:-74},
    p2:{lat:-51.4,lng:59.51},
    p3:{lat:-45.2,lng:-168.43},
    p4:{lat:-41.19,lng:-174.46},
    p5:{lat:-36.3,lng:60},
    p6:{lat:-35.15,lng:-149.08},
    p7:{lat:-34.5,lng:56.11},

    ... etc ...

    p300:{lat:-33.24,lng:70.4},
}
```

This object was loaded into the browser using another script tag, in the same way you loaded the data into the map in Chapter 2. Now, rather than creating a new request to the server, the points object contains all the points, so you only need to loop through points and determine if the current point is within the current boundary. Listing 7-14 uses the current boundary of the map from map.getBounds().

Client-Side Closest to a Common Point Method

As with the boundary method, the client-side closest to a common point method is similar to the server-side closest to common point method, but you can use the Google Maps API to accomplish the same goal on the client side if you don't have too many points. With a known latitude and longitude point, you can calculate the distance from the known point to any other point using the distanceFrom() method of the GLatLng class as follows:

```
var here = new GLatLng(lat,lng);
var distanceFromThereToHere = here.distanceFrom(there);
```

The distanceFrom() method returns the distance between the two points in meters, but remember that the Google Maps API assumes the earth is a sphere, even though the earth is slightly elliptical, so the accuracy of the distance may be off by as much as 0.3%, depending where the two points are on the globe.

In Listing 7-15 (http://googlemapsbook.com/chapter7/ClientClosest/), you can see the client-side JavaScript is very similar to the server-side PHP in Listing 7-5. The main difference (besides not sending a request to the server) is the use of point.distanceFrom() rather than the `surfaceDistance()` PHP function. Also for the example, the boundary of the data is out-lined using the `Rectangle` object, similar to the one discussed earlier.

Listing 7-15. *JavaScript for the Client-Side Closest to Common Point Method*

```
var map;
var centerLatitude = 41.8;
var centerLongitude = -72.3;
var startZoom = 8;

function init() {
    map = new GMap2(document.getElementById("map"));
    map.addControl(new GSmallMapControl());
    map.setCenter(new GLatLng(centerLatitude, centerLongitude), startZoom);

    //pass in an initial point for the center
    updateMarkers(new GLatLng(centerLatitude, centerLongitude));

    GEvent.addListener(map,'click',function(overlay,point) {
        //pass in the point for the center
        updateMarkers(point);
    });

}

function updateMarkers(relativeTo) {

    //remove the existing points
    map.clearOverlays();

    //mark the outer boundary of the data from the points object
    var allsw = new GLatLng(41.57025176609894, -73.39965820312499);
    var allne = new GLatLng(42.589488572714245, -71.751708984375);
    var allmapBounds = new GLatLngBounds(allsw,allne);
    map.addOverlay(new Rectangle(allmapBounds,4,"#F00"));

    var distanceList = [];
    var p = 0;
    //loop through points and get the distance to each point
    for (k in points) {
        distanceList[p] = {};
        distanceList[p].glatlng = new GLatLng(points[k].lat,points[k].lng);
        distanceList[p].distance = distanceList[p].glatlng.distanceFrom(relativeTo);
        p++;
    }

    //sort based on the distance
    distanceList.sort(function (a,b) {
```

```
            if(a.distance > b.distance) return 1
            if(a.distance < b.distance) return -1
            return 0
    });

    //create the first 50 markers
    for (i=0 ; i<50 ; i++) {
        var marker = createMarker(distanceList[i].glatlng);
        map.addOverlay(marker);
        if(++i > 50) break;
    }
}

function createMarker(point) {
    var marker = new GMarker(point);
    return marker;
}

window.onload = init;


/*
 * Rectangle overlay for testing to mark boundaries
 */
function Rectangle(bounds, opt_weight, opt_color) {
  this.bounds_ = bounds; this.weight_ = opt_weight || 1;
  this.color_ = opt_color || "#888888";
}
Rectangle.prototype = new GOverlay();

Rectangle.prototype.initialize = function(map) {
  var div = document.createElement("div");
  div.innerHTML = '<strong>Click inside area</strong>';
  div.style.border = this.weight_ + "px solid " + this.color_;
  div.style.position = "absolute";
  map.getPane(G_MAP_MAP_PANE).appendChild(div);
  this.map_ = map;
  this.div_ = div;
}
Rectangle.prototype.remove = function() {
  this.div_.parentNode.removeChild(this.div_);
}
Rectangle.prototype.copy = function() {
  return new Rectangle(
    this.bounds_,
    this.weight_,
    this.color_,
    this.backgroundColor_,
```

```
    this.opacity_
  );
}
Rectangle.prototype.redraw = function(force) {
  if (!force) return;
  var c1 = this.map_.fromLatLngToDivPixel(this.bounds_.getSouthWest());
  var c2 = this.map_.fromLatLngToDivPixel(this.bounds_.getNorthEast());
  this.div_.style.width = Math.abs(c2.x - c1.x) + "px";
  this.div_.style.height = Math.abs(c2.y - c1.y) + "px";
  this.div_.style.left = (Math.min(c2.x, c1.x) - this.weight_) + "px";
  this.div_.style.top = (Math.min(c2.y, c1.y) - this.weight_) + "px";
}
```

Client-Side Clustering

If your data is dense, you may still want to cluster points when there are overlapping points in proximity. As with the server-side clustering method, there are a variety of ways you can calculate which points to group. In Listing 7-16 (http://googlemapsbook.com/chapter7/ClientCluster/), we use a grid method similar to the one we used with the server-side clustering example. The biggest difference here is your grid cells will be larger and not as fine-grained, so you don't slow down the JavaScript on slower computers. If you modify the grid cells over several loops, the browser may assume that the script is taking too long and display a warning, as shown in Figure 7-10.

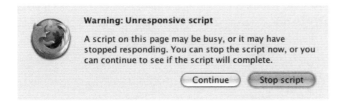

Warning: Unresponsive script

A script on this page may be busy, or it may have stopped responding. You can stop the script now, or you can continue to see if the script will complete.

Continue   Stop script

Figure 7-10. *A JavaScript warning in Firefox indicating the script is taking too long to execute*

Listing 7-16. *JavaScript for Client-Side Clustering*

```
var map;
var centerLatitude = 42;
var centerLongitude = -72;
var startZoom = 8;

//create an icon for the clusters
var iconCluster = new GIcon();
iconCluster.image = "http://googlemapsbook.com/chapter7/icons/cluster.png";
iconCluster.shadow = "http://googlemapsbook.com/chapter7/icons/cluster_shadow.png";
iconCluster.iconSize = new GSize(26, 25);
iconCluster.shadowSize = new GSize(22, 20);
iconCluster.iconAnchor = new GPoint(13, 25);
iconCluster.infoWindowAnchor = new GPoint(13, 1);
iconCluster.infoShadowAnchor = new GPoint(26, 13);
```

```
//create an icon for the pins
var iconSingle = new GIcon();
iconSingle.image = "http://googlemapsbook.com/chapter7/icons/single.png";
iconSingle.shadow = "http://googlemapsbook.com/chapter7/icons/single_shadow.png";
iconSingle.iconSize = new GSize(12, 20);
iconSingle.shadowSize = new GSize(22, 20);
iconSingle.iconAnchor = new GPoint(6, 20);
iconSingle.infoWindowAnchor = new GPoint(6, 1);
iconSingle.infoShadowAnchor = new GPoint(13, 13);


function init() {
    map = new GMap2(document.getElementById("map"));
    map.addControl(new GSmallMapControl());
    map.setCenter(new GLatLng(centerLatitude, centerLongitude), startZoom);

    updateMarkers();

    GEvent.addListener(map,'zoomend',function() {
        updateMarkers();
    });

    GEvent.addListener(map,'moveend',function() {
        updateMarkers();
    });

}

function updateMarkers() {

    //remove the existing points
    map.clearOverlays();

    //mark the boundary of the data
    var allsw = new GLatLng(41.57025176609894, -73.39965820312499);
    var allne = new GLatLng(42.589488572714245, -71.751708984375);
    var allmapBounds = new GLatLngBounds(allsw,allne);
    map.addOverlay(
        new Rectangle(
            allmapBounds,
            4,
            '#F00',
            '<strong>Data Bounds, Zoom in for detail.</strong>'
        )
    );
```

```
//get the bounds of the viewable area
var mapBounds = map.getBounds();
var sw = mapBounds.getSouthWest();
var ne = mapBounds.getNorthEast();
var size = mapBounds.toSpan(); //returns GLatLng

//make a grid that's 10x10 in the viewable area
var gridSize = 10;
var gridCellSizeLat = size.lat()/gridSize;
var gridCellSizeLng = size.lng()/gridSize;
var gridCells = [];

//loop through the points and assign each one to a grid cell
for (k in points) {
    var latlng = new GLatLng(points[k].lat,points[k].lng);

    //check if it is in the viewable area,
    //it may not be when zoomed in close
    if(!mapBounds.contains(latlng)) continue;

    //find grid cell it is in:
    var testBounds = new GLatLngBounds(sw,latlng);
    var testSize = testBounds.toSpan();
    var i = Math.ceil(testSize.lat()/gridCellSizeLat);
    var j = Math.ceil(testSize.lng()/gridCellSizeLng);
    var cell = i+j;

    if( typeof gridCells[cell] == 'undefined') {
        //add it to the grid cell array
        var cellSW = new GLatLng(
            sw.lat()+((i-1)*gridCellSizeLat),
            sw.lng()+((j-1)*gridCellSizeLng)
        );
        var cellNE = new GLatLng(
            cellSW.lat()+gridCellSizeLat,
            cellSW.lng()+gridCellSizeLng
        );
        gridCells[cell] = {
            GLatLngBounds : new GLatLngBounds(cellSW,cellNE),
            cluster : false,
            markers:[],
            length:0
        };

        //mark cell for testing
```

```
                map.addOverlay(
                    new Rectangle(
                        gridCells[cell].GLatLngBounds,
                        1,
                        '#00F',
                        '<strong>Grid Cell</strong>'
                    )
                );

            }

            gridCells[cell].length++;

            //already in cluster mode
            if(gridCells[cell].cluster) continue;

            //only cluster if it has more than 2 points
            if(gridCells[cell].markers.length==3) {
                gridCells[cell].markers=null;
                gridCells[cell].cluster=true;
            } else {
                gridCells[cell].markers.push(latlng);
            }

        }

        for (k in gridCells) {
            if(gridCells[k].cluster == true) {
                //create a cluster marker in the center of the grid cell
                var span = gridCells[k].GLatLngBounds.toSpan();
                var sw = gridCells[k].GLatLngBounds.getSouthWest();
                var marker = createMarker(
                    new GLatLng(sw.lat()+(span.lat()/2),
                    sw.lng()+(span.lng()/2))
                    ,'c'
                );
                map.addOverlay(marker);
            } else {
                //create the single markers
                for(i in gridCells[k].markers) {
                    var marker = createMarker(gridCells[k].markers[i],'p');
                    map.addOverlay(marker);
                }
            }
        }
    }
}

function createMarker(point, type) {
```

```
        //create the marker with the appropriate icon
        if(type=='c') {
            var marker = new GMarker(point,iconCluster,true);
        } else {
            var marker = new GMarker(point,iconSingle,true);
        }
      return marker;
}


window.onload = init;



/*
* Rectangle overlay for development only to mark boundaries for testing...
*/
function Rectangle(bounds, opt_weight, opt_color, opt_html) {
  this.bounds_ = bounds; this.weight_ = opt_weight || 1;
  this.html_ = opt_html || ""; this.color_ = opt_color || "#888888";
}
Rectangle.prototype = new GOverlay();

Rectangle.prototype.initialize = function(map) {
  var div = document.createElement("div");
  div.innerHTML = this.html_;
  div.style.border = this.weight_ + "px solid " + this.color_;
  div.style.position = "absolute";
  map.getPane(G_MAP_MAP_PANE).appendChild(div);
  this.map_ = map;
  this.div_ = div;
}
Rectangle.prototype.remove = function() {
  this.div_.parentNode.removeChild(this.div_);
}
Rectangle.prototype.copy = function() {
  return new Rectangle(
    this.bounds_,
    this.weight_,
    this.color_,
    this.backgroundColor_,
    this.opacity_
  );
}
Rectangle.prototype.redraw = function(force) {
  if (!force) return;
  var c1 = this.map_.fromLatLngToDivPixel(this.bounds_.getSouthWest());
  var c2 = this.map_.fromLatLngToDivPixel(this.bounds_.getNorthEast());
  this.div_.style.width = Math.abs(c2.x - c1.x) + "px";
  this.div_.style.height = Math.abs(c2.y - c1.y) + "px";
```

```
    this.div_.style.left = (Math.min(c2.x, c1.x) - this.weight_) + "px";
    this.div_.style.top = (Math.min(c2.y, c1.y) - this.weight_) + "px";
}
```

Further Optimizations

Once you have your server and JavaScript optimized for your data set, you may also want to consider some additional niceties.

Removing Load Flashing

With the examples we've presented so far, you may have noticed that your maps "flash" between redraws and requests. This occurs because the JavaScript removes all the points and then draws them all again. If you don't move the map a considerable distance, some points that are removed are then immediately replaced again. To avoid this, you can create a secondary JavaScript object to "remember" which points are currently on the map and remove only those that aren't in the new list. Using the same object, you can also add only those that aren't in the old list. Listing 7-17 (http://googlemapsbook.com/chapter7/TrackingPoints/) shows the client-side boundary method from Listing 7-14 modified to keep track of points to remove the flashing between redraws.

Listing 7-17. *Modified Client-Side Boundary JavaScript That Remembers Which Markers Are on the Map*

```
var map;
var centerLatitude = 49.224773;
var centerLongitude = -122.991943;
var startZoom = 4;

var existingMarkers = {};

function init() {
    map = new GMap2(document.getElementById("map"));
    map.addControl(new GSmallMapControl());
    map.setCenter(new GLatLng(centerLatitude, centerLongitude), startZoom);

    updateMarkers();

    GEvent.addListener(map,'zoomend',function() {
        updateMarkers();
    });
    GEvent.addListener(map,'moveend',function() {
        updateMarkers();
    });
}

function updateMarkers() {
    //don't remove all the overlays!
```

```
    //map.clearOverlays();
    var mapBounds = map.getBounds();

    //loop through each of the points in memory and remove those that
    //aren't going to be shown
    for(k in existingMarkers) {
        if(!mapBounds.contains(existingMarkers[k].getPoint())) {
            map.removeOverlay(existingMarkers[k]);
            delete existingMarkers[k];
        }
    }

    //loop through each of the points from the global points object
    //and create markers that don't exist
    for (k in points) {
         var latlng = new GLatLng(points[k].lat,points[k].lng);

        //skip it if the marker already exists
        //or is not in the viewable area
        if(!existingMarkers[k] && mapBounds.contains(latlng)) {
            existingMarkers[k] = createMarker(latlng);
            map.addOverlay(existingMarkers[k]);
        }
    }
}

function createMarker(point) {
    var marker = new GMarker(point);
    return marker;
}

window.onload = init;
```

You can apply the same fix for both server-side and client-side optimizations where the JavaScript is responsible for creating the markers.

Planning for the Next Move

If you want to be really nice and provide the ultimate user experience, you can put a little intelligence into your map and have it anticipate what the users are going to do next. From watching map users in test groups, it's our experience that most users "drag" the map in very small increments as they move around. The dragging movement of the map generally reveals only another 25% to 50% of that map in the direction opposite the drag.

Though you may assume your users will grab the map and drag around in large sweeping motions (which they still could), smaller motions offer you an advantage. You can keep track of each movement and anticipate that the next movement will take the map in generally the same direction. If you know where the users are going to go, you can request the new points for that direction and have them already waiting before they get there.

Additionally, you could also extend the requested bounds beyond the edge of the viewport to include what's just outside the edge. By extending the boundary a bit outside the viewport, your users would think the map is loading faster, as markers are appearing quickly around the edge.

Summary

In this chapter, we've presented a few optimization methods, for both your server and the browser, that allow your web application to run smoothly. By combining methods such as clustering and closest to point searches, you can further improve and create new optimization methods that will present your data in easy-to-understand and creative ways.

While working on your projects, be sure to choose the best method for the task at hand and don't base your decision on *coolness* alone. Creating your own tiles, as in the custom tile method described in this chapter, is pretty neat, but doesn't serve well for data that is generated from filtered searches, since each tile will always be different. Also, when using a feature like clustering, make sure that your icons and user interface indicate this to the user.

Once you have your web application working, be sure to go over it again and look for places that could benefit from further optimization. Check again for areas where you could reduce the amount of data transferred between the client and the server, or check places where you're looping through large amounts of data and see if you can reduce it further. Just because your web application works doesn't mean it's working as well as it could. The better optimized your map, the happier your users will be and the better experience they'll have.

At the same time you're improving your web application and optimizing it to the best of your ability, Google will continue to develop its Maps API, adding improvements and new features. In the next chapter, you'll see some of the possible things Google *may* add, but no guarantees!

CHAPTER 8

■ ■ ■

What's Next for the Google Maps API?

As this book goes to press, the Google Maps API is still very much in development; its feature set continues to change and improve. As the API increases in popularity and new methods are added, it's often necessary to alter the way things work to enable new capabilities or provide more consistency throughout the API as a whole. Version 2, for example, split the GPoint class into separate GPoint and GLatLng classes, each with enhanced capabilities corresponding to their respective roles in handling pixel coordinates and geographical locations. In reversing the zoom levels, which may have been an annoyance to developers, Google allowed the maps to support as many detail levels as the satellite photography (or your custom overlay) warrants.

So far, we've shown you a lot of really neat techniques and tricks for getting data into your application and onto a map. In the following chapters, we'll expand on that and show you some powerful tools for making complex projects. But before we dive deeper into the API, we want to mention a few things you may want to keep a lookout for as the API continues to mature. None of these things are guarantees, but they're likely possibilities, given the demand and interest in them. As developers like yourself push the API further, the demand for new capabilities—such as the free geocoder—becomes louder, and when Google consents, we get more toys and more fun.

Driving Directions

If you follow the Google Maps discussion group at http://groups.google.com/group/ Google-Maps-API, which we highly recommend you do, you'll notice a growing interest in the routing system built into http://maps.google.com, as shown in Figure 8-1.

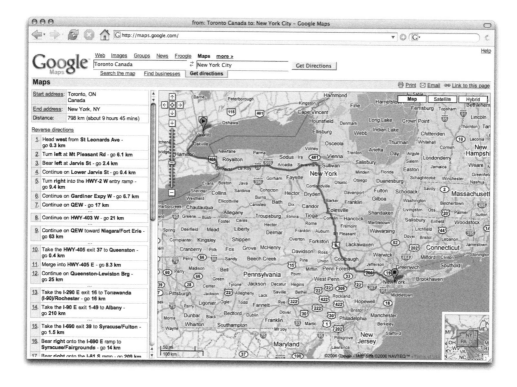

Figure 8-1. *Google Maps with a route from Toronto to New York*

Similar to the recently released geocoding service, Google could add an additional class that would allow you to retrieve the route information between arbitrary points on your map. This seems even more likely now that Google is also offering an Enterprise edition of the Maps API (http://www.google.com/enterprise/maps/) for use in closed, corporate environments. Franchises and large chains of stores or restaurants could benefit from the inclusion of routing features to service their customers and delivery personnel.

Routing is an interesting can of worms, since it begins to expose more of Google's internal road database. But road information is not a secret, of course; if you want it, you can get it from freely available sources such as the US Census Bureau's TIGER/Line files, as you will see in Chapter 11. The concern would be more with the immense computational power necessary to serve up complicated road queries in high volume, particularly to amateur API developers, who may not understand throttling or caching.

Integrated Google Services

As you've seen in Chapter 4, searching manually for data to plot and geocoding all the information yourself can be time-consuming and costly. However, vast stores of information are already available, hidden away in Google's search and service databases.

Google already offers its own business listing map web application at `http://maps.google.com`, where you can search for businesses based on their geographical location, as shown in Figure 8-2.

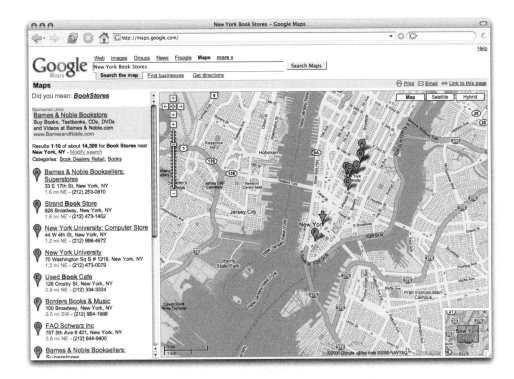

Figure 8-2. *Google Maps search for "New York Book Stores"*

If Google chose to integrate its search database into the Google Maps API, Google's servers could provide you with ready-to-use mapping information based on search terms. This would relieve you of some parsing and geocoding tasks, and eliminate the burden of collecting the information for your web application.

Imagine creating a map of bookstores in New York by asking the API for "bookstores in New York." The possibility of supplementing your map's proprietary data with Google's public data is certainly an intriguing one. As the owner of a chain of bookstores, you could not only help your customers locate your stores, but you could also offer added value by throwing up the results of a "Coffee shops within one mile of `StoreLatLng`" query.

■**Tip** Though not built into the Google Maps API, using Google's search database is actually possible now by combining some additional Google APIs such as the Google AJAX Search API and maps. For an example, check out the My Favorite Places page at `http://www.google.com/uds/samples/places.html`, where you can type in a request such as "New York Bookstores" and get mapping information.

KML Data

As you saw in Chapter 1, the `http://maps.google.com` site lets you plot any arbitrary KML data directly on your map. In that chapter, we showed you a quick sample file that marked three popular destinations in downtown Toronto. Figure 8-3 shows a similar file, which drops an arbitrary point onto southeastern Ontario.

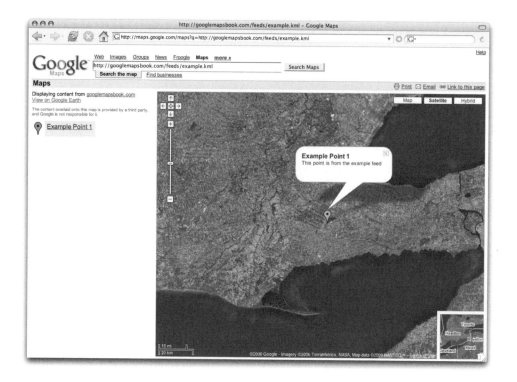

Figure 8-3. *Sample KML file in a map*

At the moment, using KML data is possible only with Google Maps itself, not directly from the API. But it certainly appears that Google has reason to expand interest in the KML data format. We expect future versions of the API to provide shortcut functions for loading and parsing this kind of information. You can do it yourself, of course, but to automate it would help bridge the gap between users of Google Maps and users of the Maps API.

More Data Layers

The satellite imagery included in the API has opened the whole world to people who may never even travel out of their hometown. With a simple click and drag of the mouse, sites such as `http://googlesightseeing.com` (Figure 8-4) can take you anywhere on the planet, and in many cases, give you a close enough look to make out cars and people.

Figure 8-4. *The Google Sightseeing home page*

So if Google can offer two layers of data (satellite and map), then why shouldn't we expect that it will begin to offer other complementary layers? The data for things like elevation, weather trends, and population density are all available, and would make excellent layers in the system. While this may tread on some of the maps we are building, it could also open up new opportunities, just as the satellite imagery did for sightseeing.

Also, Google Earth, Google's desktop mapping software, already allows you to incorporate Google SketchUp objects, so why not make these objects available to the Google Maps API, too?

Beyond the Enterprise

In building new relationships with enterprise providers, Google is edging into the corporate mapping space previously dominated by desktop products such as Microsoft MapPoint. When enterprise clients begin to require even greater performance and feature diversity, Google may provide a Google Maps Mini appliance similar to the Google Mini search appliance offered today (http://www.google.com/enterprise/mini/). A Mini appliance would provide the corporate world with a "map-in-a-box" solution that could be highly customized and branded to offer features that support the needs of specific companies and markets.

Those of us using the free mapping API may also one day see integrated advertisements in our maps. The terms of service have always provided for the eventuality of Google adding things to make money from your map. Paying enterprise customers would certainly be exempt from any integrated advertising, which would offer the rest of us a compelling reason to upgrade to the enterprise subscription.

■**Note** The API key signup page explicitly states that Google will give developers 90 days notice via the official Google Maps API blog (http://googlemapsapi.blogspot.com) before introducing advertising into third-party sites such as those you're building. If the prospect of advertising bothers you, we suggest that you follow this blog closely.

Interface Improvements

The current Google Maps interface is built entirely using XHTML, CSS, and JavaScript. It works extremely well, but is limited by the browser's ability to quickly scale images or move around large numbers of on-screen objects. Other mapping tools such as the Yahoo Mapping API offer alternative Flash clients that can benefit from the performance optimizations of that system. Though Google doesn't offer a Flash-based API, others have attempted to incorporate the Google Maps API with Flash and created unique, highly interactive, and rich web applications. Figure 8-5 shows one example: the X-Men map at http://xplanet.net.

Figure 8-5. *The X-Men Flash-based Google map*[1]

With the growing competition from Yahoo! Maps and Windows Live Local, Google may come to offer additional options such as a Flash API, or even a next-generation one based on Scalable Vector Graphics (SVG) or some other technology that can bring the browser experience closer to that of Google Earth.

Summary

In this chapter, we speculated about what might be coming up in the Google API. Along with the new services, we can expect better tools. As with any web application, Google will be continually improving on the existing components of the Maps API. Tools like the newly released geocoder will eventually expand to cover more countries and improve accuracy as more detailed information becomes available. Satellite imagery will increase in detail and will be updated continually with more and more recent images.

Now we are ready to move on to some more advancing mapping techniques. In the next part of the book, we'll cover a wide variety of complementary concepts for your mapping projects. Chapter 9 demonstrates how to make your own info windows and tool tips, as well as other overlay-related tricks. In Chapter 10, we'll cover some mathematics you may need in a professional map. Finally, in Chapter 11, we'll show you how to build your own geocoder from scratch, using a raw data set.

---

1. X-Men and XPlanet.net copyright Marvel, Fox and their related entities.

PART 3

■■■

Advanced Map Features and Methods

CHAPTER 9

∎∎∎

Advanced Tips and Tricks

Beyond what you've seen so far, the Google Maps API has a number of features that are often overlooked. Here, you'll go through a variety of examples to learn how to use some of the more advanced features of the API, such as the ability to change map tiles and the possibility of creating your own overlay objects.

In this chapter, the examples demonstrate how to do the following:

- Create an overlay for markers that acts as a tool tip.

- Promote yourself with a custom icon control.

- Add tabs to info windows.

- Construct your own info window.

- Create your own map tiles using the NASA Blue Marble images.

Debugging Maps

Before diving into the examples, let's take a quick look at debugging within the Google Maps API. With the Google Maps API version 1, the debugger's best friend was `alert()`. But as they say, "Only a Lert uses alert to debug," and if you've ever accidentally "alerted" something in a loop, you know what they mean! With Google Maps API version 2, you now have access to the wonderfully simple, yet wonderfully useful, GLog class. Now `GLog.write()` is the "new" `alert()`, but it creates a floating log window, as shown in Figure 9-1, to hold all your debugging messages.

Figure 9-1. *Empty GLog window*

For example, if you're curious about what methods and properties a JavaScript object has, such as the GMap2 object, try this:

```
var map = new GMap2(document.getElementById("map"));
for(i in map) { GLog.write(i); }
```

Voilà! The GLog window in Figure 9-2 now contains a scrolling list of all the methods and properties belonging to your GMap2 object, and you didn't need to click OK in dozens of alert windows to get to it.

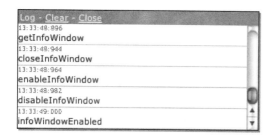

Figure 9-2. *GLog window listing methods and properties of the GMap2 object*

The GLog.write() method escapes any HTML and logs it to the window as source code. If you want to output *formatted* HTML, you can use the GLog.writeHtml() method. Similarly, to output a clickable link, just pass a URL into the GLog.writeUrl()method. The writeUrl() method is especially useful when creating your own map tiles, as you'll see in the "Implementing Your Own Map Type, Tiles, and Projection" section later in the chapter, where you can simply log the URL and click the link to go directly to an image for testing.

■Tip GLog isn't bound to just map objects; it can be used throughout your web application to debug any JavaScript code you want. As long as the Google Maps API is included in your page, you can use GLog to help debug anything from Ajax requests to mouse events.

Interacting with the Map from the API

When building your web applications using Google Maps, you'll probably have more in your application than just the map. What's outside the map will vary depending on the purpose of your project and could include anything from graphical eye candy to interactive form elements. When these external elements interact with the map, especially when using the mouse, you may often find yourself struggling to locate the pixel position of the various map objects on your screen. You may also run into situations where you need to trigger events, even mouse-related events, without the cursor ever touching the element. In these situations, a few classes and methods may come in handy.

Helping You Find Your Place

More and more, your web applications will be interacting with users in detailed and intricate ways. Gone are the days of simple requests and responses, where the cursor was merely used to navigate from box to box on a single form. Today, your web application may rely on drag-and-drop, sliders, and other mouse movements to create a more desktop-like environment. To help you keep track of the position of objects on the map and on the screen, Google has provided coordinate transformation methods that allow you to convert a longitude and latitude into X and Y screen coordinates and vice versa.

To find the pixel coordinates of a location on the map relative to the map's div container, you can use the GMap2.fromLatLngToDivPixel() method. By converting the latitude and longitude into a pixel location, you can then use the pixel location to help position other elements of your web application relative to the map objects. Take a quick look at Listing 9-1, where the mousemove event is used to log the pixel location of the cursor on the map.

Listing 9-1. *Tracking the Mouse on the Map*

```
var map;
var centerLatitude = 43.49462;
var centerLongitude = -80.548239;
var startZoom = 3;

function init() {

    map = new GMap2(document.getElementById("map"));
    map.addControl(new GSmallMapControl());
    map.addControl(new GMapTypeControl());
    map.setCenter(new GLatLng(centerLatitude, centerLongitude), startZoom);

    GEvent.addListener(map,'mousemove',function(latlng) {
        var pixelLocation = map.fromLatLngToDivPixel(latlng);
        GLog.write('ll:' + latlng + ' at:' + pixelLocation);
    });
}
window.onload = init;
```

Moving around the map, the GLog window reveals the latitude and longitude location of the cursor, along with the pixel location relative to the top-left corner of the map div, as shown in Figure 9-3.

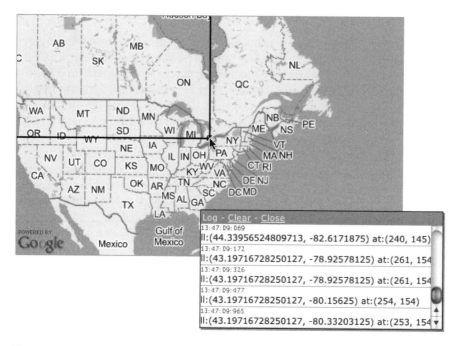

Figure 9-3. *Tracking the mouse movement relative to the map container*

Once you have the pixel location from GMap2.fromLatLngToDivPixel(), you can turn it into a location relative to the screen or window by applying additional calculations appropriate to the design and layout of your web application.

Tip For more information about JavaScript and using it to interact with your web page, pick up *DOM Scripting: Web Design with JavaScript and the Document Object Model*, by Jeremy Keith (http://www.friendsofed.com/book.html?isbn=1590595335). It covers everything you need to know when using JavaScript to add dynamic enhancements to web pages and program Ajax-style applications.

Force Triggering Events with GEvent

The GEvent object, introduced in Chapter 3, lets you run code when specific events are triggered on particular objects. You can attach events to markers, the map, DOM objects, info windows, overlays, and any other object on your map. In earlier chapters, you've used the click event to create markers and the zoomend event to load data from the server. These work great if your users are interacting with the map, but what happens if they're interacting with some *other* part of the web application and you want those objects to trigger these events? In those cases, you can use the trigger() method of the GEvent class to force the event to run.

For example, suppose you create an event that runs when the zoom level is changed on your map using the zoomend event, and it's logged to the GLog window:

```
GEvent.addListener(map,'zoomend',function(oldLevel, newLevel) {
    //some other code
    GLog.write('Zoom changed from ' + oldLevel + ' to ' + newLevel);
});
```

If you adjust the zoom level of your map, you'll get a log entry that looks something like Figure 9-4.

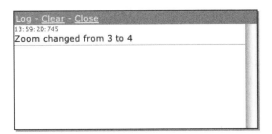

Figure 9-4. *GLog entry after changing zoom levels using the zoom control*

Notice in Figure 9-4 how the old and new zoom levels are specified. From elsewhere in your web application, you can force the zoomend event to execute by calling

```
GEvent.trigger(map,'zoomend');
```

Executing this method will cause the zoomend event to run as normal. The problem is that you'll get undefined values for both oldLevel and newLevel, as shown in Figure 9-5.

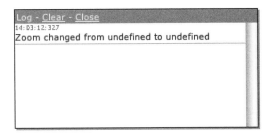

Figure 9-5. *GLog entries after triggering zoomend using GEvent.trigger(map,'zoomend')*

The same applies for any event that passes arguments into its trigger function. If the API can't determine what to pass, you'll get an undefined value.

To overcome this problem, you can pass additional arguments after the trigger() event argument, and they'll be passed as the arguments to the event handler function. For example, calling

```
GEvent.trigger(map,'zoomend',3,5);
```

would pass 3 as the oldLevel and 5 as the newLevel. But unless you changed the zoom level of the map some other way, the zoom level wouldn't actually change, since you've manually forced the zoomend event without calling any of the zoom-related methods of the map.

Creating Your Own Events

Along with triggering the existing events from the API, `GEvent.trigger()` can also be used to trigger your own events. For example, you could create an `updateMessage` event to trigger a script to execute when a message box is updated, as follows:

```
var message = document.getElementById('messageBox');
GEvent.addDomListener(message,'updateMessage',function() {
    //whatever code you want
    if(message.innerHtml != '') alert('The system reported messages.');
});
```

Then, elsewhere in your application, you can update the message and trigger the `updateMessage` event using the `GEvent.trigger()`method:

```
var message = document.getElementById('messageBox');
if (error) {
    message.innerHtml = 'There was an error with the script.';
} else {
    message.innerHtml = '';
}
GEvent.trigger(message,'updateMessage');
```

Creating Map Objects with GOverlay

In Chapter 7, you saw how to use `GOverlay` to create an image that could hover over a location on a map to show more detail. In that instance, the overlay consisted of a simple HTML `div` element with a background image, similar to the `Rectangle` example in the Google Maps API documentation (http://www.google.com/apis/maps/documentation/#Custom_Overlays). Beyond just a simple `div`, the overlay can contain any HTML you want and therefore can include anything you could create in a web page. Even Google's info window is really just a fancy overlay, so you could create your own overlay with whatever features you want.

■**Caution** Adding your own overlays will influence the limitations of the map the same way the markers did in Chapter 7. In fact, your overlays will probably be much more influential, as they will be more complicated and weighty than the simpler marker overlay.

Choosing the Pane for the Overlay

Before you create your overlay, you should familiarize yourself with the `GMapPane` constants. `GMapPane` is a group of constants that define the various layers of the Google map, as represented in Figure 9-6.

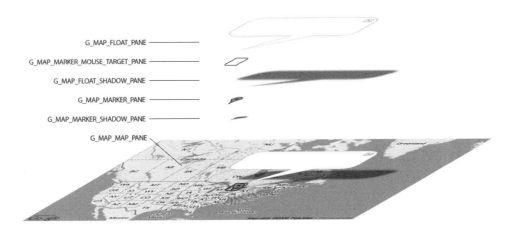

G_MAP_FLOAT_PANE

G_MAP_MARKER_MOUSE_TARGET_PANE

G_MAP_FLOAT_SHADOW_PANE

G_MAP_MARKER_PANE

G_MAP_MARKER_SHADOW_PANE

G_MAP_MAP_PANE

Figure 9-6. *GMapPane constants layering*

At the lowest level, flat against the map tiles, lies the G_MAP_MAP_PANE. This pane is used to hold objects that are directly on top of the map, such as polylines. Next up are the G_MAP_MARKER_ SHADOW_PANE and G_MAP_MARKER_PANE. As the names suggest, they hold the shadows and icons for each of the GMarker objects on the map. The shadow and icon layers are separated, so the shadows don't fall on top of the icons when markers are clustered tightly together.

The next layer above that is the G_MAP_FLOAT_SHADOW_PANE, which is where the shadow of the info window will reside. This pane is above the markers so the shadow of the info window will be cast over the markers on the map.

The next layer, G_MAP_MARKER_MOUSE_TARGET_PANE, is an ingenious trick. The mouse events for markers are not actually attached to the markers on the marker pane. An invisible object, hovering in the mouse target pane, captures the events, allowing clicks to be registered on the markers hidden in the shadow of the info window. Without this separate mouse target pane, clicks on the covered markers wouldn't register, as the info window's shadow would cover the markers, and in most browsers, only the top object can be clicked.

Finally, on top of everything else, is the G_MAP_FLOAT_PANE. The float pane is the topmost pane and is used to hold things like the info window or any other overlays you want to appear on top.

When you create your overlay object, you need to decide which of the six panes is best suited. If your overlay has a shadow, like the custom info window presented later in Listing 9-5, you'll need to target two panes.

To retrieve and target the DOM object for each pane, you can use the GMap2.getPane() method. For example, to add a div tag to the float pane, you would do something similar to this:

```
div = document.createElement('div');
pane = map.getPane(G_MAP_FLOAT_PANE);
pane.appendChild(div);
```

Obviously, your code surrounding this would be a little more involved, but you get the idea.

Creating a Quick Tool Tip Overlay

For an easy GOverlay example, let's create an overlay for markers that acts as a tool tip, containing just a single line of text in a colored box, as shown in Figure 9-7.

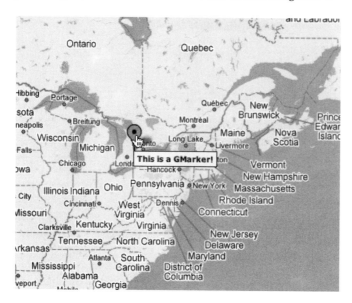

Figure 9-7. *Tool tip overlay*

Listing 9-2 shows the code for the tool tip overlay.

Listing 9-2. *ToolTip Overlay Object*

```
//create the ToolTip overlay object
function ToolTip(marker,html,width) {
    this.html_ = html;
    this.width_ = (width ? width + 'px' : 'auto');
    this.marker_ = marker;
}


ToolTip.prototype = new GOverlay();

ToolTip.prototype.initialize = function(map) {
    var div = document.createElement("div");
    div.style.display = 'none';
    map.getPane(G_MAP_FLOAT_PANE).appendChild(div);
    this.map_ = map;
    this.container_ = div;
}

ToolTip.prototype.remove = function() {
    this.container_.parentNode.removeChild(this.container_);
}
```

```
ToolTip.prototype.copy = function() {
    return new ToolTip(this.html_);
}

ToolTip.prototype.redraw = function(force) {
    if (!force) return;
    var pixelLocation = this.map_.fromLatLngToDivPixel(this.marker_.getPoint());
    this.container_.innerHTML = this.html_;
    this.container_.style.position = 'absolute';
    this.container_.style.left = pixelLocation.x + "px";
    this.container_.style.top = pixelLocation.y + "px";
    this.container_.style.width = this.width_;
    this.container_.style.font = 'bold 10px/10px verdana, arial, sans';
    this.container_.style.border = '1px solid black';
    this.container_.style.background = 'yellow';
    this.container_.style.padding = '4px';

    //one line to desired width
    this.container_.style.whiteSpace = 'nowrap';
    if(this.width_ != 'auto') this.container_.style.overflow = 'hidden';

    this.container_.style.display = 'block';
}

GMarker.prototype.ToolTipInstance = null;
GMarker.prototype.openToolTip = function(content) {
    //don't show the tool tip if there is a custom info window
    if(this.ToolTipInstance == null) {
        this.ToolTipInstance = new ToolTip(this,content)
        map.addOverlay(this.ToolTipInstance);
    }
}
GMarker.prototype.closeToolTip = function() {
    if(this.ToolTipInstance != null) {
        map.removeOverlay(this.ToolTipInstance);
        this.ToolTipInstance = null;
    }
}
```

Now let's see how it works.

Creating the GOverlay Object

To create the tool tip GOverlay, as listed in Listing 9-2, start by writing a function with the name
you would like to use for your overlay and pass in any parameters you would like to include. For
example, the arguments for the ToolTip overlay constructor in Listing 9-2 are the marker to attach
the tool tip to and the HTML to display in the tool tip. For more control, there's also an optional
width to force the tool tip to a certain size:

```
function ToolTip(marker,html,width) {
    this.html_ = html;
    this.width_ = (width ? width + 'px' : 'auto');
    this.marker_ = marker;
}
```

This function, ToolTip, will act as the constructor for your ToolTip class. Once finished, you would instantiate the object by creating a new instance of the ToolTip class:

```
var tip = new ToolTip(marker,'This is a marker');
```

When assigning properties to the class, such as html, it's always good to distinguish the internal properties using something like an underscore, such as this.html_. This makes it easy to recognize internal properties, and also ensure that you don't accidentally overwrite a property of the GOverlay class, if Google has used html as a property for the GOverlay class.

Next, instantiate the GOverlay as the prototype for your new ToolTip function:

```
ToolTip.prototype = new GOverlay();
```

Creating and Positioning the Container

For the guts of your ToolTip class, you need to prototype the four required methods listed in Table 9-1.

Table 9-1. *Abstract Methods of the GOverlay Object*

Method	Description
initialize()	Called by GMap2.addOverlay() when the overlay is added to the map
redraw(force)	Executed once when the object is initially created and then again whenever the map display changes; force will be true in the event the API recalculates the coordinates of the map
remove()	Called when removeOverlay() methods are used
copy()	Should return an uninitialized copy of the same object

First, start by prototyping the initialize() function:

```
ToolTip.prototype.initialize = function(map) {
    var div = document.createElement("div");
    div.style.display='none';
    map.getPane(G_MAP_FLOAT_PANE).appendChild(div);
    this.map_ = map;
    this.container_ = div;
}
```

The initialize() method is called by GMap2.addOverlay() when the overlay is initially added to the map. Use it to create the initial div, or other element, and to attach the div to the appropriate pane using map.getPane(). Also, you probably want to assign the map variable to an internal variable so you'll still have access to it from inside the other methods of the ToolTip object.

Next, prototype the redraw() method:

```
ToolTip.prototype.redraw = function(force) {
    if (!force) return;
    var pixelLocation = this.map_.fromLatLngToDivPixel(this.marker_.getPoint());
    this.container_.innerHTML = this.html_;
    this.container_.style.position='absolute';
    this.container_.style.left = pixelLocation.x + "px";
    this.container_.style.top = pixelLocation.y + "px";

    - cut -

    this.container_.style.display = 'block';
}
```

The redraw() method is executed once when the object is initially created and then again whenever the map display changes. The force flag will be true only in the event the API needs to recalculate the coordinates of the map, such as when the zoom level changes or the pixel offset of the map has changed. It's also true when the overlay is initially created so the object can be drawn. For your ToolTip object, the redraw() method should stylize the container_ div element and position it relative to the location of the marker. In the event that a width was provided, the div should also be defined accordingly, as it is in Listing 9-2.

Lastly, you should prototype the copy() and remove() methods:

```
ToolTip.prototype.remove = function() {
    this.container_.parentNode.removeChild(this.container_);
}

ToolTip.prototype.copy = function() {
    return new ToolTip(this.marker_,this.html_,this.width_);
}
```

The copy() method should return an uninitialized copy of the same object to the map. The remove() method should remove the existing object from the pane.

Using Your New Tool Tip Control

At the bottom of Listing 9-2 you'll also notice the addition of a few prototype methods on the GMarker class. These give you a nice API for your new ToolTip object by allowing you to call GMarker.openToolTip('This is a marker') to instantiate the tool tip; GMarker.closeToolTip() will close the tool tip.

Now you can create a marker and add a few event listeners, and you'll have a tool tip that shows on mouseover, similar to the one shown earlier in Figure 9-7:

```
var marker = new GMarker(new GLatLng(43, -80));

GEvent.addListener(marker,'mouseover',function() {
    marker.openToolTip('This is a GMarker!');
});
GEvent.addListener(marker,'mouseout',function() {
    marker.closeToolTip();
});
map.addOverlay(marker);
```

The ToolTip overlay is relatively simple but very useful. Later in the chapter, you'll revisit the GOverlay object when you create an overlay that's a little more complicated, to serve as your own customized info window (Listing 9-5).

Creating Custom Controls

Overlays are useful, but they generally apply to something on the map fixed to a latitude and longitude. When you drag the map, the overlays go with it. If you want to create a control or other object on the map that's fixed to a relative location within the map container, similar to the zoom control or the map type buttons, you'll need to implement a GControl interface.

Six controls are built into the Google Maps API, as you've seen throughout the book. Along with version 1's GSmallMapControl, GLargeMapControl, GSmallZoomControl, and GMapTypeControl, the controls GScaleControl and GOverviewMapControl (which shows a little overview window in the corner of the screen) were introduced in version 2 of the API. Depending on your application and features, you can enable or disable the controls so your users can have varying degrees of control over the map.

If these controls don't suit your needs, you can implement a custom control that replicates the functionality of one of Google's existing controls, or create something completely different. For example, the Google Maps API documentation at http://www.google.ca/apis/maps/documentation/#Custom_Controls provides an example of a textual zoom control. The Google TextualZoomControl creates the text-based Zoom In and Zoom Out buttons shown in Figure 9-8 and is an alternative to the GSmallMapControl.

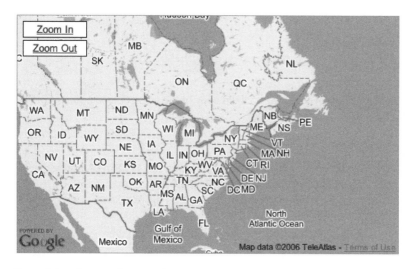

Figure 9-8. *The Google textual zoom control adds Zoom In and Zoom Out buttons.*

As an example, we'll show you how to create a custom icon control. After all the hard work you've poured into your web application, it might be nice to promote yourself a little and put your company logo down in the corner next to Google's. After all, a little promotion never hurt anyone. Implementing the icon control in Figure 9-9 is relatively simple, as you can see in Listing 9-3, and it's a great example you can further expand on.

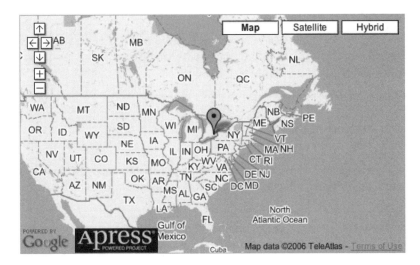

Figure 9-9. *A promotional map control, clickable to a supplied link*

Listing 9-3. *Promotional Icon PromoControl*

```
var PromoControl = function(url) {
    this.url_ = url;
};

PromoControl.prototype = new GControl(true);

PromoControl.prototype.initialize = function(map) {
    var container = document.createElement("div");
    container.innerHTML = '<img style="cursor:pointer"➡
src="http://googlemapsbook.com/PromoApress.png" border="0">';
    container.style.width='120px';
    container.style.height='32px';
    url = this.url_;
    GEvent.addDomListener(container, "click", function() {
        document.location = url;
    });
    map.getContainer().appendChild(container);
    return container;
};

PromoControl.prototype.getDefaultPosition = function() {
    return new GControlPosition(G_ANCHOR_BOTTOM_LEFT, new GSize(70, 0));
};
```

The following sections describe how Listing 9-3 works.

Creating the Control Object

To create your promo GControl object, start the same way you did with the GOverlay in the previous example. Create a function with the appropriate name, but use the prototype object to instantiate the GControl class.

```
var PromoControl = function(url) {
    this.url_ = url;
};
PromoControl.prototype = new GControl(true);
```

By passing in a url parameter, your PromoControl can be clickable to the supplied url and you can reuse the PromoControl for different URLs, depending on your various mapping applications.

Creating the Container

Next, there are only two methods you need to prototype. First is the initialize() method, which is similar to the initialize() method from the GOverlay example:

```
PromoControl.prototype.initialize = function(map) {
    var container = document.createElement("div");
    container.innerHTML = '<img src="http://googlemapsbook.com/PromoApress.png"➥
border="0">';
    container.style.width='120px';
    container.style.height='32px';
    url = this.url_;
    GEvent.addDomListener(container, "click", function() {
        document.location = url;
    });
    map.getContainer().appendChild(container);
    return container;
};
```

The difference is the GOverlay.initialize() method will be called by the GMap2.addControl() method when you add the control to your map. In the case of GControl, the container div for the control is attached to the map's container DOM object returned from the GMap2.getContainer() method. Also, you can add events such as the click event to the container using the GEvent.addDomListener() method. For more advanced controls, you can include any HTML you want and apply multiple events to the various parts of the control. For the PromoControl, you're simply including an image that links to the supplied URL, so one click event can be attached to the entire container.

Positioning the Container

Last, you need to position the PromoControl within the map container by returning a new instance of the GControlPostion class from the getDefaultPosition prototype:

```
PromoControl.prototype.getDefaultPosition = function() {
    return new GControlPosition(G_ANCHOR_BOTTOM_LEFT, new GSize(70, 0));
};
```

The GControlPosition represents the anchor point and offset where the control should reside. To anchor the control to the map container, you can use one of four constants:

- G_ANCHOR_TOP_RIGHT to anchor to the top-right corner

- G_ANCHOR_TOP_LEFT to anchor to the top-left corner

- G_ANCHOR_BOTTOM_RIGHT to anchor to the bottom-right corner

- G_ANCHOR_BOTTOM_LEFT to anchor to the bottom-left corner

Once anchored, you can then offset the control by the desired distance. For the PromoControl, anchoring to just G_ANCHOR_BOTTOM_LEFT would interfere with the Google logo, thus going against the Terms and Conditions of the API. To fix this, you offset your control using a new GSize object with an X offset of 70 pixels, the width of the Google logo.

■Caution If you plan on using the GScaleControl as well, remember that it too will occupy the space next to the Google logo, so you'll need to adjust your PromoControl accordingly.

Using the Control

With your PromoControl finished, you can add it to your map using the same GMap2.addControl() method and a new instance of your PromoControl:

```
map.addControl(new PromoControl('http://googlemapsbook.com'));
```

You'll end up with your logo positioned neatly next to the Google logo, linked to wherever you like, as shown earlier in Figure 9-9.

Adding Tabs to Info Windows

If you're happy with the look of the Google info window, or you don't have the time or budget to create your own info window overlay, there are a few new features of the Google Maps API version 2 info window that you may find useful. With version 1 of the Google Maps API, the info window was just the stylized bubble with a close box, as shown in Figure 9-10. You could add tabs, but the limit was two tabs and doing so required hacks and methods that were not "official" parts of the API.

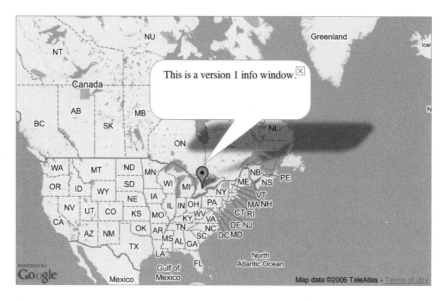

Figure 9-10. *The version 1 info window*

Creating a Tabbed Info Window

With version 2 of the API, Google has added many tab-related features to its info windows. You can have multiple tabs on each info window, as shown in Figure 9-11, and you can change the tabs from within the API using various GInfoWindow methods, as shown in Listing 9-4.

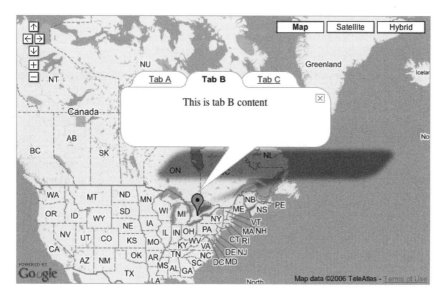

Figure 9-11. *A tabbed info window*

Listing 9-4. *Info Window with Three Tabs*

```
map = new GMap2(document.getElementById("map"));
map.addControl(new GSmallMapControl());
map.addControl(new GMapTypeControl());
map.setCenter(new GLatLng(centerLatitude, centerLongitude), startZoom);

marker = new GMarker(new GLatLng(centerLatitude, centerLongitude));
map.addOverlay(marker);

var infoTabs = [
    new GInfoWindowTab("Tab A", "This is tab A content"),
    new GInfoWindowTab("Tab B", "This is tab B content"),
    new GInfoWindowTab("Tab C", "This is tab C content")
];

marker.openInfoWindowTabsHtml(infoTabs,{
    selectedTab:1,
    maxWidth:300
});

GEvent.addListener(marker,'click',function() {
    marker.openInfoWindowTabsHtml(infoTabs);
});
```

To create the info window with three tabs in Figure 9-11, you simply create an array of GInfoWindowTab objects:

```
var infoTabs = [
    new GInfoWindowTab("Tab A", "This is tab A content"),
    new GInfoWindowTab("Tab B", "This is tab B content"),
    new GInfoWindowTab("Tab C", "This is tab C content")
];
```

Then use GMarker.openInfoWindowTabsHtml() to create the window in right away:

```
marker.openInfoWindowTabsHtml(infoTabs,{
    selectedTab:1,
    maxWidth:300
});
```

or in an event:

```
GEvent.addListener(marker,'click',function() {
    marker.openInfoWindowTabsHtml(infoTabs);
});
```

Additionally, you can define optional parameters for the tabbed info window the same way you can define options using the GMarker.openInfoWindow methods.

Gathering Info Window Information and Changing Tabs

If other parts of your web application need to interact with the various tabs on your info window, things get a little trickier. When the tabbed info window is created, the API instantiates the object for you, so you don't actually have direct access to the info window object yet. As you saw in Chapter 3, there is only one instance of an info window on a map at a time, so you can use the GMap2.getInfoWindow() method to retrieve a handle for the current info window:

```
var windowHandle = map.getInfoWindow();
```

With the handle, you can then use any of the GInfoWindow methods to retrieve information or perform various operations, such as the following:

- Retrieve the latitude and longitude of the window anchor:

```
windowHandle.getPoint();
```

- Hide the window:

```
windowHandle.hide();
```

- Switch to another tab:

```
windowHandle.selectTab(2);
```

For a full list of the GInfoWindow methods, see the API in Appendix B.

Creating a Custom Info Window

If you follow the Google Maps discussion group (http://groups.google.com/group/Google-Maps-API), you'll notice daily posts regarding feature requests for the info window. Feature requests are great, but most people don't realize the info window isn't really anything special. It's just another GOverlay with a lot of extra features. With a little JavaScript and GOverlay, you can create your very own info window with whatever features you want to integrate. To get you started, we'll show you how to create the new info window in Figure 9-12, which occupies a little less screen real estate, but offers you a starting point to add on your own features.

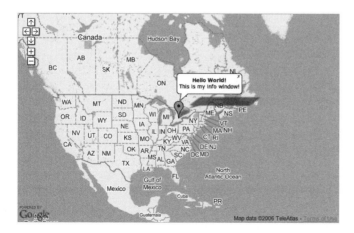

Figure 9-12. *A custom info window*

To begin, you'll need to open up your favorite graphics program and create the frame for the window. If you just need a box, then it's not much more difficult then the ToolTip object you created earlier. For this example, we used the Adobe Photoshop PSD file you'll find with the code accompanying this book, as illustrated in Figure 9-13. Once you have your info window working, feel free to modify it any way you want. You can edit the PSD file or create one of your own. For now, create a folder called littleWindow in your working directory and copy the accompanying presliced PNG files from the littleWindow folder in the Chapter 9 source code.

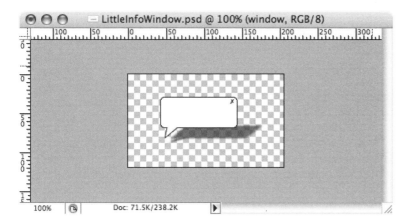

Figure 9-13. *The info window art file*

The finalized framework for the LittleInfoWindow overlay in Listing 9-5 is almost identical to the ToolTip overlay you created earlier in Listing 9-3, but the internals of each function are quite different.

Listing 9-5. *The LittleInfoWindow Object*

```
//create the LittleInfoWindow overlay onject
function LittleInfoWindow(marker,html,width) {
    this.html_ = html;
    this.width_ = ( width ? width + 'px' : 'auto');
    this.marker_ = marker;
}

//use the GOverlay class
LittleInfoWindow.prototype = new GOverlay();

//initialize the container and shadowContainer
LittleInfoWindow.prototype.initialize = function(map) {
    this.map_ = map;

    var container = document.createElement("div");
    container.style.display='none';
    map.getPane(G_MAP_FLOAT_PANE).appendChild(container);
    this.container_ = container;
```

```
    var shadowContainer = document.createElement("div");
    shadowContainer.style.display='none';
    map.getPane(G_MAP_FLOAT_SHADOW_PANE).appendChild(shadowContainer);
    this.shadowContainer_ = shadowContainer;
}

LittleInfoWindow.prototype.remove = function() {
    this.container_.parentNode.removeChild(this.container_);

    //don't forget to remove the shadow as well
    this.shadowContainer_.parentNode.removeChild(this.shadowContainer_);
}

LittleInfoWindow.prototype.copy = function() {
    return new LittleInfoWindow(this.marker_,this.html_,this.width_);
}

LittleInfoWindow.prototype.redraw = function(force) {
    if (!force) return;

    //get the content div
    var content = document.createElement("span");
    content.innerHTML = this.html_;
    content.style.font='10px verdana';
    content.style.margin='0';
    content.style.padding='0';
    content.style.border='0';
    content.style.display='inline';

    if(!this.width_ || this.width_=='auto' || this.width_ <= 0) {
        //the width is unknown so set a rough maximum and minimum
        content.style.minWidth = '10px';
        content.style.maxWidth = '500px';
        content.style.width = 'auto';
    } else {
        //the width was set when creating the window
        content.style.width= width + 'px';
    }

    //make it invisible for now
    content.style.visibility='hidden';

    //temporarily append the content to the map container
    this.map_.getContainer().appendChild(content);

    //retrieve the rendered width and height
    var contentWidth = content.offsetWidth;
    var contentHeight = content.offsetHeight;
```

```
//remove the content from the map
content.parentNode.removeChild(content);
content.style.visibility='visible';

//set the width and height to ensure they
//stay that size when drawn again
content.style.width=contentWidth+'px';
content.style.height=contentHeight+'px';

//set up the actual position relative to your images
content.style.position='absolute';
content.style.left='5px';
content.style.top='7px';
content.style.background='white';

//create the wrapper for the window
var wrapper = document.createElement("div");

//first append the content so the wrapper is above
wrapper.appendChild(content);

//create an object to reference each image
var wrapperParts = {
    tl:{l:0, t:0, w:5, h:7},
    t:{l:5, t:0, w:(contentWidth-6), h:7},
    tr:{l:(contentWidth-1), t:0, w:11, h:9},
    l:{l:0, t:7, w:5, h:contentHeight},
    r:{l:(contentWidth+5), t:9, w:5, h:(contentHeight-2)},
    bl:{l:0, t:(contentHeight+7), w:5, h:5},
    p:{l:5, t:(contentHeight+7), w:17, h:18},
    b:{l:22, t:(contentHeight+7), w:(contentWidth-17), h:5},
    br:{l:(contentWidth+5), t:(contentHeight+7), w:5, h:5}
}

//create the image DOM objects
for (i in wrapperParts) {
    var img = document.createElement('img');

    //load the image from your local image directory
    //based on the property name of the wrapperParts object
    img.src = 'littleWindow/' + i + '.png';

    //set the appropriate positioning attributes
    img.style.position='absolute';
    img.style.top=wrapperParts[i].t+'px';
    img.style.left=wrapperParts[i].l+'px';
    img.style.width=wrapperParts[i].w+'px';
```

```
        img.style.height=wrapperParts[i].h+'px';
        wrapper.appendChild(img);
        wrapperParts[i].img = img;
    }

    //add any event handlers like the close box
    var marker = this.marker_;
    GEvent.addDomListener(wrapperParts.tr.img, "click", function() {
            marker.closeLittleInfoWindow();
    });

    //get the X,Y pixel location of the marker
    var pixelLocation = this.map_.fromLatLngToDivPixel(
        this.marker_.getPoint()
    );

    //position the container div for the window
    this.container_.style.position='absolute';
    this.container_.style.left = (pixelLocation.x-3) + "px";
    this.container_.style.top = (pixelLocation.y
        - contentHeight
        - 25
        - this.marker_.getIcon().iconSize.height
    ) + "px";
    this.container_.style.border = '0';
    this.container_.style.margin = '0';
    this.container_.style.padding = '0';
    this.container_.style.display = 'block';

    //append the styled info window to the container
    this.container_.appendChild(wrapper);


    //add a shadow
    this.shadowContainer_.style.position='absolute';
    this.shadowContainer_.style.left = (pixelLocation.x+15) + "px";
    this.shadowContainer_.style.top = (pixelLocation.y
        - 10
        - this.marker_.getIcon().iconSize.height
    ) + "px";
    this.shadowContainer_.style.border = '1px solid black';
    this.shadowContainer_.style.margin = '0';
    this.shadowContainer_.style.padding = '0';
    this.shadowContainer_.style.display = 'block';

    var shadowParts = {
        sl:{l:0, t:0, w:35, h:26},
        s:{l:35, t:0, w:(contentWidth-40), h:26},
```

```
                sr:{l:(contentWidth-5), t:0, w:35, h:26}
        }

        for (i in shadowParts) {
            var img = document.createElement('img');
            img.src = 'littleWindow/' + i + '.png';
            img.style.position='absolute';
            img.style.top=shadowParts[i].t+'px';
            img.style.left=shadowParts[i].l+'px';
            img.style.width=shadowParts[i].w+'px';
            img.style.height=shadowParts[i].h+'px';
            this.shadowContainer_.appendChild(img);
        }

        //pan if necessary so it shows on the screen
        var mapNE = this.map_.fromLatLngToDivPixel(
            this.map_.getBounds().getNorthEast()
        );
        var panX=0;
        var panY=0;
        if(this.container_.offsetTop < mapNE.y) {
            //top of window is above the top edge of the map container
            panY = mapNE.y - this.container_.offsetTop;
        }
        if(this.container_.offsetLeft+contentWidth+10 > mapNE.x) {
            //right edge of window is outside the right edge of the map container
            panX = (this.container_.offsetLeft+contentWidth+10) - mapNE.x;
        }

        if(panX!=0 || panY!=0) {
            //pan the map
            this.map_.panBy(new GSize(-panX-10,panY+30));
        }
    }
}

//add a new method to GMarker so you
//can use a similar API to the existing info window.
GMarker.prototype.LittleInfoWindowInstance = null;
GMarker.prototype.openLittleInfoWindow = function(content,width) {
    if(this.LittleInfoWindowInstance == null) {
        this.LittleInfoWindowInstance = new LittleInfoWindow(
            this,
            content,
            width
        );
        map.addOverlay(this.LittleInfoWindowInstance);
    }
}
```

```
GMarker.prototype.closeLittleInfoWindow = function() {
    if(this.LittleInfoWindowInstance != null) {
        map.removeOverlay(this.LittleInfoWindowInstance);
        this.LittleInfoWindowInstance = null;
    }
}
```

The following sections describe how this code works.

Creating the Overlay Object and Containers

Similar to the Google info window, your info window will require three inputs: a marker on which to anchor the window, the HTML content to display, and an optional width. When you extend this example for use in your own web application, you'll probably add more input parameters or additional methods. You could also add the various methods and properties of the existing GInfoWindow class so that your class provides the same API as Google's info window, with tabs and an assortment of options. To keep things simple in the example, we stick to the essentials.

Like the ToolTip object you created earlier, the LittleInfoWindow object in Listing 9-5 starts off the same way. The LittleInfoWindow function provides a construction using the marker, html, and width arguments, while the GOverlay is instantiated as the prototype object. The first big difference comes in the initialize() method where you create two containers. The first container, for the info window, is attached to the G_MAP_FLOAT_PANE pane:

```
var container = document.createElement("div");
container.style.display='none';
map.getPane(G_MAP_FLOAT_PANE).appendChild(container);
this.container_ = container;
```

And the second container, for the info window's shadow, is attached to the G_MAP_FLOAT_SHADOW_PANE pane:

```
var shadowContainer = document.createElement("div");
shadowContainer.style.display='none';
map.getPane(G_MAP_FLOAT_SHADOW_PANE).appendChild(shadowContainer);
this.shadowContainer_ = shadowContainer;
```

■**Tip** A shadow isn't required for overlays, but it provides a nice finishing touch to the final map and makes your web application look much more polished and complete.

Next, the remove() and copy() methods are again identical in functionality to the ToolTip overlay, except the remove() method also removes the second shadowContainer along with the info window container.

Drawing a LittleInfoWindow

The most complicated part of creating an info window is properly positioning it on the screen with the redraw() method, and the problem occurs only when you want to position it *above* the existing marker or point.

When rendering HTML, the page is drawn on the screen top down and left to right. You can assign sizes and positions to html elements using CSS attributes, but in general, if there are no sizes or positions, things will start at the top and flow down. When you create the info window in the redraw() method, you'll take the HTML passed into the constructor, put it in a content div, and wrap it with the appropriate style. On an empty HTML page, you know the top-left corner of the content div is at (0,0), but where is the bottom-right corner? The bottom-right corner is dependent on the content of the div and the general style of the div itself.

The ambiguity in the size of the div is compounded when you want to position the div on the map. The Google Maps API requires you to position the overlay using *absolute* positioning. To properly position the info window, so the arrow is pointing at the marker, you need to know the height of the info window, but as we said, the height varies based on the content. Luckily for you, browsers have a little-known feature that allows you to access the rendered position and size of elements on a web page.

Determining the Size of the Container

When creating the redraw() function, the first thing you'll do is put the HTML into a content div and apply the appropriate base styles to the div:

```
var content = document.createElement("div");
content.innerHTML = this.html_;
content.style.font='10px verdana';
content.style.margin='0';
content.style.padding='0';
content.style.border='0';
content.style.display='inline';

if(!this.width_ || this.width_=='auto' || this.width_ <= 0) {
    //the width is unknown so set a rough maximum and minimum
    content.style.minWidth = '10px';
    content.style.maxWidth = '500px';
    content.style.width = 'auto';
} else {
    //the width was set when creating the window
    content.style.width= width + 'px';
}

//make it invisible for now.
content.style.visibility='hidden';
```

The display='inline' and the last style attribute, visibility='hidden', are important for the next step. To determine the div's rendered position and size properties, you need to access hidden properties of the div elements. When rendered on the page, browsers attach offset*XXX* properties. where the *XXX* is Left, Right, Width, or Height. These give you the position and size, in pixels, of the DOM element after it's rendered. For your info window, you're concerned with the offsetWidth and offsetHeight, as you'll need them to calculate the overall size of the window.

To access the offset variables, you'll first need to render the content div on the page. At this point in the overlay, the content DOM element exists only in the browser's memory and hasn't been "drawn" yet. To do so, append the content to the map container and retrieve the width and height before removing it again from the map container:

```
this.map_.getContainer().appendChild(content);
var contentWidth = content.offsetWidth;
var contentHeight = content.offsetHeight;
content.parentNode.removeChild(content);
content.style.visibility='visible';

//set the width and height to ensure they stay that size when drawn again.
content.style.width=contentWidth+'px';
content.style.height=contentHeight+'px'
```

The brief existence of the content div inside the map container allowed the browser to set the offset properties so you could retrieve the offsetWidth and offsetHeight. As we mentioned, the inline display and the hidden visibility are important to retrieving the correct size. When the display is inline, the bounding div collapses to the size of the actual content, rather than expanding to a width of 100%, giving you an accurate width. Setting the visibility to hidden prevents the content from possibly flashing on the screen for a moment, but at the same time, preserves the size and shape of the div.

Building the Wrapper

Now that you have the size of the content box, the rest is pretty straightforward. First, style the content accordingly and create another div, the wrapper, to contain the content and the additional images for the eye candy bubble wrapper from Figure 9-13.

```
content.style.position='absolute';
content.style.left='5px';
content.style.top='7px';
content.style.background='white';
var wrapper = document.createElement("div");
wrapper.appendChild(content);
```

To minimize the HTML required for the LittleInfoWindow, the images in the wrapper can be positioned using *absolute* positioning. The sample wrapper consists of nine separate images: four corners, four sides, and an additional protruding arm, as outlined in Figure 9-14 (along with the shadow and marker images). To give the new info window a similar feel to Google's info window, the upper-right corner has also been styled with an X in the graphic to act as the close box.

Figure 9-14. *Outlined images for the LittleInfoWindow wrapper*

To create the `wrapper` object in Listing 9-5, you could use the `innerHTML` property to add the images using regular HTML, but that wouldn't allow you to easily attach event listeners to the images. By creating each image as a DOM object:

```
var wrapperParts = {
    tl:{l:0, t:0, w:5, h:7},
    t:{l:5, t:0, w:(contentWidth-6), h:7},
    - cut -
}
```

```
//create the images
for (i in wrapperParts) {
    var img = document.createElement('img');
    - cut -
    wrapper.appendChild(img);
    wrapperParts[i].img = img;
}
```

and using the `wrapper.appendChild()` method, you can then attach event listeners directly to image DOM elements, as when you want to add a click event to the close box:

```
var marker = this.marker_;
GEvent.addDomListener(wrapperParts.tr.img, "click", function() {
    marker.closeLittleInfoWindow();
});
```

Now all that's left to do with the `LittleInfoWindow` container is position it on the map and append the `wrapper`. The design of the `LittleInfoWindow` has the arm protruding in the lower-left corner, so you'll want to position the top of the container so that the arm rests just above the marker. You can get the marker's position using the `GMap2.fromLatLngToDivPixel()` method you saw earlier in the chapter, and then use the calculated height of the `LittleInfoWindow` plus the height of the marker icon to determine the final resting position:

```
var pixelLocation = this.map_.fromLatLngToDivPixel(this.marker_.getPoint());
this.container_.style.position='absolute';
this.container_.style.left = (pixelLocation.x-3) + "px";
this.container_.style.top = ( pixelLocation.y
    - contentHeight
    - 25
    - this.marker_.getIcon().iconSize.height
) + "px";
this.container_.style.display = 'block';

this.container_.appendChild(wrapper);
```

Adding a Few Shades of Finesse

Your `LittleInfoWindow` should now be working, but a few tasks remain before we can call it complete. First, let's add a shadow to the window similar to the one on Google's info window. The shadow images are also supplied in the PSD files accompanying the book. The process for adding the shadow is similar to the wrapper you just created. We won't go through it again here, but you can take a look at the complete code in Listing 9-5 and see the example there. The shadow, in this case, expands only horizontally with the size of the wrapper, but you could easily add vertical expansion as well.

Listing 9-5 also includes some pan adjustments when your window initially opens. The nice thing about the Google's info window is when it opens off-screen, the map pans until the window is visible on-screen. You can easily add this same functionality by comparing the upper-right corner of your LittleInfoWindow with the top and right edges of the map container:

```
var mapNE = this.map_.fromLatLngToDivPixel(this.map_.getBounds().getNorthEast());
var panX=0;
var panY=0;
if(this.container_.offsetTop < mapNE.y) {
    panY = mapNE.y - this.container_.offsetTop;
}
if(this.container_.offsetLeft+contentWidth+10 > mapNE.x) {
    panX = (this.container_.offsetLeft+contentWidth+10) - mapNE.x;
}
if(panX!=0 || panY!=0) {this.map_.panBy(new GSize(-panX-10,panY+30)); }
```

Then, if necessary, you can pan the map, just as Google does, to show the open window. If you check out the online example at http://googlemapsbook.com/chapter9/CustomInfoWindow/, you can see the pan in action by moving the marker to the top or right edge and then clicking it to open the LittleInfoWindow.

Using the LittleInfoWindow

The last and final addition for your LittleInfoWindow should be the creation of the appropriate methods on the GMarker class, in the same way you created methods for the ToolTip earlier. Again, by adding open and close methods to the GMarker class:

```
GMarker.prototype.LittleInfoWindowInstance = null;
GMarker.prototype.openLittleInfoWindow = function(content,width) {
    if(this.LittleInfoWindowInstance == null) {
        this.LittleInfoWindowInstance = new LittleInfoWindow(this,content,width)
        map.addOverlay(this.LittleInfoWindowInstance);
    }
}
GMarker.prototype.closeLittleInfoWindow = function() {
    if(this.LittleInfoWindowInstance != null) {
        map.removeOverlay(this.LittleInfoWindowInstance);
        this.LittleInfoWindowInstance = null;
    }
}
```

you can access your custom info window with an API similar to the Google info window using something like this:

```
GEvent.addListener(marker,'click',function() {
    if(marker.LittleInfoWindowInstance) {
```

```
        marker.closeLittleInfoWindow();
    } else {
        marker.openLittleInfoWindow('<b>Hello World!</b>➥
<br/>This is my info window!');
    }
});
```

The difference from Google's info window is that the LittleInfoWindowInstance is attached to the GMarker, not the map, so you have the added advantage of opening more than one window at the same time. If you want to force only one window open at a time, you'll need to track the instance using the map object, rather than the marker.

Implementing Your Own Map Type, Tiles, and Projection

By default, three types of maps are built into the Google Maps API:

- *Map* (often referred to as *Normal*), which shows the earth using outlines and colored objects, similar to a printed map you might purchase for driving directions

- *Satellite*, which shows the map using satellite photos of the earth taken from space

- *Hybrid,* which is a mixture of the satellite images overlaid with information from the normal map type

Each map is an instance of the GMapType class, and each has its own constant G_NORMAL_MAP, G_SATELLITE_MAP, and G_HYBRID_MAP, respectively. To quickly refer to all three, there is also the G_DEFAULT_MAP_TYPES constant, which is an array of the previous three constants combined.

In the example in this section, you'll create your own map using a new projection and the NASA Visible Earth images (http://visibleearth.nasa.gov). But first, you need to understand how the map type, projection, and tiles work together.

GMapType: Gluing It Together

Understanding the GMapType is key to understanding how the different classes interact to create a single map. Each instance of the GMapType class defines the draggable map you see on the screen. The map type tells the API what the upper and lower zoom levels are, which GTileLayer objects to include in the map, and which GProjection to use for latitude and longitude calculations. A typical GMapType object would look similar to this:

```
var MyMapType = new GMapType(
    [MyTileLayer1, MyTileLayer2],
    MyProjection,
    'My Map Type',{
        shortName:'Mine',
        tileSize:256,
        maxResolution:5,
        minResolution:0
});
```

MyTileLayer1 and MyTileLayer2 would be instances of the GTileLayer class, and MyProjection would be an instance of the GProjection class. The third parameter for GMapType is the label to show on the map type button in the upper-right corner of the Google map. You'll also notice the fourth parameter is a JavaScript object implementing the properties of the GMapTypeOptions class, listed in Table 9-2. In this case, the short name is Mine, the tile size is 256×256 pixels, and the zoom levels are restricted to 0 through 5.

■**Caution** In your map type, all the tiles in each of the GTileLayer objects must be of equal size. You can't mix and match tile sizes within the same map type.

Table 9-2. *GMapTypeOptions Properties*

Property	Description
shortName	The short name is returned from GMapType.getName(true) and is used in the GOverviewMapControl. The default is the same as the name supplied in the GMapType arguments.
urlArg	Optional parameters for the URL of the map type; can be retrieved using GMapType.getUrlArg().
maxResolution	The maximum zoom level of this map type.
minResolution	The minimum zoom level of this map type.
tileSize	The tile size. The default is 256.
textColor	The text color returned by GMapType.getTextColor(). The default is black.
linkColor	Text link color returned by GMapType.getLinkColor(). The default is #7777cc.
errorMessage	An optional message returned by GMapType.getErrorMessage().

The GMapType object directs tasks to various other classes in the API. For instance, when you need to know where a longitude or latitude point falls on the map, the map type asks the GProjection where the point should go. When you drag the map around, the GTileLayer receives requests from the map type to get more images for the new map tiles.

In the case where you don't really need a brand-new map type, and just want to add a tile layer to an existing map (as with the custom tile method described in Chapter 7), you can simply reuse Google's existing projection and tiles, layering your own on top. Using Google's projection and tiles is easy. Creating your own GProjection and GTileLayer is where things get a bit tricky.

GProjection: Locating Where Things Are

The GProjection interface handles the math required to convert latitude and longitude into relative screen pixels and back again. It tells the map where GLatLng(-80,43) really is, and it tells your web application what latitude and longitude is at position GPoint(64,34). Besides that, it's also responsible for the biggest untruth in the map.

You may not realize it, but when you look at a map—any map—it's stretching the truth. A map printed on a piece of paper or displayed on a screen is a two-dimensional representation of a three-dimensional object. People have long understood the earth is round, but a round object can't be represented accurately in a flat image without losing or skewing some of the information.

To create the flat map, the round earth is *projected* onto the flat surface using some mathematical or statistical process, but as we said, projections do sometimes *stretch* the truth.

For example, take a look at Figure 9-15, where we've outlined the United States and Greenland. Greenland, on a round globe, covers about 836,000 square miles (2,166,000 square kilometers), and the United States covers about 3,539,000 square miles (9,166,000 square kilometers). That means Greenland is really about 20% the area of the United States, but on the Google map (and many other maps), it looks as though you could fit two of the United States inside Greenland! It also looks as though Alaska is about half the area of the United States. This is because the Google API uses the Mercator projection.

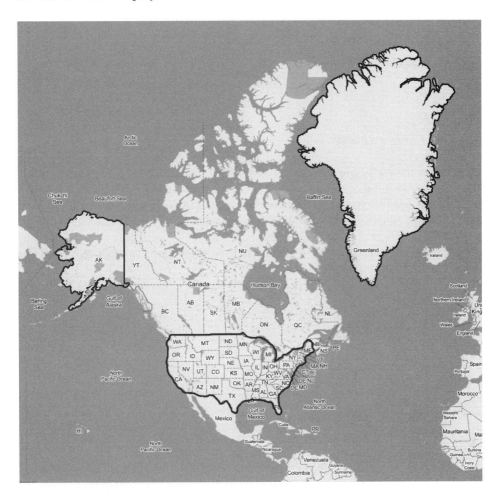

Figure 9-15. *Comparing the United States and Greenland on a Mercator projection*

Understanding Projection Types

Without going deep into mathematical theories and discussions, map projections can generally be divided into three categories—planar, conic, and cylindrical—but some projections, such as the Mollweide homolographic and the sinusoidal projection, are hybrids. Each category has dozens of different variations depending on the desired use and accuracy.

Planar: A planer map projection, often referred to as an Azimuthal projection, is created by placing a flat plane tangent to the globe at one point and projecting the surface onto the plane from a single point source within the globe, as represented in Figure 9-16. Imagine an image on a wall, created by placing a light inside a glass globe. The resulting circular image would be a planar map representing the round glass globe. The positions of the latitude and longitude lines will vary depending on the position of the plane relative to the globe, and planar projections also vary depending on where the common point is within the globe. These projections are often used for maps of the polar regions.

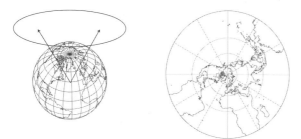

Figure 9-16. *Creating a planar projection*

Conic: Unlike the planer projection, the conic projection uses a cone, placed on the globe like an ice cream cone, tangent to some parallel, as shown in Figure 9-17. Then like the planar projection, the globe is projected into the cone using the center of the globe as the common point. The cone can then be cut along one of the meridians and placed flat. Latitude lines are represented by straight lines converging at the center; longitude lines are represented by arcs with the apex of the cone at their center. Conic projections vary depending on the position of the cone and the size of the cone.

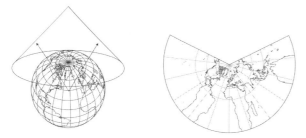

Figure 9-17. *Creating a conic projection*

Cylindrical: Cylindrical projections are similar to both the other two types of projections; however, the plane is wrapped around the globe like a cylinder, tangent to the equator, as illustrated in Figure 9-18. The globe is then projected on to the cylinder from a central point within the globe, or along a central line running from pole to pole. The resulting map has equidistant parallel longitude lines and parallel latitude lines that increase in distance as you move farther from the equator. The difficulty with cylindrical projections is that the poles of the earth can't be represented accurately.

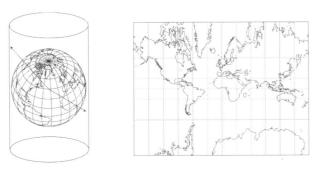

Figure 9-18. *Creating a cylindrical projection*

The Mercator projection used by the Google Maps API is a cylindrical projection; however, the latitude lines are mathematically adjusted using one of the following equations where Δ represents the longitude and Φ represents the latitude:

$$x = \lambda - \lambda_0$$

$$y = \ln\left[\tan\left(\frac{1}{4}\pi + \frac{1}{2}\phi \right) \right]$$

$$= \frac{1}{2}\ln\left(\frac{1 + \sin\phi}{1 - \sin\phi} \right)$$

$$= \sinh^{-1}(\tan\phi)$$

$$= \tanh^{-1}(\sin\phi)$$

$$= \ln(\tan\phi + \sec\phi)$$

The equations preserve more realistic shapes, as shown in Figure 9-19.

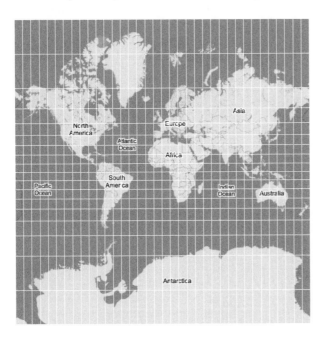

Figure 9-19. *Latitude and longitude lines of the Google Maps API's Mercator projection*

The downside with Mercator projections, as you saw in Figure 9-15, is that areas farther away from the equator are greatly exaggerated and the poles themselves can't be shown.

Using a Different Projection

By default, all of the maps in the API use the built-in GMercatorProjection class. The GMercatorProjection is an implementation of the GProjection interface using the Mercator projection. If your custom map image is using the Mercator projection, you don't have to worry about implementing your own GProjection interface, and you can just reference the GMercatorProjection class. If you would like to use a projection other than the Mercator projection, you need to create a new class for your projection and implement the methods listed in Table 9-3.

Table 9-3. *Methods Required to Implement a GProjection Class*

Method	Return Value	Description
fromLatLngToPixel (latlng,zoom)	GPoint	Given the latitude, longitude from the GLatLng object, and zoom level,returns the X and Y pixel coordinates of the location relative to the bounding div of the map.
fromPixelToLatLng (pixel,zoom,unbounded)	GLatLng	Reverse of fromLatLngToPixel. Given the pixel coordinates and zoom, returns the geographical latitude and longitude on the location. If the unbounded flag is true, the geographical longitude should *not* wrap when beyond -180 or 180 degrees.
tileCheckRange (tile,zoom,tilesize)	Boolean	Returns true if the tile index is within a valid range for the known map type. If false is returned, the map will display an empty tile. In the case where you want the map to wrap horizontally, you may need to modify the tile index to point to the index of an existing tile.
getWrapWidth(zoom)	Integer	Given the zoom level, returns the pixel width of the entire map at the given zoom. The API uses this value to indicate when the map should repeat itself. By default, getWrapWidth() returns Infinity, and the map does not wrap.

Listing 9-6 shows a generic implementation of an equidistant cylindrical projection, which you'll use in the "The Blue Marble Map: Putting it All Together" section later in the chapter to create a map using the NASA Visible Earth images as tiles. The equidistant cylindrical projection is created by plotting the latitude and longitude values from the globe in a 1:1 ratio on a plane, as shown in Figure 9-20. This creates a map whose width, unlike Google's Mercator projection, is always twice its height while latitude and longitude lines are all at equal distances. If you compare your final map with the Google map, your equidistant cylindrical map will actually be half the height and thus half the number of overall tiles per zoom level.

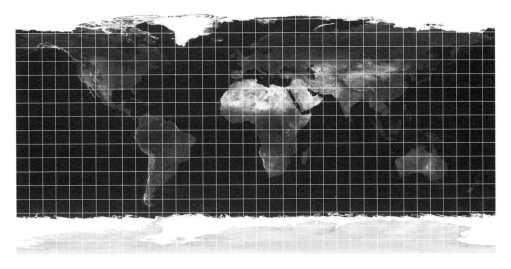

Figure 9-20. *Equidistant cylindrical projection*

You'll also notice the projection in Listing 9-6 has an additional property, EquidistantCylindricalProjection.mapResolutions, to hold the overall width of the map at each zoom level.

Caution Your implementation of the GProjection interface is dependent on the resolution of the map image you plan to use. If you want to reuse the GMercatorProjection, your map images must match the sizes discussed in the next section.

Listing 9-6. *Equidistant Cylindrical GProjection*

```
EquidistantCylindricalProjection = new GProjection();

EquidistantCylindricalProjection.mapResolutions = [256,512,1024]

EquidistantCylindricalProjection.fromLatLngToPixel = function(latlng,zoom) {
    var lng = parseInt(Math.floor((this.mapResolutions[zoom] / 360) *➥
(latlng.lng() + 180)));
    var lat = parseInt(Math.floor(Math.abs((this.mapResolutions[zoom] / 2 / 180) *➥
(latlng.lat()-90))));
    var point = new GPoint(lng,lat);
    return point;
}

EquidistantCylindricalProjection.fromPixelToLatLng =➥
function(pixel,zoom,unbounded) {
    var lat = 90-(pixel.y / (this.mapResolutions[zoom] / 2 / 180));
    var lng = (pixel.x / (this.mapResolutions[zoom] / 360)) - 180;
```

```
    var latlng = new GLatLng(lat,lng);
    return latlng;

}


EquidistantCylindricalProjection.tileCheckRange = function(tile,zoom,tileSize){
    var rez = this.mapResolutions[zoom];
    //check if it is outside the latitude range
    //the height for the Blue Marble maps are always 1/2 the width
    if(tile.y < 0 || tile.y * tileSize >= rez / 2){ return false; }

    //check if it is outside the longitude range and if so, wrap the map
    //by adjusting tile x
    if(tile.x < 0 || tile.x * tileSize >= rez){
        var e = Math.floor( rez / tileSize );
        tile.x = tile.x % e;
        if(tile.x < 0){ tile.x += e; }
    }
    return true;
}


EquidistantCylindricalProjection.getWrapWidth = function(zoom){
    return this.mapResolutions[zoom];
}
```

GTileLayer: Viewing Images

By now, you've probably already figured out that the map image, regardless of the type, is actually composed of smaller, square images referred to as *tiles*. In the Google Maps API, each of these tiles is 256×256 pixels, and at the lowest zoom level (0), the entire earth is represented in one 256×256 tile, as shown in Figure 9-21. Some maps, such as the Hybrid map in the API, use more than one layer of tiles at a time. In Chapter 7, you saw how you could use a tile layer to map large data sets, and in that instance, you added a tile layer to an existing Google map.

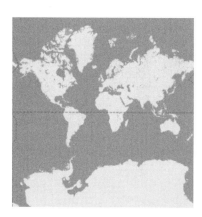

Figure 9-21. *The entire earth at zoom level 0 using one 256×256 tile*

Understanding Tiles

When creating your map with custom tiles, it's important to consider resources and the storage requirements required for the tiles. The number of tiles on a map is directly related to the zoom level of the map by:

```
Number of tiles = (2 ^ zoom) ^ 2
```

This means at zoom level 0, there is one tile, and at zoom level 17, there are 17,179,869,184 billion tiles, not to mention the accumulated total for all the zoom levels combined! Table 9-4 shows the breakdown of number of tiles, map size, and rough storage requirements for each of the zoom levels 0 through 17.

Table 9-4. *Tile Size and Storage Requirements for Each Zoom Level of the Google Mercator Projection*

Zoom	Tile Dimensions	Pixel Dimensions	Number of Tiles	Disk Space Required*
0	1×1	256×256	1	10.209KB
1	2×2	512×512	4	40.839KB
2	4×4	1024×1024	16	163.359KB
3	8×8	2048×2048	64	653.437KB
4	16×16	4096×4096	256	2.552MB
5	32×32	8192×8192	1024	10.209MB
6	64×64	16384×16384	4096	40.839MB
7	128×128	32768×32768	16384	163.359MB
8	256×256	65536×65536	65536	653.437MB
9	512×512	131072×131072	262144	2.552GB
10	1024×1024	262144×262144	1048576	10.209GB
11	2048×2048	524288×524288	4194304	40.839GB
12	4096×4096	1048576×1048576	16777216	163.359GB
13	8192×8192	2097152×2097152	67108864	653.437GB
14	16384×16384	4194304×4194304	268435456	2.552TB
15	32768×32768	8388608×8388608	1073741824	10.209TB
16	65536×65536	16777216×16777216	4294967296	40.839TB
17	131072×131072	33554432×33554432	17179869184	163.359TB
Total			22906492245	217.812TB

Based on an average file size of 10,455 bytes per tile.

Looking at Table 9-4, you quickly realize that it may not be feasible to create a large map at very high resolutions unless you have a fairly large storage facility and a lot of bandwidth to spare. Also, remember that Table 9-4 represents *one* map type and *one* tile layer. If you have a smaller map with multiple tile layers or various map images, you may also run into storage problems.

Creating Your GTileLayer

To create a tile layer for your map, you can follow the same process outlined in Chapter 7 and create a new GTileLayer object with the methods listed in Table 9-5.

Table 9-5. *Methods Required for a GTileLayer*

Method	Return Value	Description
getTileUrl (tile,zoom)	String	Returns the URL for the tile image. The URL can point to any domain, as the source of an image file is not bound by the "Same Origin" security policy.
isPng()	Boolean	Returns true if the tiles are in PNG format and could be transparent. You can still use transparent GIFs if this returns false, but if you use transparent PNGs this should be true so the API knows to fix cross-browser issues with transparent or translucent PNG files.
getOpacity()	Float	Returns the opacity to apply to the tiles: 1 is opaque and 0 is transparent. Remember that when dealing with translucent layers, performance may be degraded.

■**Caution** Two additional methods for the GTileLayer class are minResolution() and maxResolution(). These return the minimum and maximum zoom levels for the tile layer. At the time of publishing, if you try to override them, the map behaves erratically. So, you should leave them out of your custom tile layer and use the second and third arguments for the GTileLayer class to assign the maximum and minimum zoom levels.

The URL in the getTileUrl() method can point to a server-side script that generates tiles on the fly, as in the method described in Chapter 7, or you may want to preslice your image and save each tile with an appropriate name. Regardless of which method you choose, a GTileLayer simply requests the tile at the appropriate index and doesn't care how you create the image.

■**Note** In the next section of this chapter, when you build a map using the NASA Visible Earth images, you'll be preslicing the map images from the command line using ImageMagick.

As shown in Listing 9-7, there is very little code required for a tile layer. You simply define the URL for each tile and pass in the appropriate zoom level restrictions. If you want, when adding multiple layers of tiles, you can adjust the opacity of each layer as well by using the getOpacity() method.

Listing 9-7. *Creating a GTileLayer*

```
var myTiles = new GTileLayer(new GCopyrightCollection(),0,10);

myTiles.getTileUrl = function(tile,zoom){
    return 'http://example.com/tiles/' + zoom + '.' + tile.x + '.'➥
```

```
    + tile.y + '.png';
};

myTiles.isPng = function() { return true; }
myTiles.getOpacity = function() { return 1.0; }
```

The Blue Marble Map: Putting It All Together

Now that you have an idea of all the interrelating parts of the map type, projection, and tiles, you can put it all together to create your own map.

    If you don't have any readily available satellites photos lying around, you'll probably need to turn to other sources for map imagery. Luckily, NASA can provide you with just what you're looking for. The Visible Earth project at `http://visibleearth.nasa.gov`, shown in Figure 9-22, has a variety of public domain images you can download and use in your projects. Some, like the monthly Blue Marble: Next Generation images at `http://earthobservatory.nasa.gov/Newsroom/ BlueMarble/BlueMarble_monthlies.html`, are provided at a resolution of 500 meters per pixel, enough to make a Google map to zoom level 9. The images are provided free of charge. According to the Terms of Use at `http://visibleearth.nasa.gov/useterms.php`, the only thing you need to do in return is provide credits for the imagery to NASA and Visible Earth team, with a link back to `http://visibleearth.nasa.gov/`.

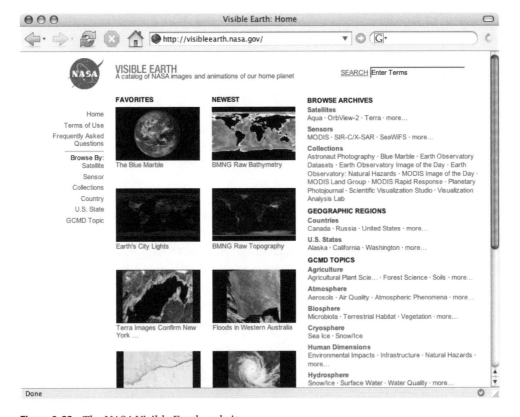

Figure 9-22. *The NASA Visible Earth website*

Conveniently, the Blue Marble monthly images and various others are created using the equidistant cylindrical projection you saw earlier (in Listing 9-6). There are other projections and image types, such as one "side" of the earth as a circle, but for this example, you'll be working with the equidistant cylindrical images. If you would like to see working examples of other projections, check out the website for this book at `http://googlemapsbook.com`.

The Images

For the final map, you'll need to create tiles for three maps, each with about five zoom levels. You'll be using these three images:

- Earth's City Lights (`http://veimages.gsfc.nasa.gov/1438/land_ocean_ice_lights_2048.tif`)

- The Blue Marble: Land Surface, Ocean Color, and Sea Ice (`http://veimages.gsfc.nasa.gov/2430/land_ocean_ice_8192.tif`)

- The Blue Marble: Land Surface, Ocean Color, and Sea Ice and Clouds (`http://veimages.gsfc.nasa.gov/2431/land_ocean_ice_cloud_8192.tif`)

The first image, Earth's City Lights, is only 2048×1024 pixels. The other images are 8192×4096 pixels. By referencing Table 9-4 earlier in the chapter, you can see the two images at 8192 pixels fit nicely into zoom level 5, whereas the City Lights image at 2048 pixels will only go to a maximum of zoom level 3. You could probably increase the dimension by one zoom level using an image-editing program, but these three images will suffice for the example.

The Blue Marble Cylindrical Projection

As we mentioned, the three Blue Marble images you're using for the example have been created using the equidistant cylindrical projection you saw earlier in Listing 9-6. The only modifications you need to make are to add the appropriate map resolutions to account for zoom levels 0 through 5, and rename the projection to `BlueMarbleProjection` so you can easily distinguish it from other projections you might make. Listing 9-8 shows the projection for this example.

Tip If you decide to integrate these, or other images, into your own maps, you could create a generic projection with a `setZoomResolution()` method that could add the various map resolutions appropriate for the given application. That way, you could easily reuse your projection without restricting it to specific zoom levels or map resolutions.

Listing 9-8. *BlueMarbleProjection for Your Custom Map Images*

```
BlueMarbleProjection = new GProjection();

BlueMarbleProjection.mapResolutions = [256,512,1024,2048,4096,8192]

BlueMarbleProjection.fromLatLngToPixel = function(latlng,zoom) {
    var lng = parseInt(Math.floor((this.mapResolutions[zoom] / 360) *➥
```

```
(latlng.lng() + 180)));
    var lat = parseInt(Math.floor(Math.abs((this.mapResolutions[zoom] / 2 / 180) *➥
(latlng.lat() - 90))));
    var point = new GPoint(lng,lat);
    return point;
}

BlueMarbleProjection.fromPixelToLatLng = function(pixel,zoom,unbounded) {
    var lat = 90 - (pixel.y / (this.mapResolutions[zoom] / 2 / 180));
    var lng = (pixel.x / (this.mapResolutions[zoom] / 360)) - 180;
    var latlng = new GLatLng(lat,lng);
    return latlng;
}

BlueMarbleProjection.tileCheckRange = function(tile,zoom,tileSize){
    var rez = this.mapResolutions[zoom];
    if(tile.y < 0 || tile.y * tileSize >= rez / 2){ return false; }
    if(tile.x < 0 || tile.x * tileSize >= rez){
        var e = Math.floor( rez / tileSize );
        tile.x = tile.x % e;
        if(tile.x < 0){ tile.x += e; }
    }
    return true;
}

BlueMarbleProjection.getWrapWidth = function(zoom){
    return this.mapResolutions[zoom];
}
```

The Blue Marble Tiles

The Google Maps API assumes a tile size of 256×256 pixels. Although you can change the tile size by using the GMapType tileSize option, the Blue Marble images divide nicely by 256, so there's no reason to change the default size for this example. Keeping the same tile size will also allow you to continue reusing most of the other examples in the book, without the need to modify code to accommodate a different tile size.

Slicing and Dicing

To serve up the tiled images for the three maps, you have a few options, including dynamically creating each tile on the fly, preslicing the images and storing them all appropriately on the server, or a combination. Taking into consideration the storage requirements discussed earlier, and the processing power you'll need to continually slice the images on the fly, you'll probably opt to spend a little money on a hard drive, if necessary, and preslice your images. The three maps, sliced for each zoom level, will occupy only about 40MB of disk space, whereas slicing the images at each request will create a huge drain on resources and slow down the server.

To slice your images, you could use Adobe Photoshop's scripting capabilities and follow the instructions at `http://www.mapki.com/index.php?title=Automatic_Tile_Cutter`, or you could install some open source image-editing utilities, such as the ImageMagick `convert` utility.

Tip To install ImageMagick, visit `http://www.imagemagick.org/script/index.php`. You'll find installation instructions and binaries for both Unix and Windows systems. If you've never used ImageMagick before, we highly recommend you browse the manual to see all the great tools it offers. Also, check out the book *The Definitive Guide to ImageMagick*, by Michael Still (`https://www.apress.com/book/bookDisplay.html?bID=10052`). If you're looking for some quick examples, check out `http://www.cit.gu.edu.au/~anthony/graphics/imagick6/`, where you'll find illustrated examples of how to use each of ImageMagick's commands. If you deal with dynamically generating images on a daily basis, you'll find ImageMagick an essential tool to add to your collection.

To tile your images with ImageMagick, first, if you haven't already done so, download the three images into a `tiles` directory, and then create subdirectories for each image's tiles. Your directory structure should look like this:

```
tiles/
    land_ocean_ice
    land_ocean_ice_8192.tif
    land_ocean_ice_cloud
    land_ocean_ice_cloud_8192.tif
    land_ocean_ice_lights
    land_ocean_ice_lights_2048.tif
```

Then it's as simple as running the following command to create each of the tiles for each of the images at each zoom level:

```
convert filename.tif -resize widthxheight -crop 256x256➥
directory/tile.zoomlevel.%d.png
```

For the resize width and height, refer back to Table 9-4.

For example, to create the tiles for the `land_ocean_ice_lights` image, you would execute the following four commands:

```
convert land_ocean_ice_lights_2048.tif -crop 256x256➥
land_ocean_ice_lights/tile.3.%d.png
convert land_ocean_ice_lights_2048.tif -resize 1024x512 -crop 256x256➥
land_ocean_ice_lights/tile.2.%d.png
convert land_ocean_ice_lights_2048.tif -resize 512x256 -crop 256x256➥
land_ocean_ice_lights/tile.1.%d.png
convert land_ocean_ice_lights_2048.tif -resize 256x256➥
land_ocean_ice_lights/tile.0.%d.png
```

Executing these four commands will create the tiles for each zoom level between 0 and 3. One tile for zoom level 0 will be created and named `tile.0.0.png`, while 32 tiles for zoom level 3 will be created and named `tile.3.0.png` through `tile.3.31.png`. The tiles you create with ImageMagick will be numbered 0 through *X*, starting with the top-left corner and reading left to right, as illustrated in Figure 9-23. It's important that you remember this pattern when you create the `getUrl` method for the `GTileLayer`.

Figure 9-23. *Tile placement produced by ImageMagick*

For the other two images, `land_ocean_ice_8192.tif` and `land_ocean_ice_cloud_8192.tif`, you can follow the same process but start a zoom level 5 and to go to 0.

■**Caution** If you are using an image that's excessively large, you may run into memory problems while running ImageMagick to create your tiles. ImageMagick tries to get as much main memory as possible when converting images so the conversion can run as fast as possible. To limit memory consumption, and leave some for other processes, you can add `-limit memory 32 -limit map 32` to the command. This will force ImageMagick to use the disk cache, rather than hog memory, but the processing time may be much slower.

Creating the GTileLayer Objects

For your Blue Marble map, you need to create three different `GTileLayer` objects, similar to the earlier generic object from Listing 9-7. For the Blue Marble tile layers, you'll need to change the generic `getUrl` method to account for the numbering scheme you used when you created the tiles, and you'll need to modify the URL to point to the actual location of your tiles for each of the three images:

```
myTiles.getTileUrl = function(tile,zoom){
    return 'http://example.com/tiles/' + zoom + '.' + tile.x + '.'➥
+ tile.y + '.png';
};
```

Each request to getTileUrl contains two arguments: the tile and the zoom. As shown in Figure 9-23, your images are numbered starting with 0 in the upper-left corner and, at zoom level 3, 31 in the lower-right corner. The corresponding tile argument for these two requests would have tile.x=0 and tile.y=0 for your tile number 0 and tile.x=8 and tile.y=4 for your tile number 31, as shown in Figure 9-24.

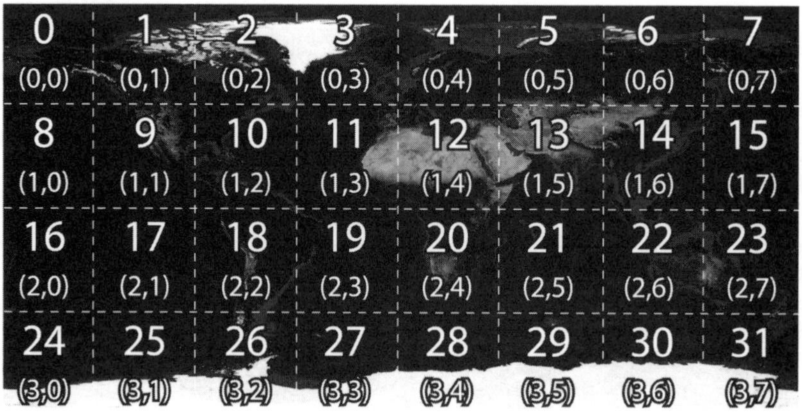

Figure 9-24. *Your tile numbering vs. Google's tile requests*

To convert the tile x and y values into your corresponding number scheme, you need to apply the simple formula:

```
x + y(2^zoom) = z
```

So, the URL you return from getTileUrl should resemble this:

```
return 'tiles/image/tile.' + zoom + '.' + (tile.x + tile.y*Math.pow(2,zoom))➡
+ '.png';
```

where *image* is replaced by the name of each of the directories you created when making your tiles.

Along with your tiles, you may want to create one extra tile that shows when the map is at a zoom level that's too close for your tiles. For example, your three images don't all have the same resolution, so if you're looking at one map at zoom level 5 and then switch map types to the land_ocean_ice_lights image, it only goes up to zoom level 3, and the map will have nothing to display. Depending on your application, you could just display an image with a message indicating to the user "There are no tiles at this zoom level; zoom out for a broader look," or you could be a little more creative, like the creators of the moon map at http://moon.google.com. That map displays tiles of cheese when you zoom in too close, as shown in Figure 9-25.

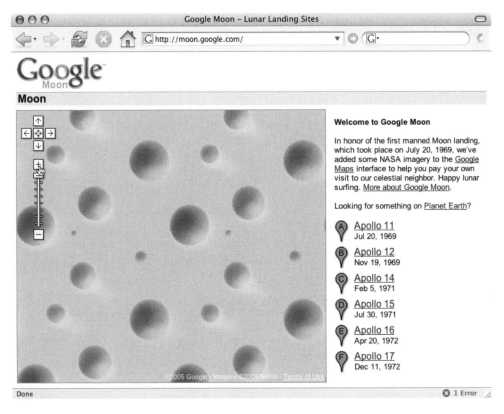

Figure 9-25. *Cheese on the moon when zoomed in too close at http://moon.google.com*

To incorporate the "too close" image, simply check the zoom level before requesting the tiles for the land_ocean_ice_lights image and request the appropriate alternate tile:

```
if(zoom > 3) return 'tiles/no_tiles_at_zoom_level.png';
else return 'tiles/land_ocean_ice_lights/tile.' + zoom + '.' +
    (tile.x + tile.y *Math.pow(2,zoom)) + '.png';
```

Don't Forget the Copyright Credits

Remember that to use the images from Visible Earth site, you must abide by the Terms of Use and give credit for the imagery to NASA and the Visible Earth team. To do so, you can easily add the appropriate copyright information to the tile layer using the GCopyright and GCopyrightCollection classes. If you use other images from different sources, you can add different or multiple copyrights to each tile layer. To do so, simply create a new GCopyrightCollection with an appropriate optional prefix:

```
copyrights = new GCopyrightCollection('Map Imagery:');
```

Then create a new GCopyright object, as per the arguments in Table 9-6, for the NASA Visible Earth team and add it to the copyright collection:

```
var visibleEarth = new GCopyright(
    'nasabluemarble',
    new GLatLngBounds(new GLatLng(-90,-180),new GLatLng(90,180)),
    0,
    '<a href="http://visibleearth.nasa.gov/">NASA Visible Earth</a>'
    copyrights.addCopyright(visibleEarth);
);
```

Table 9-6. *GCopyright Input Arguments*

Argument	Type	Description
id	Number	A unique identifier for this copyright information
minZoom	Number	The lowest zoom level at which the copyright information applies
bounds	GLatLngBounds	The boundary of the map to which the copyright applies
text	String	The copyright message

Then when creating your GTileLayer objects for each image, pass copyrights into the tile layer as the first parameter to the GTileLayer class:

```
var BlueMarbleCloudyTiles = new GTileLayer(copyrights,0,5);
```

When your map loads, you should be able to see the credit in the copyright information in the lower-right corner of the map, as shown in Figure 9-26.

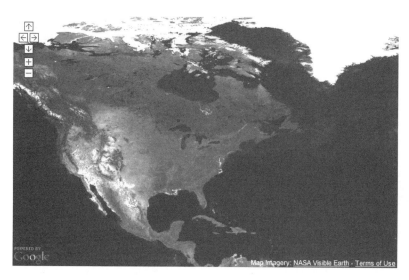

Figure 9-26. *Copyright information on the map (image courtesy of NASA Visible Earth)*

Listing 9-9 includes the copyright credits plus the three completed tiles layers, one for each image. The tile layers are named BlueMarbleTiles, BlueMarbleNightTiles, and BlueMarbleCloudyTiles, each representing one of the land_ocean_ice, land_ocean_ice_lights, and land_ocean_ice_cloud images, respectively. Also, when creating the tile layers, be sure to indicate the expected zoom levels using the second and third parameters to the GTileLayer class, so the API knows what zoom levels to expect.

Listing 9-9. *Blue Marble Copyright Credits and Tile Layers*

```
copyrights = new GCopyrightCollection('Map Imagery:');
var visibleEarth = new GCopyright(
    'nasabluemarble',
    new GLatLngBounds(new GLatLng(-90,-180),new GLatLng(90,180)),
    0,
    '<a href="http://visibleearth.nasa.gov/">NASA Visible Earth</a>'
);
copyrights.addCopyright(visibleEarth);

//tile layer for land_ocean_ice
var BlueMarbleTiles = new GTileLayer(copyrights,0,5);
BlueMarbleTiles.getTileUrl = function(tile,zoom){
    if(zoom > 5) return 'tiles/no_tiles_at_zoom_level.png';
    else return 'tiles/land_ocean_ice/tile.' + zoom + '.' +
        (tile.x + tile.y * Math.pow(2,zoom)) + '.png';
};
BlueMarbleTiles.isPng = function() { return true; }
BlueMarbleTiles.getOpacity = function() { return 1.0; }

//tile layer for land_ocean_ice_lights
var BlueMarbleNightTiles = new GTileLayer(copyrights,0,3);
BlueMarbleNightTiles.getTileUrl = function(tile,zoom){
    if(zoom > 3) return 'tiles/no_tiles_at_zoom_level.png';
    else return 'tiles/land_ocean_ice_lights/tile.' + zoom + '.' +
        (tile.x + tile.y * Math.pow(2,zoom)) + '.png';
};
BlueMarbleNightTiles.isPng = function() { return true; }
BlueMarbleNightTiles.getOpacity = function() { return 1.0; }

//tile layer for land_ocean_ice_cloud
var BlueMarbleCloudyTiles = new GTileLayer(copyrights,0,5);
BlueMarbleCloudyTiles.getTileUrl = function(tile,zoom){
    if(zoom > 5) return 'tiles/no_tiles_at_zoom_level.png';
    else return 'tiles/land_ocean_ice_cloud/tile.' + zoom + '.' +
        (tile.x + tile.y * Math.pow(2,zoom)) + '.png';
};
BlueMarbleCloudyTiles.isPng = function() { return true; }
BlueMarbleCloudyTiles.getOpacity = function() { return 1.0; }
```

The Blue Marble GMapType

Your last step is to assemble the BlueMarbleProjection and the three tile layers into their own map types. This is relatively straightforward, and you can follow the exact same process you used earlier in the chapter. Listing 9-10 contains the three map types named BlueMarble for the normal map, BlueMarbleNight for the city lights map, and BlueMarbleCloudy for the cloudy map.

Listing 9-10. *Blue Marble Map Types*

```
var BlueMarble = new GMapType(
    [BlueMarbleTiles],
    BlueMarbleProjection,
    'Blue Marble',
    {
        shortName:'BM',
        tileSize:256,
        maxResolution:5,
        minResolution:0
    }
);

var BlueMarbleNight = new GMapType(
    [BlueMarbleNightTiles],
    BlueMarbleProjection,
    'Blue Marble Night',
    {
        shortName:'BMN',
        tileSize:256,
        maxResolution:3,
        minResolution:0
    }
);

var BlueMarbleCloudy = new GMapType(
    [BlueMarbleCloudyTiles],
    BlueMarbleProjection,
    'Blue Marble Cloudy',
    {
        shortName:'BMC',
        tileSize:256,
        maxResolution:5,
        minResolution:0
    }
);
```

Using the New Blue Marble Maps

To use the new Blue Marble maps, you need to add them to your GMap2 object using the addMapType() method:

```
map = new GMap2(document.getElementById("map"));
map.addMapType(BlueMarble);
map.addMapType(BlueMarbleNight);
map.addMapType(BlueMarbleCloudy);
```

After you add the new map type to the GMap2 object, you'll see the new map type along with Google's map types, as shown in Figure 9-27.

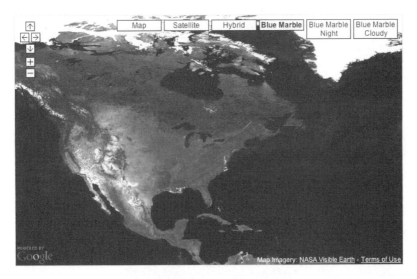

Figure 9-27. *The new map types on the map (image courtesy of NASA Visible Earth)*

If you want to show *only* the Blue Marble map types, just specify which map types to use when instantiating the GMap2 object:

```
 map = new GMap2(
    document.getElementById("map"),{
        mapTypes:[BlueMarble,BlueMarbleNight,BlueMarbleCloudy]
});
```

Now flipping back and forth between map types, you'll see the three different maps using the tiles you created. If you plot a point on the map, it will still appear in the correct location due to your new BlueMarbleProjection, as shown in Figure 9-28.

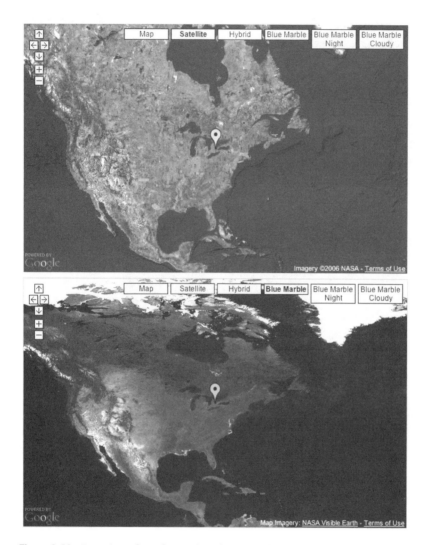

Figure 9-28. *Location plotted on a Google map (above) vs. the NASA Blue Marble map (below). Notice the difference in the map images.*

Summary

In this chapter, you've been introduced to some of the newer and more advanced features of the Google Maps API. Extending these examples further, you can create a wide variety of maps and controls that could do just about anything you wanted. For example, you could add a zoom control that works by clicking and dragging on an area, or create fancy info windows incorporating QuickTime streams, Flash, or any other plug-ins. What you put into your own overlay objects is really up to you.

Using custom tiles, you could easily create your own map using an antique hand-drawn map from the early days of exploration, or you could use the API as a high-resolution image viewer by replacing the map tiles with tiles from your high-resolution images. You could even let people comment on parts of the image using the same techniques you saw in Chapter 3.

Whatever interesting things you decide to create, it's important to keep up-to-date with the API by checking the online reference at `http://www.google.com/apis/maps/documentation/reference.html`. Google is always updating, improving, and adding new features to the Google Maps API, so be sure to check back often. We also suggest that you join the Google Maps group at `http://groups.google.com/group/Google-Maps-API` and contribute any ideas you have to the Google Maps development team. Contributing back to the community will help it prosper, and keeping up with the current topics and discussion will make you aware of all the latest additions. The group discussions also provide examples and neat ideas you might be able to use in your projects.

In the next chapter, you'll play with some other features of the API, such as polylines, finding lengths, and calculating areas on the map.

■ ■ ■

CHAPTER 10

Lines, Lengths, and Areas

All of the projects we've presented have dealt with map markers as either individual entities or as related clusters. In this chapter, we'll demonstrate some of the other ways that groups of points may be interpreted and presented.

A group of points is just that: a group of points. But a string of points in sequence may represent a line or path, which has the calculable property of *length*. Once the points form a closed loop, they may be treated as the outline of a region having *area*. Using the appropriate formulas, you can compute these distance and area values for your map projects.

The Google Maps 2.0 API includes some of this functionality, but remember that you may need to perform these kinds of calculations in your server-side scripts as well! With these mathematical tricks, as with any tools, it's good to at least have a vague understanding of their underlying principles, so you have the confidence to apply them correctly and trust their output.

In this chapter, you'll learn how to do the following:

- Compute the area and perimeter of an arbitrary region.

- Calculate angles on the earth's surface.

- Plot polygons in response to mouse clicks and allow draggable markers.

Starting Flat

When you measure quantities such as length and area on a planet's surface, what you're really measuring are properties of three-dimensional figures. A region of any significant size plotted on the surface of the earth is not flat—it contains a bulge corresponding to the earth's curvature. This bulge *increases* the amount of area over what you might measure if you plotted a region of similar perimeter on a flat (planar) surface.

An important thing to realize, though, is that you can't just generalize that *plotting it on a sphere makes it bigger*, because the results actually depend on which method you use to translate the flat object to its spherical representation.

As an example, picture a gigantic circle drawn on the earth, big enough to encompass all of Australia. This circle has two key dimensions: radius and circumference. If you plotted a flat circle with the same *circumference*, you would find that its area was smaller than the one around Australia, since it doesn't have the bonus area from the earth's bulge. But if you plotted a circle using the same *radius*, you would find quite the opposite: the flat one has a larger surface area. Why? Because forming the bulged circle is like taking a flat doily and rolling it into a cone.

Even though the "surface" radius is the same, the cone has less surface area (since some of the doily folds over on itself).

Before we discuss how to compute these distance and area values, let's quickly review the classical Euclidean stuff that applies to flat shapes on a plane.

Lengths and Angles

A cornerstone of high-school geometry is the Pythagorean theorem. In a flat system, it allows us to quickly and accurately calculate the length of the diagonal on a right-angle triangle. In practical terms, this means that given any straight line drawn on a Cartesian (X and Y) coordinate system, we can independently measure the X and Y displacements from the start to the end of the line, and then use the theorem to get the length of the line itself. You can see in Figure 10-1 how this is applied.

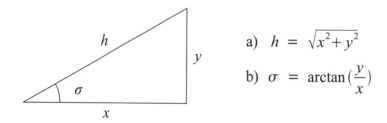

$$a) \quad h = \sqrt{x^2 + y^2}$$

$$b) \quad \sigma = \arctan\left(\frac{y}{x}\right)$$

Figure 10-1. *The Pythagorean theorem for length (a), arctangent for angle (b)*

Finding the length of a line is only half the story, though. To be able to fully describe a line, we need its length *and* its angle. And again, high-school math has us covered. The arctangent (also atan or inverse-tangent) function takes the ratio of the Y and X displacements (the slope), and gives back an angle from horizontal (also shown in Figure 10-1).

Most programming languages, however, go a step beyond providing just basic arctangent and also provide an additional function, typically called `atan2()`. With `atan2()`, you pass in the Y and X displacements separately, and it will correctly compute the angle, in the range $-\pi$ to π. Plus, it will properly handle the vertical case. (Remember that a vertical line has undefined slope because its horizontal displacement is zero; anything divided by zero is undefined.)

In JavaScript, this function takes the form of `Math.atan2()`.

RADIAN REFRESHER

You may be confused by some of the values that you get back from functions like `Math.atan2()`. Keep in mind that JavaScript, like most programming languages, does all of its trigonometric operations using *radians*. Switching between radians and degrees is a straightforward operation. But radians are the favored unit for working with circles and other curves.

A radian is defined as one *radius length* around a circle's perimeter. Since the radius and circumference of a circle are directly proportional to each other, an angle measured in radians doesn't vary with the size of the circle.

Given a circle with radius r, we know from basic principles that its circumference is π times its diameter. So the circumference of that circle is 2πr. If we want to know what percentage of the perimeter a single radian represents, we can just divide one radian's distance (r) by the total distance (2πr). And from that, it's possible to see that a radian is a little less than one-sixth of a circle. Indeed, 180 degrees is equal to exactly π radians.

$$\frac{r}{2\pi r} = \frac{x}{360°}$$

$$x = \frac{360°}{2\pi}$$

$$x \approx 57.3°$$

Radians represent a ratio, and ratios have no units. When you write an angle in degrees, you must denote it with the small circle that represents degrees. After all, degrees are an arbitrary unit; the value 360 happens to work well for a circle simply because it divides cleanly in so many ways.

Of course, sometimes it will be important to make it perfectly clear that radians are the method of measurement. In that case, you can append "rad" to the value. But this is not a unit; it's simply an indication of what the number represents.

Here's a summary of the conversion calculations:

- To convert from radians to degrees, divide by π and multiply by 180.

- To convert from degrees to radians, multiply by π and divide by 180.

Areas

In computing the area of an arbitrary region, the human method would be to break it down into simple components, such as triangles, and then sum up the individual areas of these smaller pieces. A triangle's area is just half the base times the height, and solving for the height is possible given enough of the angles and side lengths.

Breaking down a complex shape can be a tricky task, however, even for a human. In order for a computer to be able to solve for the area of an arbitrary region, a systematic approach must be developed—one that a simpleminded JavaScript function can reliably apply in all situations. To derive such a method, we'll begin by representing each point around a figure's perimeter as a coordinate pair labeled x_1 and y_1, x_2 and y_2, and so on.

The initial step is to extend each vertex of the shape to the X-axis, and then picture each line segment as being part of a quadrilateral involving two of the extension lines and a piece of the X-axis. You can see this developing in Figure 10-2.

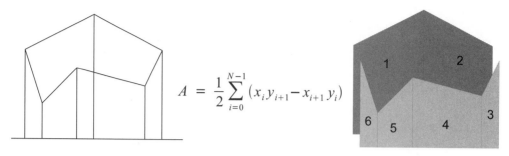

$$A = \frac{1}{2} \sum_{i=0}^{N-1} \left(x_i y_{i+1} - x_{i+1} y_i \right)$$

Figure 10-2. *Arbitrary concave polygon formula, showing the component quadrilaterals*

■**Note** Concave and convex—which is which? *Convex* describes a shape where a straight line from any point inside the shape to any other point inside the shape will never leave the shape. *Concave*, on the other hand, means that there are areas where something has been "cut out" of the shape. These definitions apply equally to three-dimensional figures. A concave lens is one that narrows toward the middle, leaving a "cave" on either side of it.

From here, it's clear that if you take the areas of all the quadrilaterals on the *far* side of the shape, and subtract the areas of those quadrilaterals on the *near* side, the area remaining is that of the shape itself.

To express this mathematically, we must use the summation operator Σ to add up the areas of the trapezoids, which are simply the average of their top and bottom lines (left and right, in our case), multiplied by the height:

$$A = \sum_{i=0}^{N-1} \frac{1}{2} \left(y_{i+1} + y_i \right) \left(x_{i+1} - x_i \right)$$

The business about adding the far-side area and subtracting the near-side area is actually one we get for free. Working under the assumption that the points are provided in clockwise order, subtracting the *x* values for the height ensures that the near and far regions have the opposite sign. The formula as given here assumes points provided in clockwise order. If you wish to accept them in either order, you can take the absolute value of the result.

This can be simplified if we bring the constant outside the summation, and expand the multiplication on the inside:

$$A = \frac{1}{2} \sum_{i=0}^{N-1} x_{i+1} y_{i+1} - x_i y_{i+1} + x_{i+1} y_i - x_i y_i$$

The observant will notice that once this summation is applied across a cyclical list of points, every $-x_{i+1}y_{i+1}$ term will *subtract out* the $x_i y_i$ term in the following iteration of the sum. After this final simplification, we're left with a straightforward formula:

$$A = \frac{1}{2}\sum_{i=0}^{N-1}\left(x_{i+1}y_i - x_i y_{i+1}\right)$$

To implement this in JavaScript is a simple matter of a loop, as shown in Listing 10-1.

Listing 10-1. *Function for an Arbitrary Shape's Area, Given by a List of Coordinate Pairs*

```
var points = [
    {'x': 1, 'y': 4 }, {'x': 4, 'y': 6 }, {'x': 6, 'y': 5 },
    {'x': 5, 'y': 1 }, {'x': 3, 'y': 3 }, {'x': 2, 'y': 2 }
];

function calculateArea(points) {
    var count = points.length;
    var tally = 0;
    var i;

    // add the first point to the end of the array
    points[points.length] = points[0];

    for(i = 0; i < count; i++) {
        tally += points[i + 1].x * points[i].y
        tally -= points[i].x * points[i + 1].y
    }

    return tally * 0.5;
}
```

■**Caution** The code in Listing 10-1 contains a "gotcha" that PHP users might not have been expecting. JavaScript passes all nonprimitives by *reference*, which means the caller's copy of the points array will get back the duplicated version with the extra element tacked on the end. If this is important, you could call the Array's pop() method to remove the final element.

You can see the Listing 10-1 code in action in Figure 10-3. Although it would work for highly localized regions, where the earth can be assumed flat, it's unsuitable as a general, global solution. You can see in the demo that we've used points plotted in pixel increments on your flat screen, and then calculated the area inside those.

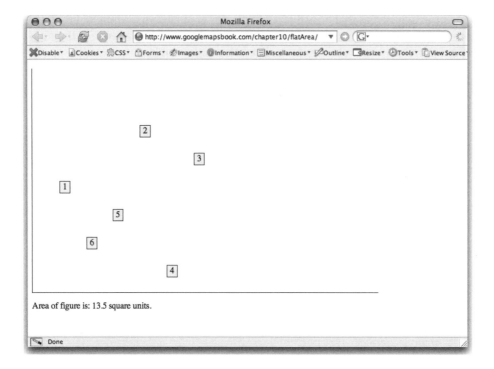

Figure 10-3. *Calculating with JavaScript the area encompassed by six flat points*

However, the formula is still important. For areas small enough to be approximated as flat, such a method is straightforward to apply and not difficult conceptually. It's helpful to see it in comparison to the spherical methods we'll develop in the next section.

Moving to Spheres

The study of spherical geometry is a field dominated by fascinating shortcuts and unusual ways of conceptualizing problems. Nothing from flat geometry can be simply applied verbatim, but there are interesting ways that aspects of spherical problems can be reduced down to planar ones.

The Great Circle

The shortest way to connect any two points on the surface of a sphere is by going *through* the sphere itself. In terms of surface routes, however, the shortest is called a *great-circle path*. It has this name because the connecting arc is *part of a circle that has the same center point as the sphere itself*, perfectly bisecting it. It's the largest possible circle that may be traced on the surface of any sphere.

All longitude lines are great circles, but of the lines of latitude, only the equator qualifies.

This can be counterintuitive at first, especially looking at maps like the New York to Paris route in Figure 10-4. When trans-Atlantic flights fly great-circle routes through the northern hemisphere, it appears—from a flat map—as though they've taken a bizarre arctic detour. But, as we explained in Chapter 7, the farther away from the equator you look on a Mercator map, the more zoomed-in your scale is. A line through the northern Atlantic is actually traveling less distance, since the scale in that location is larger. A great-circle path, when looking at a globe, makes perfect sense.

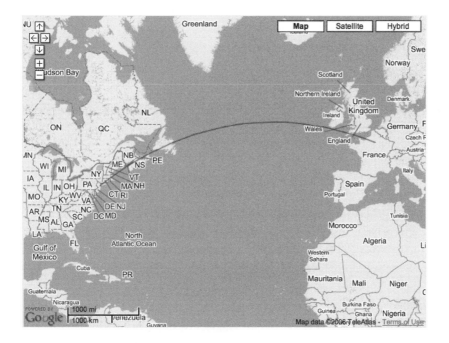

Figure 10-4. *A great-circle route from New York to Paris, similar to what Lindbergh followed on his famous 1927 hop across the Atlantic*

Note Modern New York to Paris flights likely wouldn't follow the exact path shown in Figure 10-4, but their reason for diverging from it would be to take advantage of the jet stream on eastbound flights.

In Figure 10-5, we work forward from that original shortest line—the one that joins two points by passing through the earth itself. If we imagine that we can't travel it directly, but must trace arc routes over the earth's surface, it becomes clear that the *largest* possible radius is what yields the shortest path between the points.

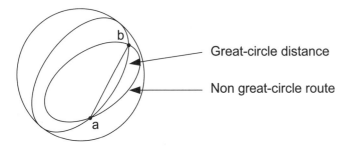

Figure 10-5. *The shortest path has the largest radius.*

Great-Circle Lengths

There are multiple possibilities for how to accurately calculate a great-circle distance between two points. We'll show two methods: the Cartesian method and the Haversine method. Both are considered very reliable. The Cartesian method is simpler to conceptualize. The Haversine method is easier to compute.

■**Note** An article from the US Census Bureau suggests that the Haversine method is the superior one in most cases. The piece has disappeared from its original location, but it has been mirrored at http://www.movable-type.co.uk/scripts/GIS-FAQ-5.1.html.

The Cartesian Method

Taking the great-circle idea and applying Euclidean geometry techniques, we can actually arrive at a perfectly valid formula for calculating the length of a great-circle path. The steps to this solution are as follows:

1. Using trigonometry and the radius of earth, transform each latitude/longitude pair into three-dimensional Cartesian coordinates.

2. Determine the distance between the two points, by calculating *x*, *y*, and *z* displacements, and then applying the Pythagorean theorem. (In three dimensions, it's exactly the same; just add the square of the Z-dimension under the root sign.)

3. Picture that distance as a chord on a "great circle" around the earth, and then using basic two-dimensional geometry, calculate the arc-length bracketed by the known straight-line length.

Although this method is accurate, unfortunately even in its simplified form, it's frighteningly complex:

$$\Delta\sigma = \arctan\left\{ \frac{\sqrt{\left[\cos\phi_2 \sin\Delta\lambda\right]^2 + \left[\cos\phi_1 \sin\phi_1 - \sin\phi_1 \cos\phi_2 \cos\Delta\lambda\right]^2}}{\sin\phi_1 \sin\phi_2 + \cos\phi_1 \cos\phi_2 \cos\phi\Delta\lambda} \right\}$$

For this reason, we turn to the Haversine formula, a non-Euclidean solution to the problem.

The Haversine Method

As with many of the mathematical tools we've used with the Google Maps API, the Haversine formula has a history with marine navigation. Although both work perfectly well, the Haversine formula has an elegant simplicity that makes it appealing. Indeed, as of version 2.0, the functionality you see here is provided in the Google Maps API, by the `GLatLng::distanceFrom()` method. Here is the Haversine formula:

$$d = 2\arcsin\left(\sqrt{\sin^2\left(\frac{\phi_2 - \phi_1}{2}\right) + \cos_1\cos_2\sin^2\left(\frac{\lambda_2 - \lambda_1}{2}\right)}\right)$$

You get surface distance by plugging in the two points' latitudes and longitudes into ϕ_1, λ_1 and ϕ_2, λ_2, respectively, and then multiplying d by the radius of the earth, 6,378,137 meters.

JavaScript exposes all of the mathematical functions required to implement an expression such as this, in the `Math` object.

■**Tip** An excellent resource for the `Math` object can be found at W3Schools: `http://www.w3schools.com/jsref/jsref_obj_math.asp`.

IS THE EARTH FLAT AFTER ALL?

It comes as a surprise to some that the earth is not *perfectly* spherical. It's flattened slightly, a shape known to mathematicians as an *oblate spheroid*.

At the equator, the earth has a radius of 6378 kilometers. Measuring from the center to the poles, however, the distance is slightly less—about 6357 kilometers. For some types of calculations, it's appropriate to use 6371 kilometers, which is the radius of a theoretical sphere having the same *volume* as the earth.

All of the formulas presented in this chapter, however, operate under the assumption that the earth *is* a sphere, having a radius of exactly 6,378,137 meters. This is, in fact, the same assumption made by the functions in version 2.0 of the Google Maps API, so any slight errors will be in good company.

Area on a Spherical Surface

Our formula from Listing 10-1 operates given a method for computing trapezoidal areas. In order to adapt this method to spherical geometry, we would need to establish a way of computing the area of a trapezoid that is now drawn on the surface of a sphere. But first, let's look at a slightly simpler problem: how to compute the area of a spherical triangle.

A Spherical Triangle

Given three points on the surface of a sphere, it's possible to join them by great-circle arcs, and then determine the surface area contained within the area. The process for doing this is an intriguing one, as it's based not around three-sided figures, but two-sided ones.

On a flat piece of paper, there is no such thing as a two-sided figure. From lines, we make the jump directly to triangles. But on a curved surface, there *is* a two-sided shape, as you can see in Figure 10-6. It's called a *lune*, and it's the orange-slice carved out when two noncoincident great circles exist in the same sphere together.

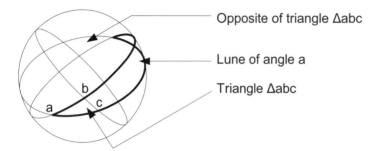

Figure 10-6. *A spherical triangle abc, with the lune formed by angle a highlighted*

Since both curves involved are great circles, determining the surface area of a lune is almost trivial:

$$A = 4\pi r^2 \left(\frac{a}{2\pi} \right) = 2r^2 a$$

It's simply the percentage of the sphere's total surface area that the angle a is of a full circle (2π, in radians).

Although Figure 10-6 has only one lune highlighted, if you look closely, you can see that there are actually six of them. Each of the points a, b, and c is the endpoint of two opposite lunes: one that encompasses the *abc* triangle, and a second one that includes not the *abc* triangle, but the "shadow" *abc*. The key to finding the area of the triangle *abc* is to realize that the surface areas of the six lunes can be summed to get an area that is the sphere's total surface area, plus the *abc* area four extra times:

$$A_{sphere} = A_a + A_b + A_c + A_{a^1} + A_{b^1} + A_{c^1} - 4A_T$$

Remember that the triangle is there twice, and there are six lunes, each of which includes the triangle's area once. The area must be subtracted four times in order to get back to just the plain old surface area. After substituting the lune surface area formula, and rearranging, we end up with the following formula:

$$4A_T = 4r^2 a + 4r^2 b + 4r^2 c - 4\pi r^2$$

A final factoring leaves us with this simpler formula:

$$A_T = r^2 (a + b + c - \pi)$$

Of course, this is not a formula that works from latitudes and longitudes. This still assumes we have the angles between the triangle lines.

Given how simple this formula is, it might be disappointing to discover just how complex a process it is to find the interior angles of the triangle—the a, b, and c values. We must express each of the three points as a vector, so that the surface point a becomes a Cartesian vector A, pointing from the center of the sphere to the location of a. Having these three vectors, the angle at a in the original triangle can be determined by the following expression of cross products and dot products (see the next section for a refresher on these vector operations):

$$a + \arctan\left(\frac{(B \times A) \bullet C}{(A \times C) \bullet (A \times B)}\right)$$

Tip For an explanation of the derivation of the expression of cross products and dot products, see http://www.ral.ucar.edu/research/verification/randy/writeups/earthareas.pdf.

This is giving us the angle we need, but it's still not starting from latitudes and longitudes. Converting latitudes and longitudes to Cartesian coordinates is not difficult given a pen and a few minutes to mull it over, and we've included the shortcut here. If the latitude and longitude of a point are known, and in ϕ and λ, then the three components of its vector are as follows:

$$x = \cos\phi \sin\lambda$$
$$y = \cos\phi \cos\lambda$$
$$z = \sin\phi$$

Listing 10-2 shows a JavaScript function that can perform this conversion directly from a GLatLng object. Notice how it uses radians, since these are the units of the JavaScript trigonometry functions. We don't have a designated class for storing three-dimensional vectors, so we'll simply return it as an array of the three elements. (Creating such a class would be a worthwhile endeavor if you were to venture too much further into this territory.)

Listing 10-2. *Cartesian Coordinates from Latitude and Longitude*

```
function cartesianCoordinates(latlng) {
    var x = Math.cos(latlng.latRadians()) * Math.sin(latlng.lngRadians());
    var y = Math.cos(latlng.latRadians()) * Math.cos(latlng.lngRadians());
    var z = Math.sin(latlng.latRadians());
    return [x, y, z];
}
```

Given these coordinates for each of the three points involved, it's just a matter of a quick refresher on how to do vector cross products and dot products, and then we'll have everything we need to cleanly implement the angle formula. And having the angles, we can find our area.

Vector Operations: Dot Products and Cross Products

When dealing with the "multiplication" of three-dimensional vectors, there are actually two separate operations that can be performed. The first of these yields a scalar (nonvector) value, and is called the *dot product*. To compute the dot product, you multiply the *x* of the first vector by the *x* of the second one, and then add that to the product of the two *y* values and the product of the two *z* values.

To see how this works, we'll simply show you our JavaScript implementation in Listing 10-3, which takes two arguments, each of which is assumed to be a three-element array representing a vector.

Listing 10-3. *Function for Calculating a Dot Product*

```
function dotProduct(a, b) {
    return (a[0] * b[0]) + (a[1] * b[1]) + (a[2] * b[2]);
}
```

The other type of vector multiplication returns another vector as its result. This is called the *cross product*, and the resulting vector has the geometric property of being perpendicular to the two initial vectors. Our function for calculating the cross product is shown in Listing 10-4.

Listing 10-4. *Function for Calculating the Cross Product*

```
function crossProduct(a, b) {
    return [(a[1] * b[2]) - (a[2] * b[1]), (a[2] * b[0]) - (a[0] * b[2]),➥
        (a[0] * b[1]) - (a[1] * b[0])];
}
```

Now we can assemble a final solver for a given angle, as in Listing 10-5.

Listing 10-5. *Function for the Angle Between Three Points on a Sphere*

```
function spherePointAngle(A, B, C) { // returns angle at B
    return Math.atan2(dotProduct(crossProduct(C, B), A),➥
        dotProduct(crossProduct(B, A), crossProduct(B, C)));
}
```

And now we have all the pieces to solve for the area of a spherical triangle. Before we get to work on that, though, there's an important thing you should know.

An Extension to Arbitrary Polygons

As it turns out, the triangle formula that we showed at the beginning of this is actually just the *n*=3 case of a general formula for shapes traced on spheres:

$$A = r^2 \left[\left(a_1 + a_2 + \ldots + a_n \right) - \left(n - 2 \right) \pi \right]$$

The *a* terms represent the angles at the vertices involved in the shape, and *n* represents the number of vertices.

From a planar geometry perspective, it seems absurd that you would be able to calculate a surface area having only angles and no lengths. But a simple thought experiment can help you persuade yourself that this works. Try to picture the smallest triangle you could draw on a sphere, and then picture the largest.

The smallest triangle is so small that the area it covers is considered flat. As a triangle on a plane, its angles must sum to 180 degrees. But the largest triangle—well, the largest possible joining of three line segments on a sphere—is going to have them all going end to end in a circle *around* it. That is, the "triangle" is simply tracing out a *great circle*, with its area being half the sphere's surface, and the three angles totaling 3 * 180° = 540°.

Clearly, there's a relationship between the total of the angles and the percentage of the sphere covered. And the general formula, derived from the Gauss-Bonnet theorem, expresses this relation.

In Listing 10-6, we've built a general function for determining the area inside a list of points, given as a list of GLatLng objects.

Listing 10-6. *General-Purpose Function for Determining Area Inside a List of Points*

```
var earthRadius = 6378137; // in meters

function polylineArea(latlngs) {
    var id, sum = 0, pointCount = latlngs.length, cartesians = [];
    if (pointCount < 3) return 0;

    for (id in latlngs) {
        cartesians[id] = cartesianCoordinates(latlngs[id]);
    }

    // pad out with the first two elements
    cartesians.push(cartesians[0]);
    cartesians.push(cartesians[1]);

    for(id = 0; id < pointCount; id++) {
        var A = cartesians[id];
        var B = cartesians[id + 1];
        var C = cartesians[id + 2];
        sum += spherePointAngle(A, B, C);
    }

    var alpha = Math.abs(sum - (pointCount - 2) * Math.PI);
    alpha -= 2 * Math.PI * Math.floor(alpha / (2 * Math.PI));
    alpha = Math.min(alpha, 4 * Math.PI - alpha);

    return Math.round(alpha * Math.pow(earthRadius, 2));
}
```

To test whether this is working properly, you could pick your favorite rectangular state, plug its corner coordinates into the function, and check if the returned value corresponds to the established measurements.

Working with Polylines

You've seen a bunch of nifty geometric qualities that we can calculate given groups of points. But it's time we took this code on the road and got it integrated with some working maps. This section's project, shown in Figure 10-7, lets the user input polygon corners, then displays the perimeter and area of the region.

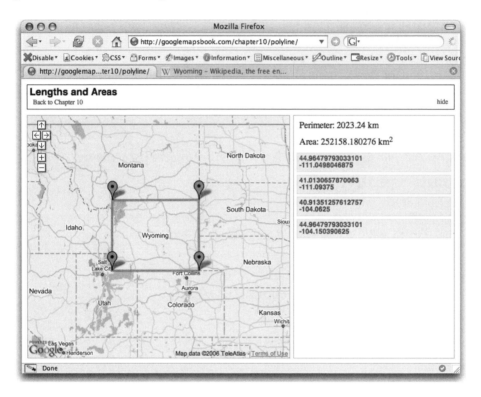

Figure 10-7. *The outline of Wyoming*

Building the Polylines Demo

Our starting setup will be pretty familiar from prior chapters. For markup and styles, establish a basic screen involving a header and flanking sidebar, as shown in Listing 10-7.

Listing 10-7. *index.php for Polylines Example*

```
<!DOCTYPE html PUBLIC "-//W3C//DTD XHTML 1.0 Strict//EN"
    "http://www.w3.org/TR/xhtml1/DTD/xhtml1-strict.dtd">
<html xmlns="http://www.w3.org/1999/xhtml" xmlns:v="urn:schemas-microsoft-com:vml">
<head>
    <script src="http://maps.google.com/maps?file=api&v=2&key=<?= $api_key ?>"➥
type="text/javascript"></script>
    <script src="map_functions.js" type="text/javascript"></script>
    <link href="style.css" rel="stylesheet" type="text/css" />
```

```
    <!--[if IE]>
    <style type="text/css"> v\:* { behavior:url(#default#VML); } </style>
    <![endif]-->
</head>
<body class="sidebar-right">
    <div id="toolbar">
        <h1>Lengths and Areas</h1>
        <ul id="sidebar-controls">
            <li><a href="#" id="button-sidebar-hide">hide</a></li>
            <li><a href="#" id="button-sidebar-show">show</a></li>
        </ul>
    </div>
    <div id="content">
        <div id="map-wrapper">
            <div id="map"></div>
        </div>
        <div id="sidebar">
            <div id="line-info">
                <p><span id="length-title">Length</span>
                <span id="length-data">0</span> km</p>
                <p>Area: <span id="area-data">0</span> km<sup>2</sup></p>
            </div>
            <ul id="sidebar-list">
            </ul>
        </div>
    </div>
</body>
</html>
```

You can see we've dropped the link element that included the `map_points.php` data. To "prove" that the calculations in this chapter are working properly, it will be more fun to feed them new data on each run. Additionally, we've added an extra XML namespace, plus a bizarre proprietary style rule contained inside a *conditional comment*. This is a special Microsoft HTML comment that reliably hides the rule from all non-Internet Explorer browsers (see `http://msdn.microsoft.com/workshop/author/dhtml/overview/ccomment_ovw.asp`). Including this rule is a prerequisite to using the `GPolyline` class, if we want our polylines to work in Internet Explorer.

Why such requirements? To render polylines on Internet Explorer, Google Maps uses Vector Markup Language (VML), an XML vector language that was ahead of its time, and sadly never got included in browsers other than Internet Explorer. For nonsupporting user agents, the API simply has Google's servers render a PNG image, which gets draped over the map. In some cases, it will try to render the polyline using Scalable Vector Graphics (SVG), a contemporary standard that occupies the same space VML once did.

We could always stick the VML rule in with all the other rules in our main `style.css` file, but because it's not standard, we should keep it separate and away from browsers that might choke on it. (Generally, it's considered good CSS practice to keep any filters or "hack" style rules separated from the main flow of the style sheet.)

The styles used in this demo are lifted verbatim from the demos in prior chapters.

And, as for the JavaScript, well, a lot of it is similar to what you've seen before, but we've made some changes, too, which are highlighted in the next few listings, starting with Listing 10-8.

Listing 10-8. *Initialization Function in map_functions.js, Containing a GEvent Call*

```
var map;
var centerLatitude = 40.6897;
var centerLongitude = -95.0446;
var startZoom = 5;
var deselectCurrent = function() {};
var removePolyline = function() {};
var earthRadius = 6378137; // in metres

var latlngs = [];

function init() {    document.getElementById('button-sidebar-hide').onclick =➥
        function() { return changeBodyClass('sidebar-right', 'nosidebar'); };
    document.getElementById('button-sidebar-show').onclick =➥
        function() { return changeBodyClass('nosidebar', 'sidebar-right'); };

    handleResize();

    map = new GMap2(document.getElementById("map"));
    map.setCenter(new GLatLng(centerLatitude, centerLongitude), startZoom);
    map.addControl(new GSmallMapControl());

    GEvent.addListener(map, 'click', handleMapClick);
}
```

Most of this should be familiar to you from earlier chapters, including the one line that attaches a click handler to the map object. But, of course, we can't just reference a map click handler function and not show it to you.

The handleMapClick() function is designed to build up a list of a GLatLng objects in an array, and on each new one added, redraw a polyline that connects the lot. Check it out in Listing 10-9.

Listing 10-9. *Handler for Map Clicks, in map_functions.js*

```
function handleMapClick(marker, latlng) {
    if (!marker) {
        latlngs.push(latlng);
        initializePoint(latlngs.length - 1);
        redrawPolyline();
    }
}
```

This function is not a tricky one. It just adds the new GLatLng to the accumulating array, initializes the new point, and then has a second function redraw the polyline that connects all the points. So what are the functions initializePoint() and redrawPolyline()?

The venerable `initializePoint()` function has undergone some slight renovations from previous versions, but large chunks of it will remain familiar in Listing 10-10. The biggest change is that a new `draggable` parameter has been enabled, so that we can move our markers around once they're down on the map.

Listing 10-10. *Function for Initializing Individual Points from a Global Array*

```
function initializePoint(id) {
    var marker = new GMarker(latlngs[id], { draggable:true });
    var listItem = document.createElement('li');
    var listItemLink = listItem.appendChild(document.createElement('a'));
    listItemLink.href = "#";
    listItemLink.innerHTML = '<strong>' + latlngs[id].lat() +➥
'<br />' + latlngs[id].lng() + '</strong>';

    var focusPoint = function() {
        deselectCurrent();
        listItem.className = 'current';
        deselectCurrent = function() { listItem.className = ''; }
        map.panTo(latlngs[id]);
        return false;
    }

    GEvent.addListener(marker, 'click', focusPoint);
    listItemLink.onclick = focusPoint;
    document.getElementById('sidebar-list').appendChild(listItem);

    map.addOverlay(marker);

    marker.enableDragging();
    GEvent.addListener(marker, 'dragend', function() {
        listItemLink.innerHTML = '<strong>' + latlngs[id].lat() +➥
'<br />' + latlngs[id].lng() + '</strong>';
        latlngs[id] = marker.getPoint();
        redrawPolyline();
    });
}
```

You can see now why it was important to keep `initializePoint()` and `redrawPolyline()` as separate entities—so that a dragged marker could *also* trigger a redrawing of the polyline. Speaking of redrawn polylines, let's take a peek at the `redrawPolyline()` function in Listing 10-11.

Listing 10-11. *Function to Redraw a Polyline from a Global Array*

```
function redrawPolyline() {
    var pointCount = latlngs.length;
    var id;
```

```
    map.removeOverlay(polyline)
    // Plot polyline, adding the first element to the end, to close the loop.
    latlngs.push(latlngs[0]);
    var polyline = new GPolyline(latlngs, 'FF6633', 4, 0.8);
    map.addOverlay(polyline);

    // Check total length of polyline (length for 2 points, perimeter > 2 points)
    if (pointCount >= 2) {
        var length = 0;
        for(id = 0; id < pointCount; id += 1) {
            length += latlngs[id].distanceFrom(latlngs[id + 1]);
        }

        if (pointCount > 2) {
            document.getElementById('length-title').innerHTML = 'Perimeter';
            document.getElementById('length-data').innerHTML =➥
Math.round(length) / 1000;
        } else {
            document.getElementById('length-title').innerHTML = 'Length';
            document.getElementById('length-data').innerHTML =➥
Math.round(length) / 2000;
        }
    }
    latlngs.pop(); // restore the array to how it was

    // Show value of area in square km.
    if (pointCount >= 3) {
        document.getElementById('area-data').innerHTML =➥
polylineArea(latlngs) / 1000000;
    }

}
```

This function may be long, but it's mostly just a sequence of mundane tasks: pad the list of points, remove the old polyline, draw the new polyline, iterate through to check length, and call our previous function to check area.

PUTTING THE GOOGLE GEOCODER TO WORK

Back in Chapter 4, we mentioned that the Google geocoder is accessible not just through a REST web service, but also directly from the JavaScript API. The polylines project in this chapter is a perfect example of a good use of this tool.

Rather than forcing users to enter points by clicking, we can provide a friendly text box that allows them to search for locations instead. The code required for this feature is not hard. The more important thing to understand is the two different mechanisms you could use to implement this feature:

- The user would submit the search box back to *your* server, and you would send out the REST request to Google, cache the response, and send out the result to your user. If the user decided to save or bookmark that point for later retrieval, you would already have it geocoded, from the first request.

- Using the JavaScript geocoder, the user's address query is submitted directly to Google, and the geocoded point is sent straight to the user's browser, without your own server as the broker between them. This means better response time for the user, but also that when the user saves that point, you need to send back the coordinates so the point doesn't need to be re-geocoded on each future request.

To add this to the polyline application of the chapter, you would need to slide in some markup for the search box, which could go anywhere, but we put ours at the top of the sidebar:

```
<div id="sidebar">
    <div id="line-info">
        <p><span id="length-title">Length</span>: <span id="length-data">0➡
</span> km</p>
        <p>Area: <span id="area-data">0</span> km<sup>2</sup></p>
    </div>
    <form id="address-search" method="get">
        <input type="text" id="s" name="s" />
        <input type="submit" id="submit" value="Add" />
        <p id="working">Working ...</p>
    </form>
    <ul id="sidebar-list">
    </ul>
</div>
```

To prevent form submissions from reloading the page, we need to hook a function to the form's onsubmit event, and return a false value, which tells the browser that the event doesn't require any further action.

```
function init() {
    ...
    document.getElementById('address-search').onsubmit = handleSearch;
}
```

And finally, the handleSearch() function contains the meat of calling the Google GClientGeocoder object. The GClientGeocoder object needs to be instantiated before the first use, but apart from that, it really couldn't be simpler: call its getLatLng() method, pass in the address string, and pass it a function to execute upon receiving the response. We've bolded the response function in the following listing, so you can see more clearly how it gets passed in.

```
function handleSearch() {
    var searchText = document.getElementById('s').value;
    if (searchText == '') {
        alert('Please enter a location to search for.');
        return false;
    }
```

```
    if (!geocoder) geocoder = new GClientGeocoder();  // initialize geocoder

    changeBodyClass('geocoder-idle', 'geocoder-busy'); // CSS hook

    geocoder.getLatLng(searchText,
        function (response) {
            changeBodyClass('geocoder-busy', 'geocoder-idle'); // clear CSS hook

            if (!response) {
                alert('Error geocoding address');
            } else {
                latlngs.push(response);
                initializePoint(latlngs.length - 1);
                redrawPolyline();
                document.getElementById('s').value = ''; // clear the search box
            }
        }
    );

    return false;
}
```

This example was a great opportunity to show you how the GClientGeocoder object works, since it's a case where the application is directly geocoding an address input by the user. It's important to realize that in any case where addresses are being sent from your server, you should geocode them on the server. But if you're receiving an address from the user, it's great to code it in JavaScript and then cache the location from there.

To see the modified version of this in action, check it out at http://googlemapsbook.com/chapter10/clientGeocoder/.

Expanding the Polylines Demo

We wanted to leave you with an example that really brims with possibilities. What could you do to expand this? Well, we've already implemented a search box where users can type in addresses to be geocoded and added to the sequence. Besides cleaning that up and clarifying its function for the user, here are a few other ideas to get you started:

- Add a way to remove points from the list.

- Find an elegant way to insert points *into* the list, rather than just assuming the user wants them at the end of it.

- Try setting up the right sidebar so that the points can be dragged up and down to reorder the list. (Sam Stephenson's Prototype library could help you out with this; see http://prototype.conio.net/.)

Plus, of course, what good is it as a tech demo? What kind of use could this be put to in the wild? Property markings, perhaps? For a realtor, it would be valuable to plot out lots on a map, particularly those spacious ones where it's important that buyers see *just how deep* the backyard is. In fact, it's applicable for boundaries of all kinds. When the Blue Team gets from the lake to the dining hall, and the Red Team gets from the path up to the service road, who defends more territory, and who has farther to search for the flag? When the phone company moves the rural area codes around, which zones are the largest?

What About UTM Coordinates?

Readers who own or have used GPS devices will know that a latitude/longitude pair is not the only way to describe a global position. Typical handheld units will also provide UTM coordinates, an *easting* and a *northing*, both in units of meters. What is UTM, and how come Google instead chose latitude and longitude for its mapping system?

UTM stands for Universal Transverse Mercator. It's a projection system designed by the US Army shortly before World War II. The primary purposes of UTM were to be highly accurate in close detail and to be a good enough flat approximation that accurate distance readings could be taken off a map, using nothing more than the Pythagorean theorem.

So how does is work? The UTM system begins by dividing the earth into narrow slices, each just 6 degrees wide. Each of these slices is then divided into 60 vertical zones, between 80° S and 84° N. As you can see in Figure 10-8, UTM has coverage of all land masses (except for inland Antarctica). Then—and here's the genius of it—each of these trapezoidal zones is presented in a *transverse* Mercator projection—it's Mercator, except rotated 90 degrees. So, instead of seeing distortion as you move farther north and south, you see it as you move east and west. Yet, because the slices are so thin, the distortion is never more than 0.1% anywhere within a zone.

If you've ever seen a government topographic map, you've seen the UTM military gridlines on it. Depending on the zoom level, each box might represent a single square meter or some multiple of meters. But they *are* perfectly square boxes, and that makes standard planar trigonometry (as described in the first section of this chapter) "work" using UTM.

You can see from this explanation how ill suited UTM would be for a global system like Google Maps. Although calculations *within* a particular zone are made very straightforward by the system, it isn't at all appropriate for performing larger-scale calculations that would span multiple zones.

Indeed, there are special cases of UTM that illustrate very clearly the work-arounds caused by this limitation. Zone 32V, which covers southwest Norway, is arbitrarily extended west to a total width of 9 degrees. This is so that it can contain the entire tip of the country and not leave a sliver alone in the otherwise empty zone 31V.

Latitude/longitude is an extremely general system. With no special cases or strange exceptions, it simply and predictably identifies any spot on the globe, and only the most basic knowledge of a protractor is required in order to "get it." UTM is a highly specialized system, designed for taking pinpoint measurements on detailed topographic maps.

It's the general system that's appropriate for the global Google Maps. But the next time you're camping with your GPS and want to plot out a trail, try switching it to UTM mode. You may find that at that level of detail, having simple readings in meters makes the system much more accessible for basic, planar geometric calculations.

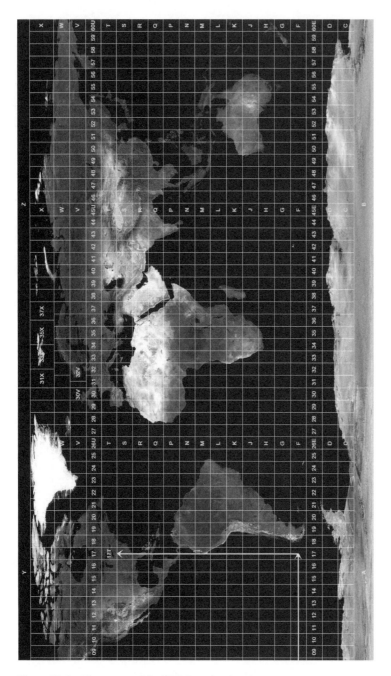

Figure 10-8. *The zones of the UTM projection system*

Running Afoul of the Date Line

In *Around the World in Eighty Days*, protagonist Phileas Fogg accounts for one extra day than his associates back home in London. In making his journey, each 15 degrees traveled east moved him one time zone *earlier*; for each zone crossed, the particular day counted was being shortened by an hour. Throughout the 80-day journey, he had logged days not as 24-hour periods, but as a sunset following a sunrise. In crossing the Pacific Ocean—and the International Date Line—he "gained" an extra day.

We aren't traveling around the world, but the International Date Line has a few implications on map-making with the Google API.

When you speak of degrees in a circle, you nearly always think in terms of all 360. A bearing of *due south* is expressed as 270 degrees, not as –90 degrees. Within circles, we think of angles as having a range from 0 to 360.

Well, with degrees of longitude, it's not from 0 to 360. It's –180 to 180. Measuring from the Prime Meridian at Greenwich, degrees eastward are positive and degrees westward are negative. So if Greenwich, England is where the zeroth degree is, that means there's a point opposite, where the 180th and –180th degrees meet. That line is the International Date Line.

Curiously enough, the International Date Line has no official path that it takes in its deviations from exactly 180 degrees. The countries through which it might pass simply declare themselves to be on the east or the west of it, and it becomes the responsibility of individual cartographers to weave the line between them accordingly. Generally, however, the line divides the Bering Strait (separating Russia from Alaska), and goes down through Oceania with Hawaii and French Polynesia on the eastern side, and nearly everything else on the western side, including New Zealand, Fiji, and the Marshall Islands.

How does this affect Google Maps? The 2.0 API is surprisingly well equipped to handle International Date Line oddities. Google uses imagery, creating an infinite equator and correctly simulating the continuous nature of a sphere. In Figure 10-9, the two maps were set to be in identical positions, each with a marker in Toronto. The one in front was then panned *right* until the marker jumped from one Toronto to the next.

The system isn't foolproof (it moves markers correctly, but it doesn't, at the moment, move the info window), but it's just another one of those trade-offs you deal with for being able to view our round globe through such a conveniently flat medium. And it's pretty elegant, even for a trade-off.

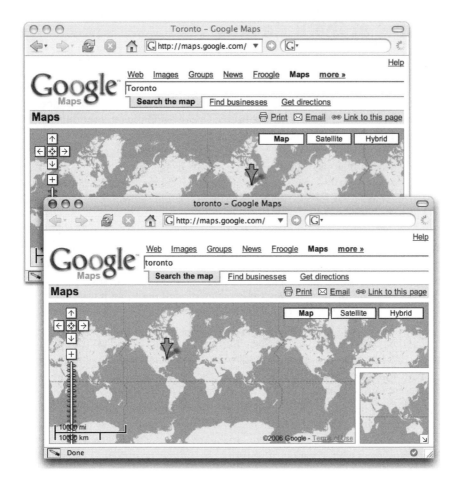

Figure 10-9. *Multiple copies of the earth's land masses, but only one marker*

Summary

This chapter provided an analysis of map regions, including area and perimeter, and described how to plot and handle GPolyline objects.

We hope this material was useful to you. Perhaps it has even given you some ideas of what's possible in and beyond the API. When that mashup opportunity comes along—the one with the voting regions, or the school districts, or the shorelines affected by an oil spill—you'll be armed with tools to get a clear and helpful visual look at the matter.

In the next, and last, chapter, we'll be discussing how a geocoder is built from scratch from two different sources of information. This will help you understand the limitations of precision in geocoding, as well as teach you the fundamentals of how to use a *very* rich data source: the US Census Bureau's TIGER/Line files.

CHAPTER 11

■■■

Advanced Geocoding Topics

In this chapter, you'll learn the basics of creating your own geocoding service. There are geocoding services already available for all sorts of data, and we covered many of them in Chapter 4. This chapter is intended for professionals and serious hobbyists who are building web applications where using third-party geocoding tools is not feasible due to cost, rate limiting, or terms of service. In these cases, developers often have no choice but to resort to getting dirty and becoming familiar with the original sources of data to do it themselves. If this describes you, then grab a pencil and paper, put on your thinking cap, and read on. We're about to get messy.

In this chapter, you'll learn how to do the following:

- Find sources of information used to create geocoding services.

- Construct a postal-code-based geocoding service for the United Kingdom. This example can be easily applied to the United States, Canada, and other countries, assuming you have access to the raw data.

- Build a more complicated and sophisticated geocoding web service for the United States, using the data from the US Census Bureau.

Where Does the Data Come From?

So where do services like Google and Yahoo get *their* data? How do they convert it into something that we can use to plot things on our maps? For graphical information systems (GIS) enthusiasts, this is a question with a really interesting answer, and the topic of most of this chapter.

Almost exclusively, this data comes from various government departments and agencies. Most often, some central authority (like the US Census Bureau) mandates that each municipality or county must provide data that is accurate to some specified degree. For many counties, meeting this requirement is not a matter of obtaining the data, but merely repurposing it. They already keep geographic information about land surveys, plot locations, and ownerships for taxation and legal purposes; converting it into maps and other GIS-related information is only a matter of time, resources, and incentive.

■**Note** This discussion applies primarily to Canada and the United States. For other areas of the world, similar kinds of information are slowly becoming available, and we are seeing more and more elaborate and complete geocoders each day, including the one introduced by Google. We hope that as the Google developers expand their road network data, they keep it's geocoder in sync; however, this chapter should help you understand how to fill in the gaps that they miss.

Sample Data from Government Sources

Figure 11-1 shows an example (a single block) of the kind of data that a typical urban planning department might have created. It shows each plot of land, the intersections, and the points where the road bends. This is a simplified example that we'll build up and use throughout the chapter, so you'll want to refer back to this page.

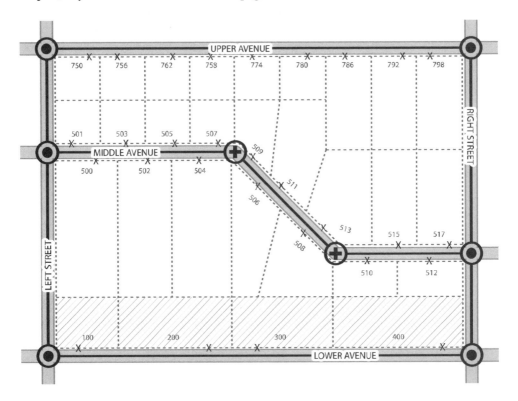

Figure 11-1. *Simplified example of a block of land in an urban planning department database*

You can see from the illustration that each plot of land is individually identified and that the roads are broken up into segments defined by intersections. Table 11-1 shows a representation of the data for each plot of land. Table 11-2 describes the sections of road. Table 11-3 holds the latitude and longitude data for each interior bend in the road, if there are any, and is associated by ID number.

Table 11-1. *A Portion of the Data for the Precise Location of Each Section of Land in Figure 11-1*

Street Name	Street No.	ZIP Code	Latitude	Longitude
Upper Ave	750	90210	43.1000	-80.1001
Upper Ave	756	90210	43.1000	-80.1003
Upper Ave	762	90210	43.1000	-80.1005
Upper Ave	768	90210	43.1000	-80.1007
Upper Ave	774	90210	43.1000	-80.1009
Upper Ave	780	90210	43.1000	-80.1011
Upper Ave	786	90210	43.1000	-80.1013
Upper Ave	792	90210	43.1000	-80.1015
Upper Ave	798	90210	43.1000	-80.1017
Middle Ave	501	90211	43.1005	-80.1001
Middle Ave	503	90211	43.1005	-80.1003
Middle Ave	505	90211	43.1005	-80.1005
Middle Ave	507	90211	43.1005	-80.1007

Table 11-2. *Road Complete Chain Endpoints*

ID No	Street Name	Start Latitude	Start Longitude	End Latitude	End Longitude
1000	Upper Ave	43.1000	-80.1000	43.1000	-80.1020
1001	Lower Ave	43.1010	-80.1000	43.1010	-80.1020
1002	Middle Ave	43.1005	-80.1000	43.1007	-80.1020
1003	West Street	43.1000	-80.1000	43.1005	-80.1000
1004	West Street	43.1005	-80.1000	43.1010	-80.1000
1005	East Street	43.1000	-80.1020	43.1007	-80.1020
1006	East Street	43.1007	-80.1020	43.1010	-80.1020

Table 11-3. *Road Complete Chain Interior Points*

ID No	SEQ	Latitude	Longitude
1002	1	43.1005	-80.1007
1002	2	43.1007	-80.1013

Of course, the Table 11-1 data is ideal for geocoding an address. It's simply a matter of looking up the street name and number, and then reading off the latitude and longitude. This data is also known as "street truth" or "ground truth" data, since it is roughly the same data you would get if you visited each address personally and used a handheld GPS device to read off the coordinates. Unfortunately, this level of data is rarely available for free, and when it is, it's only on a county-by-county basis.

The data in Tables 11-2 and 11-3, when combined, gives a very accurate picture of the streets' locations and how they intersect, and yet there is no information about the addresses of the buildings *along* those streets.

In reality, a combined set of data is what you're likely to get from a census bureau. Table 11-4 gives an amalgamated view of the records from Tables 11-1 and 11-2. This is roughly the same format that the US Census Bureau provides in its TIGER/Line data set, which we'll introduce in the next section.

Table 11-4. *Road Network Chain Endpoints*

ID No	Street Name	Start Latitude	Start Longitude	End Latitude	End Longitude	Left Addr. Start	Left Addr. End	Right Addr. Start	Right Addr. End
1000	Upper Ave	43.1000	80.1000	43.1000	80.1020			750	798
1001	Lower Ave	43.1010	80.1000	43.1010	80.1020	100	400		
1002	Middle Ave	43.1005	80.1000	43.1007	80.1020	501	517	500	512
1003	West Street	43.1000	80.1000	43.1005	80.1000				
1004	West Street	43.1005	80.1000	43.1010	80.1000				
1005	East Street	43.1000	80.1020	43.1007	80.1020				
1006	East Street	43.1007	80.1020	43.1010	80.1020				

You might be curious what left and right address start and end mean. Presume that you're standing on the intersection defined by a "start" latitude and longitude pair facing the "end" latitude longitude pair. From this reference point, you can tell that the addresses on one side are "left" and the other side are "right." This is how most GIS data sets pertaining to roads define left versus right. They cannot be correlated to east or west and merely reflect the order in which the points were surveyed by the municipalities.

By using the start and end addresses on a street segment in conjunction with the start and end latitude and longitude, you can guess the location of addresses in between. This is called *interpolation* and allows the providers of a data source to condense the data without a significant loss in resolution. The biggest problem arises when the size of the land divisions is not proportional to the numbering scheme. In our example (Figure 11-1), this occurs on the south side of Middle Avenue and also on Lower Avenue. This can affect the accuracy of your service, because you are forced to assume that all address numbers between your two endpoints exist and that they are equally spaced. We'll discuss this further in the "Building a Geocoding Service" section later in this chapter.

In cases where you cannot obtain any data based on streets, you can try to use the information used to deliver the mail. The postal services of most countries maintain a list of postal codes (ZIP codes in the United States) that are assigned to a rough geographic area. Often, a list of these codes (or at least the first portion of them) with the corresponding latitude and longitude of the center of the area is available for free or for minimal charge. Figure 11-2 shows a map with the postal codes for our sample block. Each postal code is defined by the shaded area and a letter, *A* through *E*. The small black *x* represents the latitude and longitude point recorded for each postal code.

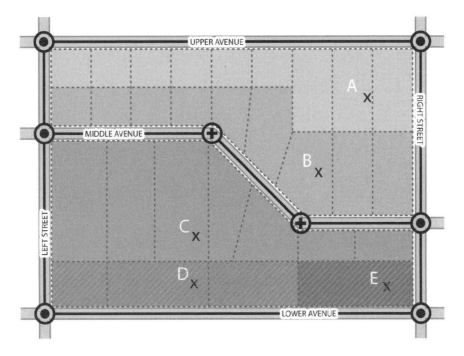

Figure 11-2. *Sample map showing only postal/ZIP codes*

In urban areas, where a small segment of a single street is represented by a unique postal code, this might be enough to geocode your data with sufficient accuracy for your project. However, problems arise when you leave the urban areas and start dealing with the rural and country spaces where mail may not be delivered directly to the houses. In these places, a single unique postal code could represent a post office (for PO boxes) or a geographical area as large as 30 square miles or more.

■**Note** In addition to the freely available data from the governments, in some cases, a private company has taken multiple sources of data and condensed them into a commercial product. Often, these commercial products also cross-reference sources of data in an attempt to filter out errors in the original sources. An example of one such product is the Geocoder.ca service discussed in Chapter 4.

Sources of Raw GIS Data

In the United States, a primary source of GIS data is the TIGER/Line (for Topologically Integrated Geographic Encoding and Referencing system) information, which is currently being revised by the US Census Bureau. This data set is huge and very well documented. As of this writing, the most current version of this data is the 2005 Second Edition data set (released in June 2006), which is available from the official website at `http://www.census.gov/geo/www/tiger/index.html`. The online geocoding service Geocoder.us relies on the TIGER/Line data, and we suspect that this data is also used (at least in part) by all of the other US-centric geocoding services, such as Google and Yahoo.

For Canada, the Road Network File (RNF) provided by the Canadian Census Department's Statistics Canada is excellent. You can find it at `http://geodepot.statcan.ca/Diss/Data/Data_e.cfm`. The current version as of this writing is the 2005 RNF. This data is available in a number of formats for various purposes. For the sake of programmatically creating a geocoder, you'll probably want the Geographic Markup Language (GML) version, since it can be processed with standard XML tools. The people who built Geocoder.ca used the RNF, combined with the Canadian Postal Code Conversion File (`http://www.statcan.ca/bsolc/english/bsolc?catno=92F0153X`) and some other commercial sources of data to create a unified data set. They attempted to remove any errors in an individual data set by cross-referencing all the sources of data.

For the United Kingdom, you can find a freely redistributable mapping between UK postal codes and crude latitude and longitude floating around the Internet. We've mirrored the information on our site at `http://googlemapsbook.com/chapter11/uk-postcodes.csv`. This information was reportedly created with the help of many volunteers and was considered reasonably accurate as of 2004. If you want to use the information for more than experimenting, you might consider obtaining the official data from the UK postal service.

For the rest of the world, you can obtain geonames data provided by the US National Geospatial Intelligence Agency (US-NGA). This data should be useful in geocoding the approximate center of most populated areas on the planet. The structure of the data provides for alternative names and permanent identifiers. For more information about this data set, see the section about geographic names (geonames) data in Appendix A.

The parsing and lookup methods used in the "Grabbing the TIGER/Line by the Tail" section later in this chapter also generally apply to the Canadian RNF and the geonames data sets, so we won't cover them with examples directly.

Note In Japan, at least in some places, the addressing scheme is determined by the order in which the buildings were constructed, rather than their relative positions on the street. For example 1 Honda Street is not necessarily next to, or even across the street from 2 Honda Street. Colleagues who have visited Japan report that navigation using handheld GPS and landmarks is much more common than using street number addresses, and that many businesses don't even list their street number on the side of the building or in any marketing material.

Geocoding Based on Postal Codes

Let's start to put some of this theory into practice. We'll begin with a geocoding solution based on the freely available UK postal code data mentioned in the previous section.

First, you'll need to get the raw CSV data from `http://googlemapsbook.com/chapter11/uk-postcodes.csv` and unpack it into a working directory on your server. This should be about 90KB uncompressed. Listing 11-1 shows a small sample of the contents of this file.

Listing 11-1. *Sample of the UK Postal Code Database for This Example*

```
postcode,x,y,latitude,longitude
AB10,392900,804900,57.135,-2.117
AB11,394500,805300,57.138,-2.092
AB12,393300,801100,57.101,-2.111
AB13,385600,801900,57.108,-2.237
AB14,383600,801100,57.101,-2.27
AB15,390000,805300,57.138,-2.164
AB16,390600,807800,57.161,-2.156
AB21,387900,813200,57.21,-2.2
AB22,392800,810700,57.187,-2.119
AB23,394700,813500,57.212,-2.088
AB25,393200,806900,57.153,-2.112
AB30,370900,772900,56.847,-2.477
AB31,368100,798300,57.074,-2.527
AB32,380800,807200,57.156,-2.317
```

The `postcode` field in this case simply denotes the forward sorting area, or *outcode*. The outcodes are used to get mail to the correct postal office for delivery by mail carriers. A full postal code would have a second component that identifies the street and address range of the destination and would look something like AB37 A5G. Unfortunately, we were unable to find a free list of full postal codes. The `x` and `y` fields represent meters relative to a predefined point inside the borders of the United Kingdom. The equation for converting these to latitude and longitude is long, involved, and not widely applicable, so we won't cover it here. Last are the fields we're interested in: `latitude` and `longitude`. They contain the latitude and longitude in decimal notation—ready and waiting for mapping on your Google map mashup.

■Note For most countries, you can find sources of data that have full postal codes mapped to latitude and longitude. However, this data is often very pricey. If you're interested in obtaining data for a specific country, be sure to check out the Geonames.org data and try searching online, but you may need to directly contact the postal service of the country you're interested in, and pay its licensing fees.

Next, you need to create a MySQL table in your experimental database. Listing 11-2 shows the table-creation statement we'll be using for this example. If you want to define a different table, you'll need to alter the code for the rest of the example accordingly.

Listing 11-2. *MySQL Table Structure for the UK Postal Code Geocoder*

```
CREATE TABLE uk_postcodes (
    outcode varchar(4) NOT NULL default '',
    latitude double NOT NULL default '0',
    longitude double NOT NULL default '0',
    PRIMARY KEY  (outcode)
) ENGINE=MyISAM;
```

Now you need to import the CSV data into this database. For this, you can use the snippet of code in Listing 11-3 and the db_credentials.php file you've built up throughout this book.

Listing 11-3. *PHP to Import the UK Postal Code CSV Data into SQL*

```php
<?php
// Connect to the database
require($_SERVER['DOCUMENT_ROOT'] . '/db_credentials.php');
$conn = mysql_connect("localhost", $db_name, $db_pass);
mysql_select_db("googlemapsbook", $conn);

// Open the CSV file
$handle = @fopen("uk-postcodes.csv","r");
fgets($handle,1024); // Strip off the header line

if ($handle) {
    while (!feof($handle)) {
        $buffer = fgets($handle, 4096);
        $line = explode(",",$buffer);
        if (count($line) == 5) {
            $result = mysql_query("INSERT INTO uk_postcodes
(outcode,latitude,longitude)➥
 VALUES ('$line[0]','$line[3]','$line[4]')");
            If (!$result) die ('Error, insert postcode failed: '.mysql_error());

        }
    }
    fclose($handle);
}
?>
```

This is a fairly simple example and uses techniques we've explored in previous chapters. Basically, we connect to the database, open the CSV file, read and convert each line into a five-element array, and then insert the three parts we're interested in into the database. (If you need a longer refresher, see Chapter 5.)

Lastly, for a public-facing geocoder, we'll need some code to expose a simple web service, allowing users to query our database from their application. Listing 11-4 outlines the basics of our UK postal code REST-based geocoder. For professional applications, you'll probably want to beef it up a bit in terms of options and error reporting, but this is a good foundation to build on later in the chapter.

Listing 11-4. *Gecoding REST Service for UK Outcodes*

```php
<?php
// Start our response
header('Content-type: text/xml');
echo '<?xml version="1.0" encoding="UTF-8"?><ResultSet>';
```

```
// Clean up the request and make sure it's not longer than four characters
$code = trim($_REQUEST['code']);
$code = preg_replace("/[^a-z0-9]/i","",$code);
$code = strtoupper($code);
$code = substr($code,0,4);

// Connect to the database
require($_SERVER['DOCUMENT_ROOT'] . '/db_credentials.php');
$conn = mysql_connect("localhost", $db_name, $db_pass);
mysql_select_db("googlemapsbook", $conn);

// Look up the provided code
$result = mysql_query("SELECT * FROM uk_postcodes WHERE outcode = '$code'");
if (!$result || mysql_num_rows($result) == 0)
    die("<Error>No Matches</Error></ResultSet>");

// Output the match that was found
$row = mysql_fetch_array($result,MYSQL_ASSOC);
echo "<Result>
    <Latitude>{$row['latitude']}</Latitude>
    <Longitude>{$row['longitude']}</Longitude>
    <OutCode>{$row['outcode']}</OutCode>
    </Result>";

// Close our response
echo "</ResultSet>";
?>
```

The comments are fairly complete, so we'll elaborate on only the parts that need a bit more explanation.

For security, safety, and sanity, the four $code = lines simply take off any whitespace around the edges, strip out characters that are not necessary (like dashes and interior spaces), convert the string to uppercase, and then reduce the length to four characters (the largest outcode in our data set), so we're not making more SQL queries than are needed.

Next, we simply query the database looking for an exact match and output the answer if we find one. That's it. After importing the data into a SQL table, it takes a mere 20 lines of code to give you a fairly robust and reliable, XML-returning REST service. A good example of how this sort of data can be used in a mapping application is the Virgin Radio VIP club members map found at http://www.virginradio.co.uk/vip/map.html. It shows circles of varying sizes based on the number of members in a given outcode. Other uses might include calculating rough distances between two people or grouping people, places, or things by region.

FUZZY PATTERN MATCHING

If you would prefer to allow people to match on partial strings, you'll need to be a bit more creative. Something like the following code snippet could replace your single lookup in Listing 11-4 and allow you to be more flexible with your user's query.

```
// Look up the provided code
$result = mysql_query("SELECT * FROM uk_postcodes WHERE outcode LIKE '$code%'");
while (strlen($code) > 0 && mysql_num_rows($result) == 0) {
    // That code was not found. Trim one character off the end and try again
    $modified_request = true;
    $code = substr($code,0,strlen($code)-1);
    $result = mysql_query("SELECT * FROM uk_postcodes WHERE outcode = '$code'");
}

// If the $code has been completely eaten, then there are no matches at all
if (strlen($code) == 0)
    die("<Error>No Matches</Error></ResultSet>");

// Output the match(es) found
while($row = mysql_fetch_array($result,MYSQL_ASSOC)) {
    echo "<Result>
    <Latitude>{$row['latitude']}</Latitude>
    <Longitude>{$row['longitude']}</Longitude>
    <OutCode>{$row['outcode']}</OutCode>
    </Result>";
}
```

Basically, you query the database table with a wildcard at the end of the requested code. This will allow you to return all results that match the prefix given. For example, if someone requests $code=AB1, there are seven matches in the database, but if their exact request yields no results, then our sample code strips one character off the end and tries again. Only if the length of the request code is zero do we give up and return an error. To return multiple results, you would simply wrap a loop around the output block.

You should be aware that with this modification to the code, it is possible for someone to harvest your entire database in a maximum of 36 requests (A,B,C,...,X,Y,Z,0,1,2,...,8,9). If this concerns you, or if you have purchased a more complete data set that you don't want to share, you might want to implement a feature to limit the maximum number of results, some rate limiting to make it impractical, or both.

Grabbing the TIGER/Line by the Tail

So what about street address geocoding? In this section, we'll discuss the US Census Bureau TIGER/Line data in detail. You can approach this data for use in a homegrown, self-hosted geocoder in two ways:

- Use the Perl programming language and take advantage of the `Geo::Coder::US` module that powers `http://www.geocoder.us`. It's free, fairly easy to use if you already know Perl (or someone who does), and open source, so it should continue to live for as long as someone finds it useful.

- Learn the structure of the data and how to parse it using PHP. This is indeed much more involved. However, it has the benefit of opening up the entire data set to you. There is much more information in the TIGER/Line data set than road and street numbers (see Appendix A). Knowing how to use this data will open a wide variety of possible mapping applications to you, and therefore we feel it is worthwhile to show you how it works.

■**Tip** If you're in a hurry, already know Perl shell scripting, and just need something quick and accurate, visit our website for an article on using `GEO::Coder::US`. We won't explicitly cover this method here, since it uses Perl and we've assumed you only have access to PHP on your server.

We'll begin by giving you a bit of a primer on the structure of the data files, then get into parsing them with PHP, and finish off by building a basic geocoder.

As we mentioned earlier in the chapter, the US TIGER/Line data is currently being revised and updated. The goal of this project is to consolidate information from many of the various sources into a widely applicable file for private and public endeavors. Among other things, the US Census Bureau is integrating the Master Address File originally used to complete the 2000 US Census, which should increase the accuracy of the address range data. The update project is scheduled to be complete in 2008, so anything you build based on these files will likely need to be kept up-to-date manually for a few years.

Understanding and Defining the Data

Before you can begin, you'll need to select a county. For this example, we selected San Francisco in California. Looking up the FIPS code for the county and state in the documentation (`http://www.census.gov/geo/www/tiger/tiger2005se/TGR05SE.pdf`), we find on page A-3 that they are 075 and 06, respectively. You can use any county and state you prefer; simply change the parameters in the examples that follow.

■**Note** FIPS stands for Federal Information Processing Standards. In our case, a unique code has been assigned to each state and county, allowing us to identify with numbers the various different entities quickly. There has been much discussion lately about replacing FIPS with something that gives a more permanent number (FIPS codes can change), and also at the same time allows you to infer proximity based on the code. We encourage you to Google "FIPS55 changes" for the latest information.

Next, you need to download the corresponding TIGER/Line data file so that you can play with it and convert it into a set of database tables for geocoding. In our case, the file is located at http://www2.census.gov/geo/tiger/tiger2005se/CA/tgr06075.zip. Place this file in your working directory for this example and unzip the raw data files.

▮Note The second edition of the 2005 TIGER/Line data files was released on June 27, 2006. Data sets are released approximately every six months. We suggest grabbing the most recent set of data, with the understanding that minor things in these examples may change if you do.

Inside the zip file, you'll find a set of text files, all with an .rt* extension. We've spent many days reading through the documentation to determine which of these files are really necessary for our geocoder. You're welcome to read the documentation for yourself, but to save you time and a whopping headache, we'll be working with the RT1, RT2, RT4, RT5, RT6, and RTC files in this example. We'll describe each one in turn here. You can delete the rest of them if you wish to save space on your hosting account.

The RT1 file contains the endpoints of each complete chain. A *complete chain* defines a segment of something linear like a road, highway, stream, or train tracks. A segment exists between intersections with other lines (usually of the same type). A *network chain* is composed of a series of complete chains (connected in order) to define the entire length of a single line.

▮Note In our case, we'll be ignoring all of the complete chains that do not represent streets with addresses. Therefore, we will refer to them as *road segments*.

The RT1 file ties everything else together by defining a field called TLID (for TIGER/Line ID) and stores the start and endpoints of the road segments along with the primary address ranges, ZIP codes, and street names. The RT2 file can be linked with the RT1 file via the TLID field and gives the internal line points that define bends in the road segment.

The RT4 file provides a link between the TLID values in the RT1 file and another ID number in the RT5 file: the FEAT (for feature) identifier. FEAT identifiers are used to link multiple names to a single road segment record. This is handy because many streets that are lined with residential housing also double as highways and major routes. If this is the case, then a single road might be referred to by multiple names (highway number, city-defined name, and so on). If someone is looking up an address and uses the less common name, you should probably still give the user an accurate answer.

The RT6 file provides additional address ranges (if available) for records in RT1. Lastly, the RTC file contains the names of the populated places (towns, cities, and so on) referenced in the PLACE fields in RT1.

■**Caution** Both RT4 and RT6 have a field called RTSQ. This represents the order in which the elements should be applied, but *cannot be used to link RT4 and RT6 together*. This means that a corresponding value of RTSQ does not imply that certain address ranges link with specific internal road segments for a higher level of positional accuracy. As tantalizing as this would be, we've confirmed this lack of correlation directly with the staff at the US Census Bureau.

We won't get into too much detail about the contents of each record type until we start talking about the importing routines themselves. What we will talk about now is the relational structure used to hold the data. Unlike with the previous postal code example, it doesn't make sense to store the street geocoder a single, spreadsheet-like table. Instead, we'll break it up into four distinct SQL tables:

- The places table stores the FIPS codes for the state, county, and place (city, town, and so on), as well as the actual name of the place. We've also formulated a place_id that will be stored in other tables for cross-linking purposes. The place_id is the concatenation of the state, county, and place FIPS codes and is nine or ten digits long (a BIGINT). This data is acquired from various FIPS files that we'll talk about shortly and the TIGER/Line RC file.

- The street_names table is primarily derived from the RT1 and RT5 records. Its purpose is to store the names, directions, prefixes, and suffixes of the streets and attach them to place_id values. It also stores the official TLID from the TIGER/Line data set, so that you can easily update your data in the future.

- The complete_chains table is where you'll store the latitude and longitude pairs that define the path of each road segment. It also stores a sequence number that can be used to sort the chain into the order that it would be plotted on a map. This data comes from the RT1 and RT2 records.

- The address_ranges table, as the name implies, holds various address ranges attached to each road segment. Most of this data will come from the RT1 records, though any applicable RT6 records will also be placed here.

The SQL CREATE statements are shown in Listing 11-5. As you'll notice, we've deliberately mixed the capitalization of the field names. Any field name appearing in all uppercase corresponds directly to the data of the same name in the original data set. Any place where we're modified the data, invented data, or inferred relationships that did not exist explicitly in the original data, we've followed the same convention as the rest of the book and used lowercase with underscores separating the English words. The biggest reason for this is to highlight at a glance the origin of the two distinct kinds of data. Assuming that you'll be importing new sets of data into your new geocoder once it's done, preserving the field names and the ID numbers of the original data set will allow for simpler updating without needing to erase and restart each time.

Listing 11-5. *SQL CREATE Statements for the TIGER-Based US Geocoder*

```
CREATE TABLE places (
  place_id bigint(20) NOT NULL default '0',
  state_fips char(2) NOT NULL default '',
  county_fips char(3) NOT NULL default '',
  place_fips varchar(5) NOT NULL default '',
  state_name varchar(60) NOT NULL default '',
  county_name varchar(30) NOT NULL default '',
  place_name varchar(60) NOT NULL default '',
  PRIMARY KEY  (place_id),
  KEY state_fips (state_fips,county_fips,place_fips)
) ENGINE=MyISAM;

CREATE TABLE street_names (
  uid int(11) NOT NULL auto_increment,
  TLID int(11) NOT NULL default '0',
  place_id bigint(20) NOT NULL default '0',
  CFCC char(3) NOT NULL default '',
  DIR_PREFIX char(2) NOT NULL default '',
  NAME varchar(30) NOT NULL default '',
  TYPE varchar(4) NOT NULL default '',
  DIR_SUFFIX char(2) NOT NULL default '',
  PRIMARY KEY  (uid),
  KEY TLID (TLID,NAME)
) ENGINE=MyISAM;

CREATE TABLE address_ranges (
  uid int(11) NOT NULL auto_increment,
  TLID int(11) NOT NULL default '0',
  RANGE_ID int(11) NOT NULL default '0',
  FIRST varchar(11) NOT NULL default '',
  LAST varchar(11) NOT NULL default '',
  PRIMARY KEY  (uid),
  KEY TLID (TLID,FIRST,LAST)
) ENGINE=MyISAM;

CREATE TABLE complete_chains (
  uid int(11) NOT NULL auto_increment,
  TLID int(11) NOT NULL default '0',
  SEQ int(11) NOT NULL default '0',
  LATITUDE double NOT NULL default '0',
  LONGITUDE double NOT NULL default '0',
  PRIMARY KEY  (uid),
  KEY SEQ (SEQ,LATITUDE,LONGITUDE)
) ENGINE=MyISAM;
```

Parsing and Importing the Data

Next, we need to determine how we are going to parse the data. The US Census Bureau has complicated our parsing a bit in order to save the nation's bandwidth. There is no need to include billions of commas or tabs in the data when you can simply define a parsing structure and concatenate the data into one long string. Chapter 6 of the official TIGER/Line documentation defines this structure for each type of record in the data set. Table 11-5 shows the simplified version we've created to aid in our automated parsing of the raw data.

■**Caution** Our dictionaries are not complete representations of each record type. We've omitted the record fields that we are not interested in to speed up the parsing when importing. Basically, we don't really care about anything more than the field name, starting character, and field width. We've left the human-readable names in for *your* convenience. We've also omitted many field definitions for information we're not interested in (like census tracts or school districts). You can download this set of dictionaries (as tab-delimited text) from http://googlemapsbook.com/chapter11/tiger_dicts.zip.

Table 11-5. *Data Dictionary for RT1*

Field Name	Start Char	Length	Description
TLID	6	10	TIGER/Line ID, Permanent 1-Cell Number
FEDIRP	18	2	Feature Direction, Prefix
FENAME	20	30	Feature Name
FETYPE	50	4	Feature Type
FEDIRS	54	2	Feature Direction, Suffix
CFCC	56	3	Census Feature Class Code
FRADDL	59	11	Start Address, Left
TOADDL	70	11	End Address, Left
FRADDR	81	11	Start Address, Right
TOADDR	92	11	End Address, Right
PLACEL	161	5	FIPS 55 Code (Place/CDP), 2000 Left
PLACER	166	5	FIPS 55 Code (Place/CDP), 2000 Right
FRLONG	191	10	Start Longitude
FRLAT	201	9	Start Latitude
TOLONG	210	10	End Longitude
TOLAT	220	9	End Latitude

Note that all of the following scripts are intended to be run in batch mode from the command line instead of via the browser. Importing and manipulation of the data will require considerable amounts of time and processing resources. If you are serious enough to need a national, street-level geocoder, then we expect that you at least have a shell account and access to the PHP command-line interface on your web server. We've optimized the following scripts to stay within the 8MB memory consumption limits of most hosts, but the trade-off is an increase in the time required to import the data. For example, importing the data for a single county (and there are hundreds per state) will take at least a few minutes. If you're just experimenting with these techniques, we suggest that you pick a single county (preferably your own, so the results are familiar), instead of working with a whole state or more.

With all of this in mind, let's get started. To parse these dictionaries as well as the raw data, we'll need a pair of helper functions, and you'll find them in Listing 11-6.

Listing 11-6. *Dictionary Helper Functions for Importing TIGER/Line Data*

```
function open_dict($type) {
    $handle = @fopen("$type.dict", "r");
    if ($handle) {
        $i = 0;
        $fields = array();
        while (!feof($handle)) {
            $buffer = fgets($handle, 1024);
            $line = explode("\t",$buffer);
            $fields[$i]['name'] = array_shift($line);
            $fields[$i]['beg'] = array_shift($line);
            $fields[$i]['length'] = array_shift($line);
            $fields[$i]['description'] = array_shift($line);
            $i++;
        } //while
        fclose($handle);
        return $fields;
    } else return false;
}

function parse_line($line_string,&$dict) {
    $line = array();
    if (is_array($dict))
        foreach ($dict AS $params)
            $line[$params['name']] = substr($line_string,➡
$params['beg']-1,$params['length']);
    return $line;
}
```

The first function, open_dict(), implements the process of opening the tab-delineated description of an arbitrary record type and creates a structure in memory used to parse individual records of that type. The second function, parse_line(), takes a dictionary structure and parses a single line of raw data into an associative array. If you need a refresher on either array_shift() or substr(), check out the official PHP documentation at http://www.php.net.

Now that we know where we are going (our SQL structure) and how to get there (our parsing helper functions), let's actually begin mining some data! Because of the design of our structure, there is no need to hold more than one type of record in memory at a time, and as such, we'll break the importer out into a separate listing for each record type. In reality, *all of these listings form a single script* (with the helpers in Listing 11-6 included at some point), but for the purposes of describing each stage of the process, it makes sense to break it into segments. Listing 11-7 covers the importing of the RT1 data file.

Listing 11-7. *Importing RT1 Records*

```php
<?php
// This will take a considerable amount of time. 5-10 minutes PER county.
set_time_limit(0);

// Connect to the database
require($_SERVER['DOCUMENT_ROOT'] . '/db_credentials.php');
$conn = mysql_connect("localhost", $db_name, $db_pass);
mysql_select_db("googlemapsbook", $conn);

// Select the state and county we're interested in
$state = "06";
$county = "075";

// Open the RT1 Dictionary file
$rt1_dict = open_dict("rt1");

// Open the RT1 Data file
$handle = @fopen("./data/TGR$state$county.RT1", "r");
$tlids = array();
if ($handle) {
    while (!feof($handle)) {
        // Grab a line from the text file and parse it into an associative array.
        $buffer = fgets($handle, 4096);
        $line = parse_line($buffer,$rt1_dict);

        // Trim up the information, while making global variables
        while(list($key, $value) = each($line)) { ${$key} = trim($value); }

        // We're not interested in the line of data in the following cases:
        // 1. Its CFCC type is not part of group A
        if (substr($CFCC,0,1) !== 'A') continue;

        // 2. There are no addresses for either side of the street
        if ($FRADDL == '' && $FRADDR == '') continue;

        // 3. If no city is associated with the road, it'll be hard to identify
        if ($PLACEL == '' && $PLACER == '') continue;

        // The latitude and longitudes are all to 6 decimal places
        $FRLAT = substr($FRLAT,0,strlen($FRLAT)-6).'.'.substr($FRLAT,➥
 strlen($FRLAT)-6,6);
        $FRLONG = substr($FRLONG,0,strlen($FRLONG)-6).'.'.substr($FRLONG,➥
 strlen($FRLONG)-6,6);
        $TOLAT = substr($TOLAT,0,strlen($TOLAT)-6).'.'.substr($TOLAT,➥
 strlen($TOLAT)-6,6);
        $TOLONG = substr($TOLONG,0,strlen($TOLONG)-6).'.'.substr($TOLONG,➥
 strlen($TOLONG)-6,6);
```

```php
            // Decide if this is a boundary of a place
            $places = array();
            if ($PLACEL != $PLACER) {
                if ($PLACEL != "") $places[] = $PLACEL;
                if ($PLACER != "") $places[] = $PLACER;
            } else {
                $places[] = $PLACEL;
            }

            // Build the queries for this TIGER/Line Item (TLID)
            $queries = array();
            foreach ($places AS $place_fips)
                $queries[] = "INSERT INTO street_names➥
(TLID,place_id,CFCC,DIR_PREFIX,NAME,TYPE,DIR_SUFFIX)➥
VALUES ('$TLID','$state$county$place_fips','$CFCC',➥
 '$FEDIRP','$FENAME','$FETYPE','$FEDIRS')";
            if ($FRADDR != '') $queries[] = "INSERT INTO address_ranges➥
 (TLID,RANGE_ID,FIRST,LAST) VALUES ('$TLID',-1,'$FRADDR','$TOADDR')";
            if ($FRADDL != '') $queries[] = "INSERT INTO address_ranges➥
 (TLID,RANGE_ID,FIRST,LAST) VALUES ('$TLID',-2,'$FRADDL','$TOADDL')";
            $queries[] = "INSERT INTO complete_chains (TLID,SEQ,LATITUDE,LONGITUDE)➥
VALUES ('$TLID',0,'$FRLAT','$FRLONG')";
            $queries[] = "INSERT INTO complete_chains (TLID,SEQ,LATITUDE,LONGITUDE)➥
VALUES ('$TLID',5000,'$TOLAT','$TOLONG')";

            foreach($queries AS $query)
                if (!mysql_query($query))
                    echo "Query Failed: $query (".mysql_error().")\n";

            // Hold on to the TLID for processing other record types
            $tlids[] = $TLID;
        }
}
fclose($handle);
unset($rt1_dict);
?>
```

Aside from opening files and the database, calling our helper functions, and creating named temporary variables, three key things are happening here:

- We're selectively ignoring lines that are irrelevant to geocoding. Structures like bridges, rivers, and train tracks, plus items like parks, bodies of water, and landmarks, are all listed in the RT1 file along with the roads. We can identify the kind of thing by looking at the CFCC field and using only items that start with an *A*. In addition to using only roads, we don't care about roads that have no address ranges (how would you identify a single point on the line?) or that are not part of a populated area like a city or a town.

- The latitude and longitude need to have their decimal symbols reinserted (they were also stripped to save bandwidth). The documentation states that all coordinates are listed to six decimal places, hence the math used in the substr() gymnastics in the middle of Listing 11-7.
- We're splitting up the data as we described for our schema. For simplicity, we remove the left and right side awareness for the address ranges and list the same segment twice if it is a boundary between two populated places. We also place the starting latitude and longitude pair into the `complete_chains` table with a sequence number of 1 and the end pair with a sequence number of 5000. We do this because the documentation states that no chain will have more than 4999 latitude and longitude pairs, and we haven't yet parsed the RT2 records to determine how many other points there may be.

■ **Caution** The TIGER/Line documentation is very careful to state that just because the latitude and longitude data is listed to six decimal places does not mean that it is *accurate* to six decimal places. In some cases, it may be, but in others it may also be third- or fourth-generation interpolated data.

This brings us nicely to parsing of the RT2 records. Listing 11-8 shows the code that follows the parsing of RT1 inline in our script.

Listing 11-8. *Parsing for RT2 Records*

```
// Open the RT2 Dictionary file
$rt2_dict = open_dict("rt2");

// Open the RT2 Data file
$handle = @fopen("./data/TGR$state$county.RT2", "r");
if ($handle) {
    while (!feof($handle)) {
        // Grab a line from the text file and parse it into an associative array.
        $buffer = fgets($handle, 4096);
        $line = parse_line($buffer,$rt2_dict);

        // Trim up the information, while making global variables
        while(list($key, $value) = each($line)) { ${$key} = trim($value); }

        // Did we import this TLID for record type 1?
        if (!in_array($TLID,$tlids)) continue;

        // Loop through the ten points, looking for one that is 0,0
        $i=1;
        $query = "INSERT INTO complete_chains (TLID,SEQ,LATITUDE,LONGITUDE)➥
 VALUES ";
        $values = array();
        while(${"LONG$i"} != 0 && ${"LAT$i"} != 0 && $i<11) {
```

```
            $LAT = ${"LAT$i"}; $LONG = ${"LONG$i"}; // convenience
            $LAT = substr($LAT,0,strlen($LAT)-6).'.'.substr($LAT,strlen($LAT)-6,6);
            $LONG = substr($LONG,0,strlen($LONG)-6).'.'.substr($LONG,➥
  strlen($LONG)-6,6);
            $SEQ = $RTSQ.str_pad($i,2,"0",STR_PAD_LEFT);
            $values[] = "('$TLID','$SEQ','$LAT','$LONG')";
            $i++;
        }

        // Use a multi-row insert to save time and server resources.
        $query = $query.implode(", ",$values).";";
        if (!mysql_query($query))
            echo "Query Failed: $query (".mysql_error().")\n";
    }
}
fclose($handle);
unset($rt2_dict);
```

Basically, we're just adding records to the complete_chains table for any TLID that we deemed important while we were parsing the RT1 records. Each RT2 record has up to ten additional interior points, and we simply keep going until we get to a pair that is listed as all zeros. Technically, the point corresponding to this special case is a valid point on the surface of the earth, but it's outside the borders of the United States, so we'll ignore this technicality.

Lastly, we need to determine the city and town names where these streets reside. For this, we'll parse the RTC file, as shown in Listing 11-9.

Listing 11-9. *Converting the RTC Records into Place Names*

```
// Open the RTC Dictionary file
$rtc_dict = open_dict("rtc");

// Open the RTC Data file
$handle = @fopen("./data/TGR$state$county.RTC", "r");
$place_ids = array();
if ($handle) {
    while (!feof($handle)) {
        // Grab a line from the text file and parse it into an associative array.
        $buffer = fgets($handle, 4096);
        $line = parse_line($buffer,$rtc_dict);

        // Trim up the information, while making global variables
        while(list($key, $value) = each($line)) { ${$key} = trim($value); }
        $place_id = "$state$county$FIPS";

        // If the FIPS 55 Code is blank or the FIPS Type
        if ($FIPS == "") continue;
        if ($FIPSTYPE != "C") continue;
        if (in_array($place_id,$place_ids)) continue;
        $place_ids[] = $place_id;
```

```
          // All looks good. Insert into places
          $query = "INSERT INTO places (place_id,state_fips,county_fips,➥
place_fips,state_name,county_name,place_name) VALUES➥
('$place_id','$state','$county','$FIPS','California','San Francisco','$NAME')";
          if (!mysql_query($query))
              echo "Query Failed: $query (".mysql_error().")\n";
     }
}
unset($rtc_dict);
fclose($handle);
```

Here, we're looking for two very simple things: the FIPS 55 code must be present, and the FIPS type must begin with *C*. If these two things are true, then the name at the end of the line should be imported into the places database table.

For the sake of brevity, we've omitted the sample code for importing alternative spellings and names for the streets, as well as importing additional address ranges. We've accounted for them in our data structures, as well as the REST service we're about to design, and we'll give you a couple hints about how you could add this easily into your own geocoder.

- For the alternative names, the basic idea is to simply keep doing more of the same parsing techniques while using the RT4 and RT5 records. For each entry in RT4 with a TLID for a record we have kept, look up the corresponding FEAT records in RT5. When inserting, simply copy the place_id from the existing record with the same TLID and replace the street name details with the new information.

- Alternative address ranges are even easier. Simply parse the RT6 file looking for matching TLID values and insert those address ranges into the address_ranges table.

Building a Geocoding Service

Now we finally get to the fun stuff: the geocoder itself. The basic idea of our geocoder will be that we are given a state, a city, a street name, and an address number for which we try to return a corresponding latitude and longitude. As a REST service, our script will expect a format like this:

```
http://googlemapsbook.com/chapter11/tiger_lookup.php?state=California&city=
San+Francisco&street=Dolores&number=140
```

When we're finished, our service for this address should return something like this:

```
<?xml version="1.0" encoding="UTF-8"?>
<ResultSet>
    <Result>
        <Latitude>37.767869</Latitude>
        <Longitude>-122.426693</Longitude>
    </Result>
</ResultSet>
```

■**Note** We've chosen this particular address because we have "street truth" data for it. For testing, we selected an address at random and had a friend of ours use his GPS device to get us a precise latitude and longitude reading. The most accurate information we have for this address is N 37.767367, W 122.426067. As you will see, the geocoder we're about to build has reasonable accuracy (to three decimal places in this example).

To achieve this, we'll start by looking up the correct `place_id` from the `places` table, and use that to limit the scope of our search. We'll then search for the street name in the `street_names` table. This should give us a `TLID` that we can use to get all of the corresponding address ranges for that street. Once we pick the correct range, we'll have a single, precise `TLID` to use to look up in the `complete_chains` table. We'll grab all of the latitude and longitude points for the segment and interpolate a single point on the line that represents the address requested. Seems simple, eh? As you'll see in Listing 11-10, the devil is in the details.

Listing 11-10. *Preliminary USA Geocoder Based on TIGER/Line Data*

```php
<?php
// Start our response
header('Content-type: text/xml');
echo '<?xml version="1.0" encoding="UTF-8"?><ResultSet>';

// Clean up the input
foreach ($_REQUEST AS $key=>$value) {
    $key = strtolower($key);
    if (in_array($key,array("state","city","street","number"))) {
        $value = trim($value);
        $value = preg_replace("/[^a-z0-9\s\.]/i","",$value);
        $value = ucwords($value);
        ${$key} = $value; // make it into a named global variable.
    }
}

// Connect to the database
require($_SERVER['DOCUMENT_ROOT'] . '/db_credentials.php');
$conn = mysql_connect("localhost", $db_name, $db_pass);
mysql_select_db("googlemapsbook", $conn);

// Try for an exact match on the city and state names
$query = "SELECT * FROM places WHERE state_name='$state' AND place_name='$city'";
$result = mysql_query($query);
if (mysql_num_rows($result) == 0) {
    // Oh well, look up the state and fuzzy match the city name
    $result = mysql_query("SELECT * FROM places WHERE state_name = '$state'");
```

```
    if (!$result || mysql_num_rows($result) == 0)
        die("<error>That state is not yet supported.</error></ResultSet>");
    $cities = array();
    for ($i=0; $i<mysql_num_rows($result); $i++) {
        $row = mysql_fetch_array($result,MYSQL_ASSOC);
        $cities['place_id'][$i] = $row['place_id'];
        $cities['accuracy'][$i] = levenshtein($row['place_name'],$city);
    }

    // Sort them by "closeness" to the requested city name and take the top one
    array_multisort($cities['accuracy'],SORT_ASC,$cities['place_id']);
    $place_id = $cities['place_id'][0];
} else {
    // We found it. Grab the place_id and continue on to phase two!
    $row = mysql_fetch_array($result,MYSQL_ASSOC);
    $place_id = $row['place_id'];
}

// Search for the street name and address
$number = (int)$number;
$query = "SELECT sn.TLID, FIRST, LAST, ($number-FIRST) AS diff
    FROM street_names AS sn, address_ranges AS ar
    WHERE ar.TLID = sn.TLID
    AND sn.place_id = $place_id
    AND sn.NAME = '$street'
    AND '$number' BETWEEN ar.FIRST AND ar.LAST
    ORDER BY diff
    LIMIT 0,1";
$result = mysql_query($query);
if (mysql_num_rows($result) == 1) $row = mysql_fetch_array($result,MYSQL_ASSOC);
else die("<Error>No Matches</Error></ResultSet>");

// We should now have a single TLID, grab all of the points in the chain
$tlid = $row['TLID'];
$first_address = $row['FIRST'];
$last_address = $row['LAST'];
$query = "SELECT LATITUDE,LONGITUDE
    FROM complete_chains
    WHERE TLID='$tlid' ORDER BY SEQ";
$result = mysql_query($query);
$points = array();
for ($i=0; $i<mysql_num_rows($result); $i++) {
    $points[] = mysql_fetch_array($result,MYSQL_ASSOC);
}

// Compute the lengths of all of the segments in the chain
$segment_lengths = array();
$num_segments = count($points)-1;
```

```php
for($i=0; $i<$num_segments; $i++) {
    $segment_lengths[] = line_length($points[$i],$points[$i+1]);
}
$total_length = array_sum($segment_lengths);

// Avoid divide by zero problems
if ($total_length == 0) {
    // The distances are too small to compute, return the start of the street.
    die("<Result>
        <Latitude>{$points[0]['LATITUDE']}</Latitude>
        <Longitude>{$points[0]['LONGITUDE']}</Longitude>
        </Result></ResultSet>");
}


// Compute how far along the chain our address is
$address_position = abs($number - $last_address);
$num_addresses = abs($first_address - $last_address);
$distance_along_line = $address_position/$num_addresses*$total_length;

// Figure out which segment our address is in, and where it is
$travel_distance = 0;
for($i=0; $i<$num_segments; $i++) {
    $bottom_address = $first_address + ($travel_distance / $total_length *➥
 $num_addresses);
    $travel_distance += $segment_lengths[$i];
    if ($travel_distance > $distance_along_line) {
        // We've found our segment, do the final computations
        $top_address = $first_address + ($travel_distance / $total_length *➥
 $num_addresses);

        // Determine how far along this segment our address is
        $seg_addr_total = abs($top_address - $bottom_address);
        $addr_position = abs($number - $bottom_address)/$seg_addr_total;
        $segment_delta = $segment_lengths[$i]*$addr_position;

        // Determine the angle of the segment
        $delta_x = abs($points[$i]['LATITUDE'] - $points[$i+1]['LATITUDE']);
        $delta_y = abs($points[$i]['LONGITUDE'] - $points[$i+1]['LONGITUDE']);
        $angle = atan($delta_y/$delta_x);

        // And you thought you'd never use trig again!
        $x = $segment_delta*cos($angle);
        $y = $segment_delta*sin($angle);
    }
}
```

```
echo("<Result>
    <Latitude>$x</Latitude>
    <Longitude>$y</Longitude>
    </Result>");

// Close our response
echo "</ResultSet>";

function line_length($point1,$point2) {
    $delta_x = abs($point1['LATITUDE'] - $point2['LATITUDE']);
    $delta_y = abs($point1['LONGITUDE'] - $point2['LONGITUDE']);
    $segment_length = sqrt($delta_x^2 + $delta_y^2);
    return $segment_length;
}

?>
```

We begin by trying to get an exact string match on the state and place name to determine the place_id. In the event that this fails, we try to get an exact match on the state name and a fuzzy match on the place name. For the fuzzy match, we grab all of the places in a given state, and then compute the Levenshtein distance between our input string and the name of the place. Once we have that, we merely sort the results and take the smallest difference as the correct place. You could also avoid sorting with a few helper variables to track the smallest distance found so far.

Note The Levenshtein distance is the number of characters that need to be added, subtracted, or changed to get from one string to another; for example, Levenshtein("cat","car") = 1 and Levenshtein ("cat","dog") = 3. You could also use the soundex() or metaphone() functions in PHP instead of (or in conjunction with) Levenshtein() if you want to account for misspellings in a less rigid way.

Next, we use a fun little feature of MySQL: the BETWEEN clause in a query. We ask MySQL to find all of the road segments with our given street name and an address range that bounds our input address. We could make use of the fuzzy search on street names here, too; however, that would require precomputing the metaphone() or soundex(), storing it in the database, and comparing against that in the query.

At this point, we should have a single TLID. Using this information, we can get the latitude and longitude coordinates of all points on the segment from the complete_chains table.

Now that we know exactly what we're dealing with, we can start calculating the information we want. We start by using Pythagoras' theorem to compute the length of each line segment in the network chain. This simple equation is implemented in the helper function at the end of Listing 11-10, and represented by l_1, l_2, and l_3 in Figure 11-3.

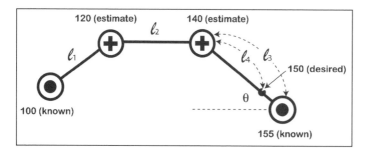

Figure 11-3. *Example of road segment calculations*

However, we immediately run into a problem: very short line segments return a length of zero due to precision problems. To avoid this, and thus increase the accuracy, you might try converting the latitude and longitudes into feet or meters before making your computations, but that conversion process also has its problems. Therefore, if we compute the total length of the chain to be zero, then we don't have much choice other than to return one of the endpoints of the line as our answer. Doing so is probably at least as accurate as geocoding based on ZIP codes, but doesn't require the users to know the ZIP code of the point they are interested in, and works for places where street numbers exist, but there is no postal service.

If we can, we next compute the approximate location of our address (150 in Figure 11-3) along the overall segment. To do this, we assume the addresses are evenly distributed, and calculate our address as a percentage of the total number of addresses and multiply by the total line length.

■**Caution** For the sake of simplicity, we're making the incorrect assumption that the last address is always larger than the first address. In practice, you'll need to account for this.

So in which segment of the line is our address located? To find out, we walk the line starting from our first endpoint, using the lengths of line segments we calculated earlier, and keep going until we pass our address. This gives us the top endpoint, and we simply take the one before it for our bottom endpoint.

Once we know which two `complete_chains` points we need to use for our calculations, we again determine (as a percentage) how far along the segment our address is. Using this new length (l_4 in Figure 11-3) and the trigonometric equations we discussed in the previous chapter, we compute the angle of the segment and the position of our address. The rest is merely outputting the proper XML for our REST service's response.

And there you have a geocoding web service. Now we need to point out some limitations you'll want to overcome before using this code in production. We've talked about things like misspellings in the street, state, and place names, as well as division by zero when the segments are very short. Here are a few more issues that we've encountered.

Address ranges that are not integers (contain alphabet characters): The TIGER/Line documentation suggests that this is a possibility that will break our SQL BETWEEN optimization. You could replace the numeric comparison in the SQL with a string-based one. This will mean that an address like 1100 will match ranges like 10–20 and 10000–50000. This is due to the natural language comparison used in string comparison. BETWEEN will still help you get a small subset of the database, but you'll need to do more work in PHP to determine which result is the best match for your query.

Street type or direction separation: We are doing no work to separate out the street type (road, avenue, boulevard, and so on) or the direction (NE, SW, and so on) in our users' input. The street type and direction are stored separately in the database and would help in narrowing down the possible address ranges considerably if we used them. The TIGER/ Line documentation enumerates each possible value for these fields, so using them is a matter of finding them in your user's input. You could ask for each part separately, as we have done with the number and street name, or you could use regular expressions, heuristics, and brute force to split a user's string into components. Google's geocoder goes to this effort to great success. It's not trivial, but might be well worth the effort.

Address spacing: We've assumed that all addresses are evenly spaced along our line segment. Since we have the addresses for only the endpoints, we have no idea which addresses actually exist. There might be as few as two actual addresses on the line, where for a range like 100–150, we are assuming there are 50. This means that simply because we are able to compute where an address *would* be, we have no idea if it is actually there.

Summary

Creating a robust geocoder is a daunting task, and could be the topic of an entire book. Offering it as a service to the general public involves significant bandwidth requirements, severe uptime expectations, and some pretty well-established competition (including Google!). However, if you're simply looking for an alternative to paying per lookup, or you've found some source of data that no one has turned into a service yet, then it's probably worth your time to build one. The techniques used for interpolating an address based on a range and a multipoint line, as well as finding the closest matching postal code can be widely reused. Even some of the basic ideas for parsing will apply to a wide variety of sources. However, keep in mind that the TIGER/Line data is organized in a rare and strange way and is in no way a worldwide standard. That said, the TIGER/Line data is probably also the most complete single source of free information for the purposes of geocoding. The GML version of the Canadian Road Network File is a distant second.

If you've made it this far, then congratulate yourself. There was some fairly involved mental lifting in this chapter, and in the many chapters that came before it. We hope that you put this information to great use and build some excellent new services for the rest of us map builders. If you do, please be sure to let us know, so that we can visit, and possibly promote it to other readers via our website.

PART 4

∎∎∎

Appendixes

APPENDIX A

■■■

Finding the Data You Want

In order to keep our book a reasonable length, we couldn't possibly use every neat idea or data source we found as an example. In Chapter 4, we used information from the Ron Jon Surf Shop chain of stores. We used the US Federal Communications Commission (FCC) Antenna Structure Registration (ASR) database in Chapters 5, 6, and 7. Also, in Chapter 5, we retrieved information on the locations of all of the capital cities in the world (through screen scraping) and used that data in our examples in Chapter 7. In Chapter 11, we used a wide range of street and address data from the US Census Bureau's TIGER/Line data set. There is much more interesting information contained in the TIGER/Line data than roads and geocoding, and we'll touch on that in this appendix.

This appendix contains some of the other interesting sources of data we found while researching this book, as well as some lessons we learned while hunting them down. We hope that this compilation will inspire you to take your new (or at least newly refined) skills and build something exciting and unique. At the very least, these links will give you more interesting data to experiment with while you wait for that killer idea to arrive.

You might consider this the exercises section of a textbook, or a problem set for you academics out there. Regardless, please drop us a line if you use this information in a map, as we would love to see what you've come up with.

Knowing What to Look For: Search Tips

We covered screen scraping at the end of Chapter 5, but we didn't discuss how to actually find the data you want to scrape or otherwise acquire. Your Googling skills are probably excellent, so we'll cover just a few tips we learned during our own research here.

Finding the Information

The data you're typically most interested in is a precompiled list of addresses or latitude/longitude points for some topic. Finding these types of lists can be tricky, and you have to ask yourself, "Besides my idea, does it make sense for anyone to have ever compiled a list like this?" If the answer is no, then don't spend too long looking for a single list, and instead focus on finding the precursor information that will help you build the list yourself.

An example would be a list of all of the veterinary clinics in Canada. You probably won't find such a list precompiled from a single source. However, you could use the address data in a phone book to geocode this kind of information, giving you the list you need. Another problem is that you probably won't find a single phone book for all of the regions in Canada, and will instead need to assemble the data from various online and CD resources. It's an involved job, but certainly not an impossible one.

Additionally, if you can find whole catalogs of data, they can be both a great source of information for an idea you have, as well as a source of inspiration for expanding on your idea. One such catalog is available from the National Center for Atmospheric Research (NCAR). The wealth of data that is available from `http://dss.ucar.edu/datasets/` is huge, though some of it will be hard to manipulate for amateurs, and other parts are not free. We present the link here as an example of yet another kind of resource you might be able to find.

Specifying Search Terms

Using the term "latitude" in your Google search terms isn't nearly as effective as using "longitude" or both. Why? Many things (such as temperature, rainfall, vegetation, and population) naturally change with your distance north or south of the equator, and people use the term *latitude* in their discussions of such phenomena.

Using "longitude" is much more likely to find you a *list* or a database of discrete points that you can use in a mapping application. This is, of course, an anecdotal assessment, but it turned out to be very consistent in our research. Another term we found useful was "locations database." Your mileage may vary.

Also, you'll probably need to keep your search fairly vague to find the information you want. This means a *lot* of results. We found that government or research-related sites were usually the best sources of information. This is typically because they are publicly funded and the raw data they collect is required to be released to support other research programs. This is definitely a Western point of view, and possibly a North American one, so again, your mileage may vary.

Watching for Errors

Lastly, as you no doubt have learned, you can't trust everything you find on the Internet. Most of the data you find will contain at least a few errors, even if they are just from the transcription process.

Sometimes, the data you find has been scraped from another source, and you'll get a much more accurate and complete set of information if you keep looking and find the original.

If accuracy is a concern, try to corroborate two sources of the same information. An example would be a list of capital cities for all of the countries of the world. Compare the latitude and longitude of the points for each city from each list, and question anything with a deviation in the first or second decimal place.

The Cat Came Back: Revisiting the TIGER/Line

The TIGER/Line data covered in depth in Chapter 11 is much more than just a compilation of roads and addresses. It's a reasonably complete database for all things related to mapping (in our case). For instance, we omitted some of the road segments in Chapter 11 because they either had no addresses or no name associated with them. However, if we pay careful attention to the CFCCs (Census Feature Class Codes), we find that TIGER gives us mappable information for everything from roads that are accessible only via an all-wheel-drive vehicle, to walking trails, to railroads and rail-transfer yards.

But wait, it gets better. There is also data on landmarks such as parks, churches, prisons, military installations, and hospitals. Table A-1 contains a list of the ones we thought would be most interesting, and page 3-25 in the official TIGER/Line documentation starts off nearly 20 pages of additional options.

Table A-1. *CFCCs for Other Interesting Data in the TIGER/Line Files*

CFCC	Description
A51	Vehicular trail; road passable only by four-wheel-drive vehicle; unseparated
A67	Toll booth barrier to travel
A71	Walkway or trail for pedestrians, usually unnamed
B11	Railroad main track, not in tunnel or underpassing
B14	Abandoned/inactive rail line with tracks present
B19	Railroad main track, bridge
B3*x*	Railroad yard (multiple subclasses exist)
C20	Power transmission line; major category used alone
D10	Military installation or reservation; major category used alone
D21	Apartment building or complex
D23	Trailer court or mobile home park
D24	Marina
D27	Hotel, motel, resort, spa, hostel, YMCA, or YWCA
D28	Campground
D31	Hospital, urgent care facility, or clinic
D33	Nursing home, retirement home, or home for the aged
D35	Orphanage
D36	Jail or detention center
D37	Federal penitentiary or state prison
D42	Convent or monastery
D43	Educational institution, including academy, school, college, and university
D44	Religious institution, including church, synagogue, seminary, temple, and mosque
D45	Museum, including visitor center, cultural center, and tourist attraction
D46	Community center
D47	Library
D51	Airport or airfield
D52	Train station including trolley and mass transit rail system
D53	Bus terminal
D54	Marine terminal
D61	Shopping center or major retail center

Continued

Table A-1 *(Continued)*

CFCC	Description
D64	Amusement center, including arena, auditorium, stadium, coliseum, race course, theme park, and shooting range
D71	Lookout tower
D72	Transmission tower, including cell, radio, and TV
D73	Water tower
D74	Lighthouse beacon
D78	Monument or memorial
D81	Golf course
D82	Cemetery
D83	National Park Service land
D84	National forest or other Federal land
D85	State or local park or forest
D86	Zoo
D87	Vineyard, winery, orchard, or other agricultural or horticultural establishment
D88	Landfill, incinerator, dump, spoil, or other location for refuse
E23	Island, identified by name
E27	Dam
F*xx*	Nonvisible boundaries, such as political divisions and property lines
H*xx*	Water-related polygon (lake), line (river), or point (small ponds)

In Chapter 11, we used mostly data from record type 1, and this is where you'll find all of the data (or at least the start of the data) for CFCCs in class A, B, or C. For the rest of the landmark features, you'll need to use record types 7, 8, and P. The parsing strategies in Chapter 11 should serve you well in extracting this data into a database for your own use, so if you don't care about building your own geocoder, you might still be interested in reading the first few parts of the chapter so you can get a better handle on how to extract this data.

Lastly, there is one more source of census-related data that we found (we're sure there are some we've missed). It's the summary files for the US 2000 census, located at http://www.census.gov/prod/cen2000/. These contain condensed information like population, number of houses per city, economic data, and other general demographics. They are undoubtedly easier to work with if all you're looking for are these simple statistics. The summary files won't help you find all of the zoos or lighthouses in the United States, but they'll tell you the number of people per house for a given city.

More on Airports

While we did find that the TIGER/Line CFCC D51 denotes an airfield or airport, the TIGER/Line covers only the United States; therefore, we have a few other sources of worldwide information to pass along for this category.

The Global Airport Database is a simple database listing nearly 10,000 airports (both large and small) from around the world. More important, it is explicitly *free*, just like the government data we've been primarily working with here. It can be found at `http://www.partow.net/miscellaneous/airportdatabase/`. It makes no claims to be complete, and we're not sure what the underlying source of the information is, so you might want to cross-reference this with the TIGER/Line data for points inside the United States.

Another interesting source of data related to the US airports can be found at the Federal Aviation Administration's site at `http://www.faa.gov/ATS/ata/ata100/120/stdatafiles.html`. The information here ranges from the polygons that define the airspace for each airport to the inter-airport routes that constitute the nation's highways in the sky.

The Government Standard: The Geonames Data

When various US government departments and agencies need to refer to geographic entities by name or location, they check the databases maintained by the US Board on Geographic Names. The US Board on Geographic Names is a federal body organized in 1890 and created in its present form by law in 1947. The Board's database provides a way to maintain a uniform geographic name usage throughout the US Federal Government. The Board comprises representatives of federal agencies concerned with geographic information, population, ecology, and management of public lands. These include, but are not limited, to the Federal Bureau of Investigation (FBI), Central Intelligence Agency (CIA), US Geological Survey (USGS), and US Census Bureau.

This database is very useful for mapping purposes, as it provides (among other things) latitudes and longitudes for many of the world's cities, along with population data. Like the TIGER/Line data, the US Board of Geographic Names data includes churches, schools, monuments, and landmarks. Unlike with the TIGER/Line data, many of these are located outside the United States.

We think this database would make a great cross-reference resource for data found in other places. For example, comparing a list of the locations for cities in Canada with one supplied by the Canadian government would likely weed out any strange anomalies.

The home page for the domestic database is located at `http://geonames.usgs.gov/`. The foreign data is available in raw downloadable form from `http://earth-info.nga.mil/gns/html/index.html`. The folks at `geonames.org` have gone a long way in converting this data into something you can use quite easily. They also seem to have found and integrated a few other sources of data, like postal codes for many European countries. They have even done some inspiring Google Maps version 2 mashups, such as the one of the world's most populated cities, found at `http://www.geonames.org/maps/cities.html`.

Shake, Rattle, and Roll: The NOAA Goldmine

While zooming around the satellite images in Google Maps and Google Earth, we occasionally spotted an active steam or smoke plume coming from a volcano (check out Hawaii's Kilauea), and that led us to hunt for a source of names and locations of current volcanoes. We found a database of more than 1500 worldwide volcanoes and volcano-related features from the National Geophysical Data Center (NGDC), which is part of the National Oceanographic and Atmospheric Administration (NOAA). Little did we know that this was just the tip of the iceberg of raw, map-oriented data that was available for free download and analysis.

The databases that are available from the various NOAA departments cover everything from volcanoes and earthquakes to hot springs, hurricanes, and hail. They even have a high-resolution data set for the elevation above sea level of each square kilometer of the world's land masses!

We won't talk about each individual data source since they are all fairly well documented. Instead, we'll simply provide a list of links for you to discover what we've uncovered. If you would like to avoid typing each link in to your browser, you can simply visit `http://googlemapsbook.com/appendixa/links.html` and browse from there instead. The first link in each list is the official starting point for the data from the NOAA. The rest are either maps we've found that are based on the same data (Google-based or otherwise) or data we've found for the same topic from other sources. You might want to use secondary sources of data for cross-referencing to weed out errors.

Volcanoes:

- `http://www.ngdc.noaa.gov/seg/hazard/volcano.shtml` (data)

- `http://www.volcano.si.edu/world/globallists.cfm` (data)

- `http://www.geocodezip.com/volcanoBrowser.asp` (map)

Earthquakes:

- `http://www.ngdc.noaa.gov/seg/hazard/earthqk.shtml` (data)

- `http://earthquake.usgs.gov/eqcenter/recenteqsww/catalogs/` (data)

Tsunami-related:

- `http://www.ngdc.noaa.gov/seg/hazard/tsu.shtml` (data)

- `http://map.ngdc.noaa.gov/website/seg/hazards/viewer.htm` (map)

Wildfires:

- `http://www.ngdc.noaa.gov/seg/hazard/wildfire.shtml` (data)

Hot springs:

- `http://www.ngdc.noaa.gov/seg/geotherm.shtml` (data)

- `http://www.acme.com/jef/hotsprings/` (map)

Hurricanes:

- `http://hurricane.csc.noaa.gov/hurricanes/download.html` (data)

- `http://www.nhc.noaa.gov/` (data)

- `http://www.hurricane.com/hurricane-season/hurricane-season-2005.html` (data)

- `http://flhurricane.com/cyclone/stormlist.php?year=2005` (data and maps)

Hail, tornados, and high winds:

- `http://www.spc.noaa.gov/archive/` (data)

- `http://www.ems.psu.edu/~nese/` (volatile link, research data up to 1995)

- `http://www.stormreportmap.com/` (map)

Geomagnetism and gravity:

- `http://www.ngdc.noaa.gov/seg/geomag/geomag.shtml` (data)

- `http://www.ngdc.noaa.gov/seg/gravity/welcome.shtml` (data)

Weather prediction and forecasting:

- `http://www.weather.gov/organization.php` (data)

- `http://www.spc.noaa.gov/` (data)

- `http://www.cpc.noaa.gov/` (data)

- `http://www.ncep.noaa.gov/` (data)

- `http://api.weatherbug.com/api/` (data)

Worldwide elevations:

- `http://www.ngdc.noaa.gov/mgg/topo/globe.html` (data)

Everything else:

- `http://www.ngdc.noaa.gov/ngdcinfo/onlineaccess.html` (data)

One idea we had was to use a variety of the destructive weather databases to create a historic map combining references to encyclopedic articles for many (or all) of the items on the map. It would take some research to find or write the articles and cross-reference the names, but it would be a neat map. This might make a good high-school multidisciplinary project—computer science, geography, and writing skills would all be required. You could even throw in some environmental sciences and math, too.

Another idea would be to combine the databases on tourist-attraction-style features like hot springs with some other travel-related material. You might even be able to make some money using AdSense or other contextual advertising programs.

For the Space Aficionado in You

We're geeks, we admit it. This led us to some interesting ideas for a satellite mashup of the earth's crater impacts, as well as more fiction-related maps like those of UFO/UAP sightings.

Crater Impacts

We managed to dig up some data that is absolutely screaming to be mashed up. In a sense, it already has been mashed, just not using Google's maps, but rather using the vaguely competing World Wind project. The World Wind project is an open source analogue of Google Earth. It takes satellite imagery and topographical data, and works them into a desktop application that allows the browser to "fly" around the maps. It was originally started as a project at the National Aeronautics and Space Administration (NASA) and has medium-resolution data (15 meters) driving it. For more information, visit `http://www.worldwindcentral.com`.

The data found at `http://www.worldwindcentral.com/hotspots/` is a lot like the Google sightseeing forum at `http://googlesightseeing.com/`. Visiting the craters category (`http://www.worldwindcentral.com/hotspots/index.php?cat=54`) yields a list of latitude and longitude coordinates, as well as a short blurb submitted by the poster. You might request permission to use this data as the starting point for your own visitor-annotated map using the Google Maps API.

UFO/UAP Sightings

Okay, so this is part science and part science fiction/wishful thinking, but we did consider taking the various unidentified flying object (UFO)—alternatively, unidentified aerial phenomena (UAP)—reporting sites and mashing them up using the Google Maps API.

Most of these reporting sites have at least a city and country associated with them. Using the US Board of Geographic Names data discussed earlier in this appendix, you could easily create a mashup of the individual sightings to at least the accuracy of a city/town. You might even create an "outbreak" style map that adds markers over time based on the sighting date(s). If you find enough data, using an overlay (see Chapters 7 and 9) might be interesting as well.

The first site we found was the Mutual UFO Network's site at `http://www.mufon.com`. Using the data search tool, we were able to find out about reports on a wide range of criteria. They seem to be limited to state/country location information, but often have images associated with them and long descriptions of the circumstances surrounding the event being reported.

The second was the obvious National UFO Reporting Center at `http://www.nuforc.org/`. This site has a lot of data (hundreds of items per month); however, most of it appears to be uncorroborated. And the site developers state that they have been experiencing problems with falsified reports coming from bored students. The data is also only for the United States apparently, though it does include date, time, city, state, type, duration, and eyewitness.

Another database we found was a result of looking for some data outside the United States that had city-level accuracy. The best (though not great) source we found covers a portion of the United Kingdom and seems to stop abruptly in May of 2003. We include it here since it does appear to have some interesting data that could be used to cross-reference the data we were not able to find, on the chance that you do. The link is `http://www.uform.org/sightings.htm`. Again, this link should be treated as volatile since the most recent data is several years old.

As you can see, there is a huge and wide-ranging array of information that can be used to make your mashup ideas a reality. This list is very US-centric, but it should give readers in (or building maps for) other countries a sense of where they might find the same data in their own governments. Many Western governments have a freedom of information policy that should allow you to obtain some or all of the data, even if they haven't yet made it available online. We wish you luck and success in all of your Google Maps endeavors, and hope that this list of resources can at least provide some inspiration.

■■■

Google Maps API

This appendix provides a detailed explanation of all the methods, classes, constants, and objects available through the Google Maps API as of version 2.58. For the most up-to-date list from the API, visit `http://www.google.com/apis/maps/documentation/reference.html`.

Note The class, method, and function arguments listed within square brackets are optional.

---

class GMap2

GMap2 (aka GMap) is the central class in the API. If you've loaded the API using the v=2 flag, you may also use GMap to refer to the GMap2 class; however, GMap is provided only for better backward-compatibility, and Google recommends that you modify your code to call GMap2 to conform with the most current API.

GMap2 Constructor

Constructor	Description
GMap2(containerDomElement, [opts])	Instantiating this object creates a new map inside the given DOM element, usually a DIV. The optional opts argument should be an instance of GMapOptions. If no map types are defined in opts, the default G_DEFAULT_MAP_TYPES set is used. Likewise, if no size is defined in opts, the size of the containerDomElement is used. If a size has been defined in opts, the containerDomElement will be resized accordingly.

GMap2 Methods

Configuration

Method	Returns	Description
enableDragging()		Enables the dragging of the map (dragging is enabled by default).
disableDragging()		Disables the dragging of the map.
draggingEnabled()	Boolean	Returns true if the map is draggable.
enableInfoWindow()		Enables the info window operations for the map (the info window is enabled by default).
disableInfoWindow()		Disables the opening of a new info window, and if one is already open, closes the existing one.
infoWindowEnabled()	Boolean	Returns true if the info window is enabled.
enableDoubleClickZoom()		Enables double-click to zoom. If enabled, double-clicking with the left mouse button will zoom in on the map, and double-clicking with the right mouse button will zoom out on the map. This overrides the initial functionality of double-clicking to recenter the map. It is disabled by default.
disableDoubleClickZoom()		Disables double-click to zoom. See enableDoubleClickZoom().
doubleClickZoomEnabled()	Boolean	Returns true if double-click to zoom is enabled; otherwise, returns false.
enableContinuousZoom()		Enables a smooth zooming transition, similar to the Google Earth desktop software, for Firefox and Internet Explorer browsers running under Windows. By default, this is disabled.
disableContinuousZoom()		Disables the smooth zooming transition. See enableContinuousZoom().
continuousZoomEnabled()	Boolean	Returns true if smooth zooming transitions are enabled; otherwise, returns false.

Controls

Method	Returns	Description
addControl(control, [position])		Adds the given GControl object to the map. The optional position argument should be an instance of the GControlPosition class and is used to determine the position of the control on the map. If no position is given, the position of the control will be determined by the GControl.getDefaultPosition() method. You can add only one instance of each control to a map.
removeControl(control)		Removes the control from the map.
getContainer()	Node	Returns the HTML DOM object that contains the map (usually a DIV). Called by GControl.initialize().

Map Types

Method	Returns	Description
getMapTypes()	Array of GMapType	Returns, as an array, all of the GMapType objects registered with the map.
getCurrentMapType()	GMapType	Returns the GMapType object for the currently selected map type.
setMapType(type)		Sets the map type for the map. The GMapType object for the map type must have been previously added using the addMapType() method.
addMapType(type)		Adds a new GMapType object to the map. See Chapter 9 and the GMapType class for more on how to define custom map types.
removeMapType(type)		Removes the GMapType object from the map.

Map State

Method	Returns	Description
isLoaded()	Boolean	Returns true if the map has been initialized by setCenter().
getCenter()	GLatLng	Returns the geographical coordinates for the center point of the current viewport.
getBounds()	GLatLngBounds	Returns the geographical boundary of the map represented by the visible viewport.
getBoundsZoomLevel(bounds)	Number	Returns the zoom level at which the given GLatLngBounds object will fit entirely in the viewport. The zoom level may vary depending on the active map type.
getSize()	GSize	Returns the size of the map viewport in pixels.
getZoom()	Number	Returns the current zoom level.

Map State Modifications

Method	Returns	Description
setCenter(center, [zoom], [type])		Loads the map centered on the given GLatLng with an optional zoom level as an integer and an instance of a GMapType object. The map type must have been previously added using the addMapType() method and be available in the allowed list defined in the constructor. This method must always be called first after instantiation of the GMap object to set the initial state of the map.
panTo(center)		Changes the center location of the map. If the given GLatLng is already visible elsewhere in the viewport, the pan will be animated as a smooth slide.
panBy(distance)		Starts a pan animation, sliding the map by the given GSize object.
panDirection(dx, dy)		Starts a pan animation, sliding the map by half the width and height in the given direction. +1 is right and down, and -1 is left and up.

Method	Returns	Description
setZoom(level)		Changes the zoom level of the map.
zoomIn()		Increases the zoom level by one. Larger zoom levels are closer to the earth's surface.
zoomOut()		Decreases the zoom level by one. Smaller zoom levels are farther away from the earth's surface.
savePosition()		Tells the map to internally store the current map position and zoom level for later retrieval using returnToSavedPosition().
returnToSavedPosition()		Restores the map position and zoom level saved by savePosition().
checkResize()		Notifies the map of a change of the size of its container. You must call this method if you change the size of the containing DOM element so that the map can adjust itself to fit the new size.

Overlays

Method	Returns	Description
addOverlay(overlay)		Adds a GOverlay object to the map.
removeOverlay(overlay)		Removes a GOverlay object from the map. The removeoverlay() event is triggered only if the GOverlay object existed on the map.
clearOverlays()		Removes all GOverlay objects from the map.
getPane(pane)	Node	Returns the DIV DOM element that holds the object in the given GMapPane layer.

Info Window

Method	Returns	Description
openInfoWindow (latlng, dom, [opts])		Opens an info window at the given GLatLng location. If the info window is not fully visible on the map, the map will pan to fit the entire window in the viewport. The content of the info window must be defined using a DOM node.
openInfoWindowHtml (latlng, html, [opts])		Opens an info window at the given GLatLng location. If the info window is not fully visible on the map, the map will pan to fit the entire window in the viewport. The content of the info window must be defined using an HTML string.
openInfoWindowTabs (latlng, tabs, [opts])		Opens a tabbed info window at the given GLatLng location. If the info window is not fully visible on the map, the map will pan to fit the entire window in the viewport. The content of the info window must be defined using a DOM node.
openInfoWindowTabsHtml (latlng, tabs, [opts])		Opens a tabbed info window at the given GLatLng location. If the info window is not fully visible on the map, the map will pan to fit the entire window in the viewport. The content of the info window must be defined using an HTML string.

Method	Returns	Description
showMapBlowup (latlng, [opts])		Opens an info window at the given GLatLng, which contains a close-up view on the map centered on the given GLatLng.
closeInfoWindow()		Closes the current info window.
getInfoWindow()	GInfoWindow	Returns the info window object of this map. If no info window exists, it is created but not displayed. enableInfoWindow() does not affect the result of getInfoWindow().

Coordinate Transformations

Method	Returns	Description
fromLatLngToDivPixel(latlng)	GPoint	Returns the GPoint pixel coordinates of the given GLatLng geographical location, relative to the DOM element that contains the draggable map.
fromDivPixelToLatLng(pixel)	GLatLng	Returns the GLatLng geographical coordinates of the given GPoint pixel coordinates, relative to the DOM element that contains the draggable map.
fromContainerPixelToLatLng(pixel)	GLatLng	Returns the GLatLng geographical coordinates of the given GPoint pixel coordinates, relative to the DOM element that contains the map on the page.

Events

Event	Arguments	Description
addmaptype	maptype	Fired when a map type is added to the map using addMapType().
removemaptype	maptype	Fired when a map type is removed from the map using removeMapType().
click	overlay, latlng	Fired when the map is clicked with the mouse. If the click is on a GOverlay object such as a marker, the overlay is passed to the event handler through the overlay argument and the overlay's click event is fired. If no overlay is clicked, the GLatLng location of the click is passed in the latlng argument.
movestart		Fired when the map tiles begin to move. This will fire when dragging the map with the mouse, in which case a dragstart is also fired, or by invoking the movement using one of the GMap methods.
move		Fired while the map is moving. This event may fire repeatedly as the map moves.
moveend		Fired when the map stops moving.
zoomend	oldLevel, newLevel	Fired when the map reaches a new zoom level.
maptypechanged		Fired when another map type is selected.
infowindowopen		Fired when the info window opens.

Event	Arguments	Description
infowindowclose		Fired when the info window closes. If a currently open info window is reopened at a different point using another call to openInfoWindow*(), then infowindowclose will fire first.
addoverlay	overlay	Fired when an overlay is added using addOverlay(). The overlay is passed to the event handler.
removeoverlay	overlay	Fired when a single overlay is removed by the method removeOverlay(). The overlay that was removed is passed as an argument to the event handler.
clearoverlays		Fired when all overlays are removed by clearOverlays().
mouseover	latlng	Fired when the mouse moves into the map from outside the map. A GLatLng location is passed to the event handler.
mouseout	latlng	Fired when the user moves the mouse off the map. A GLatLng location is passed to the event handler.
mousemove	latlng	Fired when the user moves the mouse inside the map. This event is repeatedly fired while the user moves around the map. A GLatLng location is passed to the event handler.
dragstart		Fired when the user starts dragging the map.
drag		Repeatedly fired while the user drags the map.
dragend		Fired when the user stops dragging the map.
load		Fired when everything on the map has loaded, with the exception of the image tiles, which load asynchronously.

class GMapOptions

The GMapOptions class, instantiated as an object literal, is used to provide optional arguments to the GMap class constructor.

GMapOptions Properties

Property	Type	Description
size	GSize	Sets the size of the map container. If the container is of a different size, the container will be resized to the given GSize. If no size is passed, the map will assume the current size of the container.
mapTypes	Array of GMapType	Array of GMapType constants to allow for the map. If no mapTypes are defined, the constant G_DEFAULT_MAP_TYPES is used. See also GMap2.addMapType().

enum GMapPane

As discussed in Chapter 9, the GMapPane constants define the various layers of the map used to place overlays and their complementary icons and shadows.

GMapPane Constants

Constant	Description
G_MAP_MAP_PANE	The bottom layer, directly on top of the map. Used to hold overlays such as polylines.
G_MAP_MARKER_SHADOW_PANE	The pane containing the shadow of the markers. Lies directly beneath the markers.
G_MAP_MARKER_PANE	The pane containing the markers.
G_MAP_FLOAT_SHADOW_PANE	The pane containing the shadow of the info window. It lies above the G_MAP_MARKER_PANE to allow the markers to appear in the shadow of the info window.
G_MAP_MARKER_MOUSE_TARGET_PANE	The pane that holds transparent objects that react to the DOM mouse events registered on the overlays. It lies above the G_MAP_FLOAT_SHADOW_PANE to allow all the markers on the map to be clickable, even if they lie in the shadow of the info window.
G_MAP_FLOAT_PANE	The topmost layer. This pane contains any overlays that appear above all others but under the controls, such as the info window.

class GKeyboardHandler

You can instantiate a GKeyboardHandler to add your own keyboard bindings to a map.

GKeyboardHandler Bindings

Key Action	Description
up, down, left, right	Continuously moves the map while the key is pressed. If two nonopposing keys are pressed simultaneously, the map will move diagonally.
page down, page up, home, end	Triggers an animated pan by three-quarters of the height or width in the corresponding direction.
+, -	Adjusts the zoom level of the map by one level closer (+) or farther away (-).

GKeyboardHandler Constructor

Constructor	Description
GKeyboardHandler(map)	Creates a keyboard event handler for the given map.

interface GOverlay

As discussed in detail in Chapters 7 and 9, the GOverlay interface is implemented by the GMarker, GPolyline, and GInfoWindow classes, as well as any custom overlays you create. The GOverlay instance must be attached to the map using the GMap2.addOverlay() method. Upon addition, the map will call the GOverlay.initialize() method. Whenever the map display changes, the map will call GOverlay.redraw().

GOverlay Constructor

Constructor	Description
GOverlay()	Creates the default implementation of the GOverlay methods and should be used when inheriting from the class.

GOverlay Static Method

Static Method	Returns	Description
getZIndex(latitude)	Number	Returns the CSS z-index value for the given latitude. By default, overlays that are farther south have higher z-index values, so that the overlays will appear stacked when close together.

GOverlay Abstract Methods

Method	Returns	Description
initialize(map)		Called by GMap2.addOverlay() so the overlay can draw itself into the various panes of the map.
remove()		Called by GMap2.removeOverlay() and GMap2.clearOverlays(). The overlay should use this method to remove itself from the map.
copy()	GOverlay	Returns an uninitialized copy of itself.
redraw(force)		Called when the map display changes. force will be true only if the zoom level or the pixel offset of the map view has changed.

class GInfoWindow

GInfoWindow is always created by the GMap or GMarker class and accessed by their methods.

GInfoWindow Methods

Method	Returns	Description
selectTab(index)		Selects the tab with the given index.
hide()		Makes the info window invisible but does not remove it from the map.
show()		Makes the info window visible if it's currently invisible.
isHidden()	Boolean	Returns true if the info window is hidden or closed.
reset(latlng, tabs, size, [offset], [selectedTab])		Resets the state of the info window to the given arguments. If the argument value is null, that item will maintain its current value.
getPoint()	GLatLng	Returns the geographical point at which the info window is anchored. The default info window points to this point, modulo the pixel offset.
getPixelOffset()	GSize	Returns the offset, in pixels, of the tip of the info window from the anchor point.
getSelectedTab()	Number	Returns the index of the selected tab. The first left-most tab is index 0.

GInfoWindow Event

Event	Arguments	Description
closeclick		Fired when the info window's close button (X) is clicked.

class GInfoWindowTab

Instances of GInfoWindowTab are passed as an array to the tabs argument of GMap2.openInfoWindowTabs(), GMap2.openInfoWindowTabsHtml(), GMarker.openInfoWindowTabs(), and GMarker.openInfoWindowTabsHtml().

GInfoWindowTab Constructor

Constructor	Description
GInfoWindowTab(label, content)	Creates a tab object that can be passed to the tabs argument for all openInfoWindowTabs*() methods. The label is the text that appears on the tab. The content can be either an HTML string or a DOM node, depending on which openInfoWindowTabs*() method you plan to use.

class GInfoWindowOptions

The GInfoWindowOptions class, instantiated as an object literal, is used to provide optional arguments for the GMap and GMarker methods: openInfoWindow(), openInfoWindowHtml(), openInfoWindowTabs(), openInfoWindowTabsHtml(), and showMapBlowup().

GInfoWindowOptions Properties

Property	Type	Description
selectedTab	Number	Sets the window to open at the given tab. The first leftmost tab is index 0. By default, the window will open on tab 0.
maxWidth	Number	Maximum width, in pixels, of the info window content.
onOpenFn	Function	Called after the info window has finished opening and the content is displayed.
onCloseFn	Function	Called when the info window has been closed.
zoomLevel	Number	Applies only when using showMapBlowup(). The zoom level of the blowup map in the info window.
mapType	GMapType	Applies only when using showMapBlowup(). The map type of the blowup map in the info window.

class GMarker

An instance of the GMarker class is used to mark a geographical location on a map. It implements the GOverlay interface and is added to the map using the GMap2.addOverlay() method.

GMarker Constructor

Constructor	Description
GMarker(latlng, [opts])	Creates a new marker at the given GLatLng with optional arguments specified by GMarkerOptions.

GMarker Methods

Method	Returns	Description
openInfoWindow (content, [opts])		Opens the info window over the icon of the marker. The content of the info window must be defined using a DOM node. Optional arguments are passed using the GInfoWindowOptions class.
openInfoWindowHtml (content, [opts])		Opens the info window over the icon of the marker. The content of the info window must be defined using a string of HTML. Optional arguments are passed using the GInfoWindowOptions class.
openInfoWindowTabs (tabs, [opts])		Opens the tabbed info window over the icon of the marker. The content of the info window must be defined as an array of GInfoWindowTab instances that contain the tab content as DOM nodes. Optional arguments are passed using the GInfoWindowOptions class.
openInfoWindowTabsHtml (tabs, [opts])		Opens the tabbed info window over the icon of the marker. The content of the info window must be defined as an array of GInfoWindowTab instances that contain the tab content as a string of HTML. Optional arguments are passed using the GInfoWindowOptions class.
showMapBlowup([opts])		Opens the info window over the icon of the marker. The content of the info window becomes a close-up of the area around the info window's anchor. Optional arguments are passed using the GInfoWindowOptions class.
getIcon()	GIcon	Returns the GIcon associated with this marker as defined in the constructor.
getPoint()	GLatLng	Returns the GLatLng geographical coordinates of the marker's anchor. The anchor is set by the constructor or modified by setPoint().
setPoint(latlng)		Sets the geographical coordinates of the marker's anchor to the given GLatLng instance.

GMarker Events

Event	Arguments	Description
click		Fired when the marker is clicked with the mouse. The GMap's click event will also fire with the marker passed as the overlay argument.
dblclick		Fired when the marker icon is double-clicked.
mousedown		Fired when the DOM mousedown event is fired on the marker icon.

Event	Arguments	Description
mouseup		Fired for the DOM mouseup on the marker.
mouseover		Fired when the mouse moves into the area of the marker icon.
mouseout		Fired when the mouse moves out of the area of the marker icon.
infowindowopen		Fired when the info window of the map is opened using one of the GMarker info window methods.
infowindowclose		Fired when the info window, opened using GMarker.OpenInfoWindow*(), is closed or if the info window is opened on another marker.
remove		Fired when the marker is removed from the map.

class GMarkerOptions

The GMarkerOptions class, instantiated as an object literal, is used to provide optional arguments for the GMarker class.

GMarkerOptions Properties

Property	Type	Description
icon	GIcon	An instance of the GIcon class. If not specified, G_DEFAULT_ICON is used.
clickable	Boolean	If set to false, the marker becomes inert and consumes fewer resources. Inert markers will not respond to any events. By default, this option is true and markers are clickable.
title	String	The title will appear as a tool tip on the marker, like the title attribute on HTML elements.

class GPolyline

If available, the GPolyline class draws a polyline on the map using the browser's built-in vector-drawing facilities. Otherwise, the polyline is drawn using an image from Google servers.

GPolyline Constructor

Constructor	Description
GPolyline(points, [color], [weight], [opacity])	Creates a polyline from the array of GLatLng instances. Optionally, the color of the line can be defined as a string in the hexadecimal format RRGGBB; the weight can be defined in pixels; and the opacity can be defined as a number between 0 and 1, where 0 is transparent and 1 is opaque.

GPolyline Methods

Method	Returns	Description
getVertexCount()	Number	Returns the number of vertices in the polyline.
getVertex(index)	GLatLng	Returns the vertex with the given index in the polyline starting at 0 for the first vertex.

GPolyline Event

Event	Arguments	Description
remove		Fired when the polyline is removed from the map.

class GIcon

The GIcon class specifies the image to display as the icon for the GMarker on the map. If no icon is specified, G_DEFAULT_ICON is used.

GIcon Constructor

Constructor	Description
GIcon([copy], [image])	Creates a new GIcon object. Existing GIcon's properties can be copied by passing the existing icon into the copy argument. The optional image argument can be used as a shortcut to the image property.

GIcon Constant

Constant	Description
G_DEFAULT_ICON	The default icon used by markers.

GIcon Properties

Property	Type	Description
image	String	URL for the foreground image.
shadow	String	URL for the shadow image.
iconSize	GSize	The pixel size of the foreground image.
shadowSize	GSize	The pixel size of the shadow image.
iconAnchor	GPoint	The pixel coordinates of the image's anchor relative to the top-left corner of the image.
infoWindowAnchor	GPoint	The pixel coordinates of the point where the info window will be anchored, relative to the top-left corner of the image.
printImage	String	URL of the foreground image used for printed maps. It must be the same size as the image property.
mozPrintImage	String	The URL of the foreground icon image used for printed maps in Firefox/Mozilla. It must be the same size as the image property.
printShadow	String	The URL of the shadow image used for printed maps. Most browsers can't accurately print PNG transparency, so this property should be a GIF.

Property	Type	Description
transparent	String	Used to represent the clickable part of the icon in Internet Explorer. This should be a URL to a 24-bit PNG version of the main icon image with 1% opacity and the same shape and size as the image property.
imageMap	Array of numbers	Used to represent the clickable part of the icon in browsers other than Internet Explorer. This should be an array of integers representing the X/Y coordinates of the clickable image area.

class GPoint

In version 1 of the API, a GPoint represented a geographical latitude and longitude. In version 2 of the API, a GPoint represents a point on the map by its *pixel coordinates*. Now, for geographical latitude and longitude, see the GLatLng class.

Unlike regular HTML DOM elements, the map coordinates increase to the left and down, so the X coordinate increases as objects are farther west, and the Y coordinate increases as objects are farther south.

Note Although the x and y properties are accessible and modifiable, Google recommends you always create a new GPoint instance and avoid modifying an existing one.

GPoint Constructor

Constructor	Description
GPoint(x, y)	Creates a GPoint object.

GPoint Properties

Property	Type	Description
x	Number	X coordinate, increases to the left.
y	Number	Y coordinate, increases downwards.

GPoint Methods

Method	Returns	Description
equals(other)	Boolean	Returns true if the other given GPoint has equal coordinates.
toString()	String	Returns a string that contains the X and Y coordinates, separated by a comma and surrounded by parentheses, in the form (x,y).

class GSize

A GSize is a width and height definition, in pixels, of a rectangular area on the map. Note that although the width and height properties are accessible and modifiable, Google recommends that you always create a new GSize instance and avoid modifying an existing one.

GSize Constructor

Constructor	Description
GSize(width, height)	Creates a GSize object.

GSize Properties

Property	Type	Description
width	Number	The width in pixels.
height	Number	The height in pixels.

GSize Methods

Method	Returns	Description
equals(other)	Boolean	Returns true if the other given GSize has exactly equal components.
toString()	String	Returns a string that contains the width and height coordinates, separated by a comma and surrounded by parentheses, in the form (*width*,*height*).

class GBounds

A GBounds instance represents a rectangular area of the map in pixel coordinates. The GLatLngBounds class represents a rectangle in geographical coordinates.

GBounds Constructor

Constructor	Description
GBounds(points)	Constructs a rectangle that contains all the given points in the points array.

GBounds Properties

Property	Type	Description
minX	Number	The X coordinate of the left edge of the rectangle.
minY	Number	The Y coordinate of the top edge of the rectangle.
maxX	Number	The X coordinate of the right edge of the rectangle.
maxY	Number	The Y coordinate of the bottom edge of the rectangle.

GBounds Methods

Method	Returns	Description
toString()	String	Returns a string containing the northwest and the southeast corners of the area separated by a comma, surrounded by parentheses, in the form (*nw*,*se*).
min()	GPoint	The point at the upper-left corner of the box.

Method	Returns	Description
max()	GPoint	The point at the lower-right corner of the box.
containsBounds(other)	Boolean	Returns true if the other GBounds is entirely contained in this GBounds.
extend(point)		Increases the size of the bounds so the given GPoint is also contained in the bounds.
intersection(other)	GBounds	Returns a new GBounds object that represents the overlapping portion of this and the given GBounds.

class GLatLng

A GLatLng instance represents a geographical longitude and latitude on the map projection.

Note Although longitude is representative of an X coordinate on a map, and latitude with the Y coordinate, Google has chosen to follow customary cartography terminology where the latitude coordinate is written first, followed by the longitude as represented in the GLatLng constructor arguments.

GLatLng Constructor

Constructor	Description
GLatLng(lat, lng, [unbounded])	Creates a new GLatLng instance. If the unbounded flag is true, the latitude and longitude will be used as passed. Otherwise, latitude will be restricted to between -90 degrees and +90 degrees, and longitude will be wrapped to lie between -180 degrees and +180 degrees.

GLatLng Methods

Method	Returns	Description
lat()	Number	Returns the latitude coordinate in degrees.
lng()	Number	Returns the longitude coordinate in degrees.
latRadians()	Number	Returns the latitude coordinate in radians, as a number between $-PI/2$ and $+PI/2$.
lngRadians()	Number	Returns the longitude coordinate in radians, as a number between $-PI$ and $+PI$.
equals(other)	Boolean	Returns true if the other GLatLng has equal components (within an internal round-off accuracy).
distanceFrom(other)	Number	Returns the distance, in meters, from this GLatLng to the other GLatLng. Google's API approximates the earth as a sphere, so the distance could be off by as much as 0.3%.
toUrlValue()	String	Returns a string representation of this point that can be used as a URL parameter value. The string is formatted with the latitude and the longitude in degrees rounded to six decimal digits, separated by a comma, without whitespace.

GLatLng Properties

There are a few GLatLng properties; however, they exist only for backward-compatibility with version 1 of the API. Therefore, we do not list them here. If you would like to reference them, see Google's online documentation at http://www.google.com/apis/maps/documentation/reference.html#GLatLng.

class GLatLngBounds

A GLatLngBounds instance represents a rectangle in geographical coordinates. The GBounds class represents a rectangle in pixel coordinates.

GLatLngBounds Constructor

Constructor	Description
GLatLngBounds([sw], [ne])	Creates a new instance of GLatLngBounds with a boundary defined by the southwest and northeast corners.

GLatLngBounds Methods

Method	Returns	Description
equals(other)	Boolean	Returns true if the other GLatLngBounds has equal components (within an internal round-off accuracy).
contains(latlng)	Boolean	Returns true if the geographical coordinates of the given GLatLng lie within the boundary.
intersects(other)	Boolean	Returns true if the given GLatLngBounds intersects this GLatLngBounds.
containsBounds(other)	Boolean	Returns true if the given GLatLngBounds is contained entirely within this GLatLngBounds.
extend(latlng)		Increases the size of the bounds so the given GLatLng is also contained in the bounds. When calculating the longitude change, the bounds will enlarged in the smaller of the two possible ways given the wrapping of the map. If both directions are equal, the bounds will extend at the eastern boundary.
getSouthWest()	GLatLng	Returns the latitude and longitude at the southwest corner of the rectangle.
getNorthEast()	GLatLng	Returns the latitude and longitude at the northeast corner of the rectangle.
toSpan()	GLatLng	Returns a GLatLng with latitude and longitude degrees representing the height and width, respectively.
isFullLat()	Boolean	Returns true if this boundary extends the full height of the map, from the south pole to the north pole.
isFullLng()	Boolean	Returns true if this boundary extends fully around the earth.
isEmpty()	Boolean	Returns true if this boundary is empty.
getCenter()	GLatLng	Returns the center point of the rectangle.

interface GControl

As discussed in Chapter 9, the GControl interface is implemented by all control objects, and implementations must be added to the maps using the GMap2.addControl() method.

GControl Constructor

Constructor	Description
GControl([printable], [selectable])	Creates the prototype instance for a new control class. If the printable flag is true, the control will appear when printed. Use the selectable argument to indicate if the control contains text that should be selectable.

GControl Methods

Method	Returns	Description
printable()	Boolean	Returns true to the map if the control should be printable; otherwise, returns false.
selectable()	Boolean	Returns true to the map if the control contains selectable text; otherwise, returns false.
initialize(map)	Node	Will be called by GMap2.addControl() so the control can initialize itself and attach itself to the map container.
getDefaultPosition()	GControlPosition	Returns to the map the GControlPosition representing where the control appears by default. This can be overridden by the second argument to GMap2.addControl().

class GControl

The following are existing instances of the GControl interface.

GControl Constructors

Constructor	Description
GSmallMapControl()	Creates a control with buttons to pan in four directions, and zoom in and zoom out.
GLargeMapControl()	Creates a control with buttons to pan in four directions, and zoom in and zoom out, and a zoom slider.
GSmallZoomControl()	Creates a control with buttons to zoom in and zoom out.
GScaleControl()	Creates a control that displays the map scale.
GMapTypeControl()	Creates a control with buttons to switch between map types.

class GControlPosition

The GControlPosition class describes the position of a control in the map container. A corner from one of the GControlAnchor constants and an offset relative to that anchor determine the position.

GControlPosition Constructor

Constructor	Description
GControlPosition(anchor, offset)	Creates a new control position.

enum GControlAnchor

The GControlAnchor constants are used to reference the position of a GControl within the map viewport. You will need these if you are creating your own control objects, as discussed in Chapter 9.

GControlAnchor Constants

Constant	Description
G_ANCHOR_TOP_RIGHT	Anchored in the top-right corner of the map.
G_ANCHOR_TOP_LEFT	Anchored in the top-left corner of the map.
G_ANCHOR_BOTTOM_RIGHT	Anchored in the bottom-right corner of the map.
G_ANCHOR_BOTTOM_LEFT	Anchored in the bottom-left corner of the map.

class GMapType

As discussed in Chapter 9, the GMapType is the grouping of a map projection and tile layers.

GMapType Constructor

Constructor	Description
GMapType(layers, projection, name, [opts])	Creates a new GMapType instance with the given layer array of GTileLayers, the given GProjection, a name for the map type control, and optional arguments from GMapTypeOptions.

GMapType Methods

Method	Returns	Description
getSpanZoomLevel (center, span, viewSize)	Number	Returns the zoom level at which the GLatLng span, centered on the GLatLng center, will fit in the GSize defined by viewSize.
getBoundsZoomLevel (latlngBounds, viewSize)		Returns the zoom level at which the GLatLngBounds will fit in the GSize defined by viewSize.
getName(short)	String	Returns the name of the map type. If short is true, the short name will be returned; otherwise, the full name will be returned.
getProjection()	GProjection	Returns the GProjection instance.
getTileSize()	Number	Returns the tile size in pixels. The tiles are assumed to be quadratic, and all tile layers have the same tile size.

Method	Returns	Description
getTileLayers()	Array of GTileLayer	Returns the array of tile layers.
getMinimumResolution ([latlng])	Number	Returns the lowest zoom level.
getMaximumResolution ([latlng])	Number	Returns the highest zoom level.
getTextColor()	String	Returns the color that should be used for text, such as the copyright, overlaid on the map.
getLinkColor()	String	Returns the color that should be used for a hyperlink overlaid on the map.
getErrorMessage()	String	Returns the error message to display on zoom level where this map type doesn't have any map tiles.
getCopyrights (bounds, zoom)	Array of strings	Returns the copyright messages appropriate for the given GLatLngBounds bounds at the given zoom level.
getUrlArg()	String	Returns a value that can be used as a URL parameter value to identify this map type in the current map view. Useful for identifying maps and returning to the same location via hyperlinks in web applications.

GMapType Constants

Constant	Description
G_NORMAL_MAP	The normal street map type.
G_SATELLITE_MAP	The Google Earth satellite images.
G_HYBRID_MAP	The transparent street maps over Google Earth satellite images.
G_DEFAULT_MAP_TYPES	An array of G_NORMAL_MAP, G_SATELLITE_MAP, and G_HYBRID_MAP.

GMapType Event

Event	Argument	Description
newcopyright	copyright	Fired when a new GCopyright instance is added to the GCopyrightCollection associated with one of the tile layers contained in the map type.

class GMapTypeOptions

The GMapTypeOptions class, instantiated as an object literal, is used to provide optional arguments for the GMapType constructor.

GMapTypeOptions Properties

Property	Type	Description
shortName	String	The short name that is returned from GMapType.getName(true). The default is the same as the name from the constructor.
urlArg	String	The URL argument that is returned from GMapType.getUrlArg(). The default is an empty string.
maxResolution	Number	The maximum zoom level. The default is the maximum from all tile layers.
minResolution	Number	The minimum zoom level. The default is the minimum from all tile layers.
tileSize	Number	The tile size for the tile layers. The default is 256.
textColor	String	The text color returned by GMapType.getTextColor(). The default is "black".
linkColor	String	The text color returned by GMapType.getLinkColor(). The default is "#7777cc".
errorMessage	String	The error message returned by GMapType.getErrorMessage(). The default is an empty string.

interface GTileLayer

As explained in Chapters 7 and 9, you use the GTileLayer interface to implement your own custom tile layers.

GTileLayer Constructor

Constructor	Description
GTileLayer(copyrights, minResolution, maxResolution)	Creates a new tile layer instance. The arguments for the constructor can be omitted if instantiated as a prototype for your custom tile layer. copyrights is an array of GCopyright objects. minResolution and maxResolution refer to the minimum and maximum zoom levels, respectively.

GTileLayer Methods

Method	Returns	Description
minResolution()	Number	Returns the lowest zoom level for the layer.
maxResolution()	Number	Returns the highest zoom level for the layer.
getTileUrl(tile, zoom)	String	Abstract, must be implemented in custom tile layers. Returns the URL of the map tile. tile is a GPoint representing the x and y tile index. zoom is the current zoom level of the map.
isPng()	Boolean	Abstract, must be implemented in custom tile layers. Returns true if the tiles are PNG images; otherwise, GIF is assumed.
getOpacity()	Number	Abstract, must be implemented in custom tile layers. Returns the layer opacity between 0 and 1, where 0 is transparent and 1 is opaque.

GTileLayer Event

Event	Argument	Description
newcopyright	copyright	Fired when a new GCopyright instance is added to the GCopyrightCollection of this tile layer.

class GCopyrightCollection

The GCopyrightCollect is a collection of GCopyright objects for the current tile layer(s).

GCopyrightCollection Constructor

Constructor	Description
GCopyrightCollection([prefix])	Creates a new copyright collection. If the prefix argument is defined, the copyright messages all share the same given prefix.

GCopyrightCollection Methods

Method	Returns	Description
addCopyright(copyright)		Adds the GCopyright object to the collection.
getCopyrights(bounds, zoom)	Array of strings	Returns all copyrights for the given GLatLng bounds at the given zoom level.
getCopyrightNotice(bounds, zoom)	String	Returns the prefix concatenated with all copyrights for the given GLatLng bounds at the given zoom level, separated by commas.

GCopyrightCollection Event

Event	Argument	Description
newcopyright	copyright	Fired when a new GCopyright is added to the GCopyrightCollection.

class GCopyright

The GCopyright class defines which copyright message applies to a boundary on the map, at a given zoom level.

GCopyright Constructor

Constructor	Description
GCopyright(id, bounds, minZoom, copyrightText)	Creates a new GCopyright object with the given id, the given GLatLng bounds, and the minimum zoom level with which the copyright applies.

GCopyright Properties

Property	Type	Description
id	Number	A unique identifier.
minZoom	Number	The lowest zoom level at which this information applies.
bounds	GLatLngBounds	The latitude and longitude boundary for the copyright.
text	String	The copyright message.

interface GProjection

As explained in Chapter 9, the GProjection interface is responsible for all the mathematical calculations related to placing objects on the map. The GMercatorProjection, for example, is used by all predefined map types and calculates geographical positions based on the Mercator mapping projection.

GProjection Methods

Method	Returns	Description
fromLatLngToPixel (latlng, zoom)	GPoint	Returns the map coordinates in pixels from the given GLatLng geographical coordinates and the given zoom level.
fromPixelToLatLng (point, zoom, [unbounded])	GLatLng	Returns the geographical coordinates for the given GPoint and the given zoom level. The unbounded flag, when true, prevents the geographical longitude coordinate from wrapping when beyond the -180 or +180 degrees meridian.
tileCheckRange (tile, zoom, tilesize)		Returns true if the index of the tile given in the tile GPoint is in a valid range for the map type and zoom level. If false is returned, the map will display an empty tile. In some cases where the map wraps past the meridian, you may modify the tile index to point to an existing tile.
getWrapWidth(zoom)		Returns the number of pixels after which the map repeats itself in the longitudinal direction. The default is Infinity, and the map will not repeat itself.

class GMercatorProjection

This GMercatorProjection class is an implementation of the GProjection interface and is used by all the predefined GMapType objects.

GMercatorProjection Constructor

Constructor	Description
GMercatorProjection(zoomlevels)	Creates a GProjection object based on the Mercator projection for the given number of zoom levels.

GMercatorProjection Methods

Method	Returns	Description
fromLatLngToPixel (latlng, zoom)	GPoint	See GProjection.
fromPixelToLatLng (pixel, zoom, [unbounded])	GLatLng	See GProjection.
checkTileRange (tile, zoom, tilesize)		See GProjection.
getWrapWidth(zoom)		See GProjection. Returns the width of the map for the entire earth, in pixels, for the given zoom level.

namespace GEvent

The GEvent namespace contains the methods you need to register and trigger event listeners on objects and DOM elements. The events defined by the Google Maps API are all custom events and are fired internally using GEvent.triggerEvent().

GEvent Static Methods

Static Method	Returns	Description
addListener (object, event, handler)	GEventListener	Registers an event handler for the event on the object. Returns the GEventListener handle that can be used to deregister the handler with GEvent.removeListener(). When referencing 'this' from within the supplied handler function, 'this' will refer to the JavaScript object supplied in the first argument.
addDomListener (dom, event, handler)	GEventListener	Registers an event handler for the event on the DOM object. Returns the GEventListener handle that can be used to deregister the handler with GEvent.removeListener(). When referencing 'this' from within the supplied handler function, 'this' will refer to the DOM object supplied in the first argument.
removeListener(handler)		Removes the handler. The handler must have been created using addListener() or addDomListener().
clearListeners (source, event)		Removes all handlers on the given source object or DOM, for the given event, that were registered using addListener() or addDomListener().
clearInstanceListeners (source)		Removes all handlers on the given object or DOM for all events that were registered using addListener() or addDomListener().
trigger (source, event, ...)		Fires the given event on the source object. Any additional arguments after the event are passed as arguments to the event handler functions.

Static Method	Returns	Description
bind(source, event, object, method)		Registers the specified method on the given object as the event handler for the custom event on the given source object. You can then use the trigger() method to execute the event.
bindDom(source, event, object, method)		Registers the specified method on the given object as the event handler for the custom event on the given source object. Unlike bind(), the source object must be an HTML DOM element. You can then use the trigger() method to execute the event.
callback(object, method)		Calls the given method on the given object.
callbackArgs (object, method, ...)		Calls the given method on the given object with the given arguments.

GEvent Event

Event	Argument	Description
clearlisteners	event	Fired for the object when clearListeners() or clearInstanceListeners() is called on that object.

class GEventListener

The GEventListener class is opaque. There are no methods or constructor. Instances of the GEventListener are returned only from GEvent.addListener() and GEvent.addDomListener(). Instances of GEventListener can also be passed back to GEvent.removeListener() to disable the listener.

namespace GXmlHttp

The GXmlHttp namespace provides a browser-agnostic factory method to create an XmlHttpRequest (Ajax) object.

GXmlHttp Static Method

Static Method	Returns	Description
create()	GXmlHttp	Factory to create a new instance of XmlHttpRequest.

namespace GXml

The GXml namespace provides browser-agnostic methods to handle XML. The methods will function correctly only in browsers that natively support XML.

GXml Static Methods

Static Method	Returns	Description
parse(xmlString)	Node	Parses the given XML string into a DOM representation. In the event that the browser doesn't support XML, the method returns the DOM node of an empty DIV element.
value(xmlDom)	String	Returns the text value of the XML document fragment given in DOM representation.

class GXslt

The GXslt class provides browser-agnostic methods to apply XSLT to XML. The methods will function correctly only in browsers that natively support XSL.

GXslt Static Methods

Static Method	Returns	Description
create(xsltDom)	GXslt	Creates a new GXslt instance from the DOM representation of an XSLT stylesheet.
transformToHtml (xmlDom, htmlDom)		Boolean Transforms the xmlNode DOM representation of the XML document using the XSLT from the constructor. The resulting HTML DOM object will be appended to the htmlDom. In the event that the browser does not support XSL, this method will do nothing and return false.

namespace GLog

The GLog namespace is not directly related to the mapping functions of the map but is provided to help you debug your web applications. As discussed in Chapter 9, you can use the write*() methods to open a floating log window and record and debug messages.

GLog Static Methods

Static Method	Returns	Description
write(message, [color])		Writes a message to the log as plaintext. The message text will be escaped so HTML characters appear as visible characters in the log window.
writeUrl(url)		Writes a URL to the log as a clickable link.
writeHtml(html)		Writes HTML to the log as rendered HTML (not escaped).

enum GGeoStatusCode

The GGeoStatusCode constants are returned from the geocoder.

GGeoStatusCode Constants

Constant	Description
G_GEO_SUCCESS	The supplied address was successfully recognized and no errors were reported.
G_GEO_SERVER_ERROR	The server failed to process the request.
G_GEO_MISSING_ADDRESS	The address is null.
G_GEO_UNKNOWN_ADDRESS	The supplied address could not be found.
G_UNAVAILABLE_ADDRESS	The address was found; however it could not be exposed by Google for legal reasons.
G_GEO_BAD_KEY	The supplied API key is invalid.

class GClientGeocoder

Use the GClientGeocoder class to geocode addressees using Google's geocoding service.

GClientGeocoder Constructor

Constructor	Description
GClientGeocoder([cache])	Creates a new instance of a geocoder. You may optionally supply your own client-side GFactualGeocodeCache object.

GClientGeocoder Methods

Method	Returns	Description
getLatLng (address, callback)		Retrieves the latitude and longitude of the supplied address. If successful, the callback function receives a populated GLatLng object. If the address can't be found, the callback receives a null value.
getLocations (address, callback)		Retrieves one or more geocode locations based on the supplied address and passes them as a response object to the callback function (see Chapter 10). The response contains a Status property (response.Status) that can be examined to determine if the response was successful.
getCache()	GGeocodeCache	Returns the cache in use by the geocoder instance.
setCache(cache)		Tells the geocoder instance to discard the current cache and use the supplied GGeocodeCache cache object. If null is passed, caching will be disabled.
reset()		Resets the geocoder and the cache.

class GGeocodeCache

Use the GGeocodeCache class to create a cache for GClientGeocoder requests.

GGeocodeCache Constructor

Constructor	Description
GGeocodeCache()	Creates a new cache object for storing encoded address. When instantiated, the constructor calls reset().

GGeocodeCache Methods

Method	Returns	Description
get(address)	Object	Retrieves the stored response for the given address. If the address can't be found, it will return null.
isCachable(reply)	Boolean	Determines if the given address should be cached. This method is used to avoid caching null or invalid responses and can be extended in your custom cache objects to provide more control of the cache.
put(address, reply)		Stores the given reply/address combination in the cache based on the results of the isCacheable() and toCanonical() methods.
reset()		Empties the cache.
toCanonical(address)	String	Returns a canonical version of the address by converting the address to lowercase and stripping out commas and extra spaces.

class GFactualGeocodeCache

The GFactualGeocodeCache class is a stricter version of the GGeocodeCache class. It restricts the cache to replies that are unlikely to change within a short period of time.

GFactualGeocodeCache Constructor

Constructor	Description
GFactualGeocodeCache()	Creates a new instance of the cache.

GFactualGeocodeCache Method

Method	Returns	Description
isCachable(reply)	Boolean	Implementation of GGeocodeCache.isCachable() whereby the status of the response is validated against GGeoStatusCode constants. Only successful (G_GEO_SUCCESS) requests or known invalid requests are cached.

Functions

Along with the classes and objects, the API includes a few functions that don't require you to instantiate them as new objects.

Function	Returns	Description
GDownloadUrl(url, onload)		Retrieves the resource from the given URL, and calls the onload function with the results of the resource as the first argument and the HTTP response status code as the second. The URL should be an absolute or relative path. This function is a simplified version of the GXmlHttp class and discussed in Chapter 3. It is subject to the same-origin restriction of cross-site scripting and, like the GXmlHttp class, it is executed asynchronously.
GBrowserIsCompatible()	Boolean	Returns true if the browser supports the API. Use this function to determine if the browser is compatible with the Google Maps API.
GUnload()		Dismantles the map objects to free browser memory and avoid leaks and bugs. Call this function in the unload event handler for your web page to free up browser memory and help clean up browser leaks and bugs. Calling this function will disable all the map objects on the page.

Index

You Need the Companion eBook

Your purchase of this book entitles you to buy the companion PDF-version eBook for only $10. Take the weightless companion with you anywhere.

We believe this Apress title will prove so indispensable that you'll want to carry it with you everywhere, which is why we are offering the companion eBook (in PDF format) for $10 to customers who purchase this book now. Convenient and fully searchable, the PDF version of any content-rich, page-heavy Apress book makes a valuable addition to your programming library. You can easily find and copy code—or perform examples by quickly toggling between instructions and the application. Even simultaneously tackling a donut, diet soda, and complex code becomes simplified with hands-free eBooks!

Once you purchase your book, getting the $10 companion eBook is simple:

❶ Visit **www.apress.com/promo/tendollars/**.

❷ Complete a basic registration form to receive a randomly generated question about this title.

❸ Answer the question correctly in 60 seconds, and you will receive a promotional code to redeem for the $10.00 eBook.

2560 Ninth Street • Suite 219 • Berkeley, CA 94710

eBookshop

Offer valid through 2/14/07.